News from the Front

SANDY GALL

News from the Front

The Life of a Television Reporter

HEINEMANN : LONDON

First published in Great Britain 1994
by William Heinemann Ltd
an imprint of Reed Consumer Books Ltd
Michelin House 81 Fulham Road London SW3 6RB

Reprinted 1994

A CIP catalogue record for this book
is held by the British Library
ISBN 0 434 00087 6

Picture Credits
Plate 1 ITN
Plate 2 (top): Pakistan Government
        (bottom): Rex Features
Plate 3: Hugh Thomson
Plate 4 (top): Charles Morgan
        (bottom): Sandy Gall
Plate 5: Sandy Gall
Plate 6 (top left and right): Sandy Gall
        (bottom): Steven Harrow
Plate 7: Chris Bannister
Plate 8 (top): ITN
        (bottom): Royal Society for Asian Affairs

Typeset by CentraCet Limited, Cambridge
Printed and bound in Great Britain
by Mackays of Chatham plc, Chatham, Kent

An Irish Blessing

May the road rise to meet you
May the wind be always at your back
May the sun shine warm upon your face
The rain fall soft upon your fields
And, until we meet again
May God hold you in the palm of his hand

Chapter
1

About nine o'clock on the evening of 5 July 1977, as I sat at the *News at Ten* desk in ITN's old building in Wells Street, a Reuter flash dropped in front of me. It was datelined Islamabad and said a relatively little-known general called Zia ul-Haq had just overthrown the government of the Prime Minister of Pakistan, Zulfikar Ali Bhutto, and put him and the rest of his ministers under house arrest. There had been no bloodshed and the country, which had been in turmoil for weeks, was now calm.

I leant across the desk and said to David Nicholas, sitting opposite me, 'Have you seen the coup story from Pakistan? Well, I know this chap, this new general. He's a friend of mine.'

David, now Sir David, was in fact the editor of ITN but for some reason was in the producer's chair that night. He looked up briefly and said, 'Why don't you try and do a phono with him?' A phono is journalese for a phoned interview, which we would run on *News at Ten* with a couple of stills: one of Zia, and another of me holding a telephone. I immediately alerted the ITN switchboard, but it was by then after midnight in Islamabad and we failed to reach the new master of Pakistan. I did, however, write a brief story about the coup, using library footage. We had very little film of Zia, but quite a lot of Bhutto, a flamboyant, westernised

1

figure, educated at Oxford, who had been his country's president, and then prime minister, as well as holding the Foreign and Defence portfolios from 1971 to 1977. The coup made headlines the next day, but in the absence of any serious disturbances, was quickly relegated to the inside pages.

To most Britons, Pakistan was not of much immediate concern, not even being in the Commonwealth any more: Bhutto had walked out following the Bangladesh débâcle in 1971. On the other hand, Pakistan had once been part of India and thus of the British Empire. Every schoolboy of my generation had read some Kipling, even if it was only 'The Ballad of East and West' – 'Oh, East is East, and West is West, and never the twain shall meet . . .' Thanks to television and M. M. Kaye's *The Far Pavilions*, the concept of the Raj was still strong, and names like the Khyber Pass and the North-West Frontier still echoed like a bugle call, even if faintly. Personally, as a journalist, I was fascinated: it is not every day, after all, that someone you know makes a coup and takes over a country.

About a week later, the phone rang in the kitchen of my cottage thirty miles south of London, in Kent. There was a gabble of heavily accented English from the other end which I took a moment to comprehend.

'Mr Sandy Gall?'

'Speaking.'

'Stand by for Chief Martial Law Administrator, Pakistan.' It was clearly an order. I waited, listening to the whine of the static. Then a very relaxed, friendly voice came on the line.

'Sandy? Zia here. How are you? How's the family?' It was always the first question he asked.

I stammered. 'Fine, fine, how are you, Zia?'

'I'm very well. Sandy, I want you to come out to Pakistan, as my guest. I'll send you a ticket. I want to talk to you and explain just what has been happening here. When can you come?'

2

I hesitated, caught slightly off balance. 'I don't know. I'll have to ask the office. It depends on whether I can get away from *News at Ten*.' My journalistic senses recovered. 'If I do come, I'd like to bring a camera crew with me. Would that be all right?'

It was Zia's turn to hesitate. 'I think it would be best if you just came yourself, initially. You can bring the cameras later.' I said I would let him have an answer as soon as possible and he rang off.

I stared out of the window, but for once the beauty of the garden failed to register. I was thinking of the first time I had met Zia ul-Haq, seven years before, in Amman, when he was a brigadier attached to the Pakistani military mission to Jordan. It was shortly after Black September when, following a great deal of provocation, King Hussein's Beduin army took on and finally crushed the Palestinian resistance. The battle had been fought in the refugee slums of Amman, which the PLO had heavily fortified and tried to turn into no-go areas. The relatively lightly-armed Palestinian guerrillas turned out to be no match for the tanks and artillery of one of the best-trained armies in the Middle East. Yasser Arafat and his propagandists were talking of 40,000 dead. That was a wild exaggeration: the real figure was closer to 400. Zia, a tank expert, was said to have given the King crucial advice during the battle for Amman, something the Palestinians never forgave.

We were introduced by an American friend, Ed Hughes, the Middle East correspondent of *Time* magazine, in the lobby of the Intercontinental Hotel. Zia was extremely hail-fellow-well-met and, as Ed had predicted, immediately asked us to dinner.

'Why don't you both come and have a curry at my house tomorrow?' He smiled his famous, brilliantly white-toothed smile and we accepted, willingly. Amman was not the most social of places, and Zia was undoubtedly well informed. It turned out to be an excellent dinner. Zia was a good host, plying us with beer, but did not, as far as I remember, drink himself: he was always a devout Moslem. He asked me if I was getting all the help I needed from the Jordanian Ministry of Information. I said, frankly no, I wasn't: it was virtually impossible to see anyone of importance, let alone the minister. While this made my job more difficult it also meant that in the battle of words with Arafat and the PLO, the Jordanian Government's case was going by default. Zia grasped this point immediately and said, casually, he might be able to help. I did not set much store by his offer, but next evening, the bell rang in the bullet-scarred Royal Suite at the top of the Intercontinental, where we were staying. I opened the door to find a mysterious figure standing before me in the shadows: most of the bulbs in the corridor had been shot out in the recent fighting.

He did not introduce himself and refused to come in, but after establishing my identity, said, 'I hear you feel you are not getting as much help as you would like from the authorities here?'

'Well, yes, that's true.'

'Are you free tomorrow morning?'

'Yes, of course.'

'Then I think we can help you. I will send a car for you at eight o'clock.'

With that the mysterious stranger withdrew, still without saying who he was. I did not ask, entering into the cloak and dagger spirit of the thing, and knowing, instinctively, he must be important. It was only later I discovered that my visitor was King Hussein's private secretary, Moraiwid Tel, younger brother of Wasfi Tel, the tough prime minister during Black September, who was later assassinated by the PLO in Cairo. Moraiwid was as good as his word, sending a Palace car with a crown on the number plate to take us to the military side of the airport. An hour later we took off in one of the royal fleet of Alouette helicopters and spent most of the day flying around northern Jordan, following the

4

king. It was his first visit to his troops in the field since the fighting, and they gave him a tremendous reception, going wild with excitement, hoisting him on their shoulders and carrying him round for several minutes in an astonishing demonstration of Beduin tribal loyalty. The story led *News at Ten* that night and helped Alan Downes win the Cameraman of the Year award. It was also, for me, the start of a fascinating relationship with both the king and Zia.

About a week after Zia's telephone call I left London in the first-class cabin of a Pakistan Airlines 747, to find the red carpet waiting for me at Islamabad airport next morning. I was whisked through the VIP lounge, driven to the Intercontinental Hotel near the airport and a little later, after a wash and a change, taken to see Zia. As Chief of Army Staff, he occupied a large, comfortable house, next to the Presidential Palace, which had once been the residence of the British general commanding Rawalpindi. Although in the centre of the city, its high walls kept out the sound of the traffic; the garden, through which Zia liked to stroll, was immaculate. The whole place, I imagine, had hardly changed since the days of the Raj.

I now found myself in the curious journalistic position of being handed a scoop on a plate, but not being allowed to use it. Zia proceeded to tell me the inside story of the coup which no other outsider, let alone journalist, was privy to, but at the same time did not want me to publish it. I could only guess at his intentions, and I came to two conclusions. The obvious one was that he wanted to give his version of events to the western journalist he probably knew best; the other was that in a curious way he wanted to explain and justify himself as a friend, perhaps anticipating the criticism that was to follow. Whatever the reasons, it made riveting listening, and for the next few days I listened hard.

The story really started six years earlier, on 3 December 1971, with the outbreak of the war between India and Pakistan, the second since Partition in 1947. Most of the

5

fighting took place in East Pakistan, now Bangladesh, where the Pakistan army was accused of great brutality in trying to put down the Bengali independence movement. The turning-point came when Indira Gandhi, quick to seize the opportunity to score off the old enemy, sent her army across the border in support of the secessionists. The numerically superior Indians inflicted a crippling defeat on Pakistan, which ended up suffering the double ignominy of losing the eastern half of its territory as well as having 90,000 of its soldiers taken prisoner. On 17 December Pakistan surrendered. Humiliation was total. Next day, President Yahya Khan, who was responsible for the débâcle, was deposed and Bhutto, then Foreign Minister, was recalled from the United Nations in New York to take over.

I had been sent by ITN to report the war in West Pakistan – we already had a team in the East – but apart from some fighting in Azad [Lower] Kashmir, there was little real action. The most exciting aspect of it for me was actually getting there. Since Pakistan had closed its airspace, I was forced to fly to the Afghan capital, Kabul, where I hired a taxi and drove 200 miles through the mountains to the Khyber Pass and Peshawar, reaching Rawalpindi next day. I stayed in the Intercontinental, where a day or two later, by chance, I bumped into Zia in the American-style coffee shop. He had been recalled from Jordan because of the crisis and promoted general. But he looked depressed, haunted almost, completely shattered by the news of the rout of the Pakistan army in the east.

I stayed on to witness Bhutto's triumphant return from New York. He was given a tremendous reception at the airport, cheered by thousands lining his route as his motorcade drove into town, and mobbed like a conquering hero when he appeared in the ballroom of the Intercontinental to give a press conference. After the nightmare of defeat, here was something to cheer about: it was almost as if he had won the war. Certainly, after the bumbling generals who

6

had dominated Pakistan since Partition, the new leader cut a dashing figure. The son of a rich, landowning family from Sind, he had been brought up in feudal splendour with servants galore before being sent to America and England to be educated. Like so many successful politicians before and after him, he became president of the Oxford Union and man about town. Unlike Zia, the unassuming general he was to appoint much later as his Chief of Army Staff, Bhutto was very much at home in the West; he liked his glass of whisky and the company of pretty women. But beneath the charm, there was a ruthless streak. A contemporary of his at Oxford told me how, one summer's day, when they were all watching some procession from an upstairs balcony – probably during one of the May Day balls – Bhutto in effect raped a girl undergraduate who was standing in front of him. According to a contemporary who was also on the balcony and witnessed the scene the girl was not strong enough to fight off her unwanted admirer and too frightened, or ashamed, to cry out.

There was a neat irony in the Bhutto-Zia relationship. Bhutto promoted Zia above a number of more senior generals in the belief that he would be less ambitious and more pliable – subservient even – than his rivals. Since Zia owed his preferment to Bhutto, he not unnaturally expected him to be loyal. There is very little doubt that Zia would have been, too, had Bhutto played the game according to the rules, the rules which Zia had learnt from the British as a young officer in the Guides, a crack Indian Army cavalry regiment. Zia was commissioned into the Guides in 1945, serving first in Burma and the Far East during the war and later at home until Partition in 1947. He was always proud of the British connection.

Benazir Bhutto described him at the time of his appointment as Chief of Army Staff as an insignificant little man who was shy to the point of gaucheness. No doubt this is exactly why Bhutto favoured Zia, being mindful, like all

Pakistani politicians, that the army had made a habit of intervening in politics since Field Marshal Ayub Khan had appointed himself president in 1958, eleven years after the birth of Pakistan and ten years after the death of the country's founder, Mohammed Ali Jinnah. Ayub Khan had been followed by another soldier, General Yahya Khan, Bhutto's predecessor.

Sitting now in his comfortable, rather English study, as if he had all the time in the world, Zia began by talking about his early devotion to the man he always referred to as Mr Bhutto, or the Prime Minister. He had always been in such awe of him, he said, that even now he could hardly believe he had dared to challenge him politically. Zia had been brought up in the British tradition that the army was above politics. Whatever his own views, it was a soldier's duty to carry out his political masters' bidding without argument. The sudden, dramatic change in what seems to have been an exemplary relationship – at least on Zia's side – came after the elections of March 1977, which were to prove even more disastrous for Bhutto than Watergate had been for Richard Nixon in 1972. At least Nixon escaped with his life.

In the previous general election, Bhutto had won a landslide victory and now he still looked the likely winner, although with a reduced majority. But, driven by very much the same motives as the Republicans in the United States in the 1972 campaign, Bhutto's Pakistan's People's Party [PPP] indulged in absurd overkill. Officials rigged the vote in such a blatant way that the PPP's predicted small majority was transformed into a veritable avalanche, winning 255 of the 300 seats in the National Assembly. One peculiarly Pakistani dirty trick, quoted by the opposition, occurred at the segregated, women-only polling booths. Since Pakistani women always go veiled in public, the opportunity for multiple voting and other forms of fraud was virtually limitless. Public opinion reacted with astonishing vigour, the opposition organising demonstrations and general strikes and

8

calling for new elections. Bhutto's reaction, predictably, was as high-handed as Marie Antoinette's; but whereas she offered the mob cake, Bhutto gave them a diet of lead. As rioting swept the country, he sent first the police and then, as the situation deteriorated, the army into the streets. By 20 May, when there was a lull, 350 people had been killed, thousands wounded and thousands more thrown into jail.

When talks between Bhutto, now fighting for survival, and the opposition Pakistan National Alliance [PNA] broke down in June, civil war looked inevitable. It was at this point that Zia ceased being a docile Chief of Staff and began to show that he had a mind of his own. Summoning his fellow generals to dinner at his house in Rawalpindi on a Saturday night at the end of June, Zia outlined his concern. Not that he needed to explain the explosiveness of the situation. His colleagues understood as well as he did that it was one thing for the army to act, however drastically, in support of the civil power in places like Sind and the North-West Frontier, but quite another when Punjabi soldiers had to open fire on Punjabi demonstrators in Lahore, the capital of Pakistan's biggest and richest province.

The Punjabis had always been the backbone of the army, and Zia and most of his fellow generals were Punjabis. Naturally, their concern, above all else, was for the well-being of the army. They saw it as the most stable element in a young country with strong, centrifugal tendencies; if the army disintegrated, the whole country would fall apart. Public opinion must not be allowed to turn against the army. At the end of dinner it was agreed that Zia, as the senior soldier in Pakistan, should request an immediate interview with the Prime Minister and present him with an ultimatum: unless he brought the situation under control within a week, the army would take over. When Zia described the ultimatum to me, I was astonished both by its directness and its naivety.

'Weren't you frightened that by giving him notice of

exactly what you planned to do, you would find yourself under arrest?'

Zia laughed. 'He did go round a lot of the other generals in the week that followed, trying to get them to take my job, but they all turned him down.'

First of all, however, Bhutto tried to do a deal with Zia.

'He said to me, "Look here, Zia. We'll run the country between us. I'll control the government and you control the army. Together we'll put a stop to these demonstrations." I said, "Prime Minister, I can't do that. This is a political crisis and you will have to solve it politically." But he was determined to use force. We knew he was distributing arms to his party workers. He wanted a showdown. If he had his way, there was going to be a lot more bloodshed. So I gave him an ultimatum, until the following Saturday.

'By the end of the week, things were worse, the police could not control the situation. The army was having to open fire and shoot more and more people. This was something we could not allow to go on any longer. Mr Bhutto still refused to contemplate a political solution – the resignation of his government, another election, or whatever other means to defuse the crisis. He was still determined to brazen it out. The next Saturday, the same generals came to my house for dinner again and we decided we had to intervene. We had no option. The strain on the army was now intolerable. Any further delay would seriously prejudice the security of the nation.'

That weekend, Zia gave orders for the arrest of Bhutto and various other senior ministers who were taken to the hill station of Murree, forty miles from the twin city of Islamabad-Rawalpindi and placed under house arrest. On Tuesday 5 July Zia imposed martial law and assumed the title of Chief Martial Law Administrator. Demonstrations stopped; the country was quiet. It had been a bloodless coup. A few days later, Bhutto and the other ministers were released and allowed to go home.

10

Zia and I had several more long talks over the next two or three days, fitted into gaps in his busy schedule. He also encouraged me to go and talk to other people. 'Go and see anyone you want,' he said, 'including Mr Bhutto.'

'Really? You mean that?'

'Of course I mean it.' He flashed the famous smile. 'I have nothing to hide.'

I took him at his word and next day, accompanied by a middle-ranking and extremely helpful official from the Ministry of Information, went to Bhutto's house in the diplomatic quarter of Islamabad, a pleasant, shady suburb on the northern side of the city, facing the Magala Hills. There were dozens of people milling about outside and as we forced our way up the path, Bhutto's daughter, Benazir, then aged about seventeen, passed us surrounded by a posse of bodyguards. Eventually we managed to get inside the house and after asking to see the former prime minister, we were shown to his study. Bhutto was sitting at a desk. He glanced up and asked, curtly, 'What do you want?'

He looked preoccupied and bad tempered. I introduced myself, explaining that I was from ITN, that I had come to Pakistan without a crew, but was going round talking to people about the situation. He listened without much show of interest and then said abruptly, 'It's absolutely intolerable. They follow me everywhere, even into my own house.'

I asked, 'Who do you mean, who's following you?'

Bhutto glared at me, balefully. 'The police, of course, who do you think I mean?' Then, his voice venomous, 'Where have you come from, then? The moon?'

My official escort started to say something placatory. Bhutto rounded on him like a tiger. 'Who are you? What's your name?'

'I'm Hussain, sir, from the Ministry of Information. I'm helping Mr Sandy Gall . . .'

'How dare you come into my house?' Bhutto's face

contorted with rage. 'Who gave you permission to come in here? Get out at once. Leave this room immediately. Go!'

Hussain rose, without a word, and left the room. There was an awkward silence. I started to explain that the man had been told to take me round, that he was only trying to do his job. Bhutto was not listening. He seemed to have withdrawn into some private world. After a few moments of embarrassing silence, I got up and left.

Outside, I found Hussain waiting. As we walked out of the gate, I asked, 'Is he often like that?'

Hussain said carefully, 'Mr Bhutto has the reputation of being a very difficult man. Sometimes, like you saw, he can be very rude, very bad tempered.'

'He looks a worried man.'

'A very frightened man, in my opinion,' Hussain said.

Next day I flew to Lahore, a journey of about an hour in a jet. Lahore is Pakistan's second-largest city after Karachi and its most attractive, the broad, tree-lined boulevards and handsome old houses virtually unchanged since Kipling's day. This is where his best novel, *Kim*, is set and, at the entrance to the bazaar you can still see the huge old cannon on which the young Kim used to sit. There were one or two journalists I wanted to see, but the main purpose of my visit was to talk to Air Marshal Mohammed Asghar Khan, a retired air force officer who had gone into politics and founded the small Tehrik-i-Istiqlal Party, part of the PNA. Zia suggested I talk to him, I imagine, because he had been an active opponent of Bhutto for many years and had been frequently jailed by his secret police.

The Air Marshal, a rather good-looking man, received me affably, his civilian clothes so well cut and pressed he contrived, somehow, to make them look like a uniform. I explained what I was doing and told him I had met Bhutto the day before. When I recounted how Bhutto had complained bitterly of being followed everywhere by the police, he gave a wry laugh.

12

'He doesn't like it when it happens to him, but of course when he was in power, he had his police watching and following everyone who was in opposition.'

'They followed you?'

'Not just followed me. They used to pick me up, put me in their car and drive out of Lahore, maybe ten or twenty miles, and then just stop the car and tell me to get out. In the middle of nowhere, right out in the country. Even, sometimes, at night. They would arrive at the house, tell me to get in the car and then just drive out of the city. Day or night, it didn't matter to them. The first time they did it – stopped the car and told me to get out – I asked them, "How am I going to get back to Lahore?" They just shrugged their shoulders and said, "You can walk back." That happened to me so many times, I lost count. At first I used to ask them, "Why are you doing this, what right have you to arrest me like this?" and so on. In the end, I didn't bother.'

'Did they ever beat you up?'

'No. They were insulting and arrogant but they didn't use physical violence.'

I asked the Air Marshal what he thought the purpose behind this sort of behaviour was.

'Oh, harassment, plain and simple. It was a way of wasting your time and energy, of disrupting your life and making you less effective, especially as a politician. They also wanted to let you know they had absolute power, that they could do anything they liked. In the end, it was intimidation, of course. They wanted to break you down, make you give up.'

I tried another tack. 'Wasn't it simply a display of vindictiveness by some petty, local official?'

'Oh, no, not at all. It was all organised from the very top. The orders came from Bhutto himself.'

'Really? I find that extraordinary. After all, you were doing nothing illegal.'

'That's not the point. Bhutto could not tolerate opposition.

13

Any opposition. He is a very vindictive person. In the end he was paranoiac.'

It was the Air Marshal who provided the next piece in the jigsaw. 'There is one man who, if you haven't seen him, you must talk to!'

I waited, intrigued.

'Kasuri!'

I had never heard of him. But the Air Marshal was right. As I would later find out, he was the key to the fall of Bhutto.

Chapter
2

In one of our talks, Zia claimed that it was only after he started going through state papers and began to discover in detail how Bhutto had run the country that the scales fell from his eyes.

'You see, to me, Mr Bhutto had always been a great man. I respected his talent and his record. He had had the best education that the West could provide – Christ Church, Oxford; the University of California, Berkeley; and called to the Bar at Lincoln's Inn. He had a brilliant career, first as Foreign Minister and later as Prime Minister. After the war and the loss of Bangladesh, he put the country back on its feet again. In my eyes, he was the most distinguished living Pakistani. If anyone had told me that one day I would have to depose him and then find that he had betrayed the trust the country had placed in him, I simply wouldn't have believed them.'

Zia said that not long after he became Chief of Army Staff, Bhutto raised with him the issue of the improper use of army transport. 'It was quite a minor affair. Someone had used a lorry or vehicle of some sort to take guests to a wedding. Bhutto made a tremendous fuss about it. He went on and on, shouting and banging his fist on the table, saying it was totally unacceptable that public property should be used for private purposes and that he simply would not tolerate this sort of thing.

'Of course I agreed with him one hundred per cent. I too had been taught in the army to treat public property with the utmost respect. I was just as much against any kind of corruption or malpractice as he was. So you can imagine my surprise, or shock rather, when I discovered that the man who had made such a fuss about the improper use of an army lorry had been using state funds as if they were his own private property. As if it was his own bank account. To the tune of millions! This was the man who I had held in the highest respect and who I had always looked up to!'

I asked if he was saying that Mr Bhutto was guilty of fraud, or embezzlement, on a huge scale.

'I have seen the evidence with my own eyes. It's all there in black and white. He simply used public money as his own, as if there was no distinction.'

Bhutto was nothing if not controversial, arousing admiration and anathema in equal proportions. But as I made the rounds of various ministries, including the Ministry of Information, I quickly discovered that he was highly unpopular among senior civil servants. Admittedly, now that he was down and apparently out, plenty of people were willing to come forward and say what they thought of him. Many senior civil servants who had been so frightened of his authoritarian behaviour that they would never have dared to criticise him when he was prime minister, were quite willing to tell me, although guardedly, just in case he made a comeback, what an unpleasant character he really was. As I had seen briefly myself, with my friend Mr Hussain, he could cut up very rough even from a position of weakness.

But most civil servants were lucky enough not to have to deal very often with him personally. It was his closest associates who had to suffer the full weight of his biting

16

sarcasm and paranoiac rages; and who could have been closer than the members of his cabinet. 'He treated them,' one civil servant who had worked in the cabinet office told me, 'like dirt.' He then related the story of how one day, in his presence, Bhutto had humbled one minister in a particularly cruel and public manner. In front of the entire cabinet, Bhutto told the wretched man to his face, 'Your wife is a tart. She's cuckolding you. Do you know how I know?' As his victim cringed, Bhutto glanced round triumphantly to make sure everyone was listening.

'No? Well, I'll tell you how I know, because I've slept with her myself!' And such was the terror he inspired, my informant added, that no one dared to say anything. 'They just stood there in silence, shuffling their feet. Bhutto thought it was a tremendous joke. That is what he was like. He liked destroying people!'

Thus, when Zia came to power, there was a lot of support for him, not only in the army, but among civil servants and all sorts of people in public and private life who had felt the weight of Bhutto's displeasure. One of the officials the Information Ministry arranged for me to see was the Chief Returning Officer of the 1977 election, who cited a long list of malpractices which he said he had known about but had been helpless to prevent. I asked him what sort of illegalities had taken place.

'There were so many. PPP supporters were allowed to vote twice or three times, ballot boxes from opposition constituencies simply disappeared, others – from areas where the Bhutto party was strong – were counted twice and so on. In some instances,' the official told me, 'police sealed off polling stations and, acting under the orders of local PPP officials, simply turned away people who were known to be members or supporters of opposition parties.' The whole thing was done with such blatancy that the whole country knew there had been fraud. But it was not until the results were announced that the scale of the fraud

17

became apparent; and it was only then that the scandal blew up in Bhutto's face.

Diplomats in the British Embassy were convinced that Bhutto would have won the election without too much difficulty. 'The idiotic thing is that he didn't need to cheat,' one of them told me. 'We reckon he would have won fairly comfortably. But his officials wanted to make doubly sure. He should have stopped them, but he didn't.'

In our talks, I found Zia virtually unchanged. He radiated energy and optimism, but had not lost his modesty, which was engaging. 'I am a simple soldier,' he would say, flashing a big smile. 'I have no ambition to be president or anything like that. I've got the only job I ever wanted and I'd like to keep it. I have no ambitions apart from that and no desire to be rich. When I retire, it will be to a modest place in the country where I can do a little shooting.'

In support of his claim to have no political ambitions, Zia expressed his intention of returning the country to civilian rule as soon as possible. At a small dinner party he gave for me one night, to which he invited a number of well-known Pakistani journalists, including a few editors, the subject of elections soon came up. Some of the guests were quite clearly unsympathetic, if not hostile, to the military takeover and pressed him about his plans. Zia was, as always, disarmingly frank. 'We are going to hold elections within ninety days,' he said categorically. He told his cabinet the same thing and I believe he sincerely meant to carry out his promise. Much later, one of his civilian ministers told me that he had 'lied' to the cabinet, which assumes that Zia had no intention of holding elections. My own view is that, originally, he did mean what he said, but in the end found it impossible to deliver.

Certainly, as the days passed, and as the advice flowed in from supporters who were much more hardline than himself, his views began to change. I had flown back to London by then, but it is clear from his public statements that the

18

early euphoria and the simpleness – some would say naivety – of his views soon began to evaporate. He became aware that if he did hold elections within three months, the formidable Bhutto political machine, despite its recent loss of face, might very possibly deliver a genuine victory. Bhutto had used his years in power to good effect; the opposition was weak and divided. Even to someone as easy-going and self-confident as Zia, an election must have begun to look an unacceptably risky undertaking. A triumphant and vindictive Bhutto would, without the slightest doubt, instantly seek revenge. Zia would find himself under arrest, charged with treason, facing court-martial and the firing squad.

Like many soldiers, Zia despised politicians; not all politicians, but certainly most Pakistani politicians. He thought highly of Mrs Thatcher, admiring her tough, straight-from-the-shoulder style, but there were not many like Mrs Thatcher in Pakistan. He therefore set about the daunting task of trying to reshape the political map of Pakistan, by destroying or at least neutering the PPP, which he saw as typical of the corrupt, Tammany Hall style of Pakistani politics, and putting in its place a new, 'clean' system of non-party government, based on an orthodox, Islamic code. This would include strict application of Koranic, or Shariat law; in other words, convicted thieves would have their hands cut off, women caught in adultery would be stoned to death, and petty criminals would be flogged.

When I pointed out on a later occasion that these extreme forms of punishment were considered unacceptable in the West, he simply smiled and said, 'This is what is written in the Koran, but so far we haven't cut off anyone's hands or stoned anyone to death.' He defended flogging, however – and the death penalty – with the argument that life in Pakistan was very different from life in Britain. 'In England you don't have the death penalty. You are not a violent people. But here, in Pakistan, we are a very violent society and we do have the death penalty.

19

'When I took over from Mr Bhutto, there were seventy death sentences sitting on his desk, waiting for his decision. I went through each and every one, very carefully, to see if there were any extenuating circumstances; to see, for example, if any of them was either very young, or had suffered terribly, or if there was any other reason for considering a pardon. And you know, I couldn't find a single case where I felt there was a good reason for commuting the death sentence. There were some terrible crimes; a gang, for example, that had kidnapped a boy, buggered him, tortured him, and then murdered him. That was one case. How could you pardon someone who had committed a crime like that?'

Flogging was widespread after the coup, and served to make the army highly unpopular. If Zia was aware of this – and it was always hard to know just how much he knew and how much was kept from him – he no doubt considered it one of the prices that had to be paid for the creation of a truly Islamic state. Previous military dictators, like Presidents Ayub Khan and Yahya Khan, had served in the Indian Army, with its very British tradition of the officers' mess, where a considerable intake of alcohol was considered not only normal, but almost obligatory. Ayub is said to have drunk a bottle of whisky a day and Bhutto, Westernised as he was, tended to take the precepts of the Koran fairly lightly. He once told a British diplomat's wife that after a long day in the office, he saw no reason why he should not relax over a glass of whisky in the evening, in the privacy of his own house.

This was not the way Zia saw things. Although he also served in the Indian Army, he never adopted the habits of the mess and rarely, if ever, drank alcohol. He was a devout Moslem and accepted, without qualification, that Pakistan had been founded as an Islamic state, with the express purpose of nurturing and upholding the Islamic virtues. His natural constituency was the Islamic right, represented

20

politically by the ultra conservative Jamaat-Islami (Society of Islam) party. Jamaat were sticklers for strict adherence to the fundamental tenets of Islam and totally at odds with the creeping secularisation of Pakistan, which had begun under the generals and accelerated under Bhutto. In Zia's sudden access to power, they saw the perfect opportunity to reverse the trend and gave him the political backing he needed. Influential as Jamaat was, many Pakistanis found its views at once too extreme and too provincial. They rebelled against the harshness of the regime, with its floggings and military courts, its insistence on Shariat law and the banning of alcohol, and denied Zia the popularity he felt he deserved.

I do not know at what point Zia ul-Haq came to the conclusion that he and Zulfikar Ali Bhutto were locked in a mortal struggle, but I suspect it was only a matter of weeks after the coup. To the journalists and diplomats whose job it was to report on Zia's Pakistan, it seemed inevitable that the trial of strength between Zia and the former prime minister would last as long as they were both alive, since even if Bhutto were exiled, he would undoubtedly continue to work for the overthrow of his hated usurper. It was a frequent topic of conversation among the small group of foreign correspondents who spent many weeks covering the early period of Zia's rule: Mark Tully of the BBC, Peter Niesewand of the *Guardian*, Bruce Loudon of *The Daily Telegraph* and myself. Everyone involved in the country's affairs was fascinated to know how this puzzle would be resolved. The answer was provided by that well-known ingredient of every classical play, a *deus ex machina*. In the case of Bhutto, this particular god appeared in the unlikely shape of a former Bhutto protégé called Ahmed Raza Kasuri, accused the former prime minister of being responsible for his father's murder. Although the original complaint had been buried as long as Bhutto was in power, Zia's prosecuting officials, once they found out about it, lost no time in resurrecting it.

It was an extraordinary story, not least because Mr Kasuri, a member of the National Assembly, had been the head of the youth section of the PPP, and one of Bhutto's most fervent supporters. Then, for some reason, he turned against Bhutto and started to attack him as publicly and vociferously as he had once eulogised him. On a famous occasion in the National Assembly in 1974 Bhutto, who had been forced to listen to Kasuri's diatribes once too often and who had a venomous tongue himself, snarled in rage, 'I have had enough of you. I will not tolerate your nuisance.' The words duly found their way into the local Hansard.

Mr Kasuri I eventually ran to ground in Islamabad, and he told me that some time after that confrontation in the National Assembly he had gone to Lahore, where his family lived, to attend a wedding. Afterwards, in the evening, he drove his parents home, his father sitting beside him in front, his mother in the back. 'We came to a big roundabout on the way home and as we started to go round it, suddenly, without warning, a number of people standing in the middle of the roundabout opened fire on us with automatic weapons. I couldn't see who they were, because it was dark. All I saw were the flashes of their guns. There were several of them, that's all I could tell. A lot of bullets hit the car, one of them wounding my father, who was right beside me, but by some miracle, none of them hit my mother, or me.

'It all happened very suddenly but, luckily, the car didn't stall. Somehow I managed to keep going, otherwise we'd all have been killed. As soon as I realised my father had been hit, I drove straight to the hospital. By the time we got there my father was dead. So I went from the hospital to the police station and reported the incident. They wrote down the details and then they asked me, "Have you any idea who might be responsible for this?"

'I said, "Yes, I do, the Prime Minister, Mr Bhutto."'

'What made you say that?' I asked.

'I knew. I knew he was trying to kill me, after that occasion in the Assembly. There was an attempt in Islamabad, when they shot at my car. Everyone knew that Bhutto got rid of people who were in his way. There were plenty of examples of him having his political opponents assassinated. They simply disappeared, were found shot, or had a car accident.'

I asked what the reaction of the Lahore police had been to the sensational allegation that he was accusing the prime minister of murder.

'They refused to write it down. Of course, they were not going to do anything as long as Mr Bhutto was prime minister.'

Having failed to get any satisfaction from the police, Kasuri tried to bring a private case, but since Pakistan law was based largely on British law, private citizens could not bring murder charges. That was the prerogative of the state. So no action was taken in the case of Kasuri Senior until after General Zia's coup. Then, things started to move quickly. On 3 September, less than two months after the coup, Bhutto was charged with 'conspiracy to murder'. In an interview with the *New York Times*, published three days later, Zia described Bhutto as 'Machiavelli in 1977'. He was, he said, 'an evil genius who had been running the country on more or less Gestapo lines, misusing public funds, blackmailing people, detaining them illegally, and even, perhaps, ordering them to be killed.' On another occasion, Zia referred to Bhutto as 'a cheat and a murderer'.

The trial of the former prime minister and four members of the Federal Security Force [FSF], which the opposition described as Bhutto's private army, opened on 11 October before four judges of the Lahore High Court. The key prosecution witness, Masud Mahmoud, the former head of FSF who had turned state evidence, testified that he had ordered the attempted assassination of Ahmed Raza Kasuri on Bhutto's instructions. The proof was alleged to lie in a note to Mahmoud, telling him to take action against Kasuri, in Bhutto's own writing. This key accusation, needless to say, was hotly disputed by the defence. Bhutto's lawyers wanted a well-known British barrister to defend him but the Pakistani authorities refused to accept his credentials. In the event, Bhutto was defended by his former Attorney General, Yahya Bakhtiar, a tall, lugubrious-looking man expert at keeping the foreign media abreast of every twist and turn in the case. Bhutto refused to take part in the proceedings, alleging that the charge was a frame-up.

On 18 March 1978, Bhutto and the other four defendants were all found guilty and sentenced to death. The senior judge commented that Bhutto was 'a compulsive liar' and that the case had been 'proved to the hilt'. The news produced riots in Pakistan, put down quickly by the army, and an outcry in the Moslem world and in the West. Bhutto's lawyers promptly appealed and the hearing was set down for January 1979, before the Supreme Court in Rawalpindi.

At the request of John Mahoney, perhaps the best Foreign Editor ITN ever had, I left London for Pakistan on 24 January to cover the appeal. Although I was then regularly co-presenting *News at Ten* with the unflappable Andrew Gardner and the inimitable Reginald Bosanquet, the other member of the team, Leonard Parkin, and I took it in turns to go abroad on major stories. In the eighteen months since the coup, I had done virtually all ITN's reporting from Pakistan, and the outcome of the Bhutto appeal was clearly going to represent the end of this particular chapter, one way or the other.

Arriving in Islamabad next day, I rang Zia's office and arranged to see him that evening. Since the passing of the death sentence, Zia had been deluged with threats as well as appeals for clemency. If he was shaken by the reaction, he did not show it. One of my first questions to him was, 'If the Supreme Court rejects Bhutto's appeal, will you intervene to commute the death sentence? A lot of people are saying that as a former prime minister, he should be pardoned.'

Zia looked me straight in the eye. 'How can I interfere with the course of justice?' he asked. 'Who am I to overrule the carefully considered opinion of the Supreme Court, unless there is some overriding reason to do so? It is up to the judges. If they uphold the appeal, Mr Bhutto will walk from the court a free man. If on the other hand they reject the appeal, he will have to face the full rigour of the law.' Zia spread his hands. 'Look, Mr Bhutto has had all the advantages life can offer: education, wealth, rank, fame. How can I make an exception for a man who has enjoyed all the advantages he has had, when I would not do the same for someone lower down the scale. Privilege carries with it certain responsibilities. As a former prime minister, Mr Bhutto must be judged by the highest of standards, the strictest of standards. With his background and all his advantages, shouldn't he be setting an example to the rest of us?'

I said there were reports that he, Zia, was putting pressure on the judges to reject the appeal. He denied it vehemently. 'I have never tried to influence the court and I have no intention of doing so in the future. They will make their own decision without any interference from me. Here in Pakistan we have the rule of law, British law, which we inherited from you. We are proud of our system and I have no intention of tampering with it.'

I came away convinced that if the Supreme Court rejected the appeal, Zia had not the slightest intention of stepping in to save Bhutto from the hangman. I also detected, perhaps for the first time, the iron hand which was always so well hidden in the velvet glove, the steely will which had confronted Bhutto in the first place and then, when he ignored the generals' ultimatum, removed him from power. Listening to Zia that day, I realised he was utterly convinced of the rightness of his case; there was no room in his mind for even a flicker of doubt.

For the next ten days or so, I and the handful of other Western journalists covering the appeal spent much of our time at the Supreme Court building, a charmless, modern structure. To reach it you drove along the Mall, a wide, tree-lined avenue laid out in the days of the British Raj with on one side, shimmering in the winter sunshine, the smooth, brown-green oval of the Maidan where once the British, and now the Pakistanis, played cricket and polo. On the other, behind a few elegant shops like the military outfitters where in the space of a few hours they could run you up a handsome puggree (military turban) in raw silk, sprawled the tightly-packed rabbit warren of old Rawalpindi. Also on that side of the Mall, half-screened by trees, reposed another venerable relic, the long low white-washed, tin-roofed shape of Flashman's Hotel.

Here, Bhutto's barrister, Yahya Bakhtiar, more harassed and lugubrious-looking than ever, held court after each new stage of the appeal. He insisted that General Zia was putting relentless pressure on the court to reject it, citing as proof the resignation, half-way through the hearing, of one of the judges. That reduced the bench from eight to seven, which may well have had far-reaching consequences.

A few days later, on 6 February, the Supreme Court voted by four to three to reject Bhutto's appeal; the previous outcry, after the Lahore verdict, was nothing to the storm that broke now. As the appeals for clemency poured in – almost every head of state and government in the world sent one; James Callaghan, the Labour Prime Minister, sent no less than three – everyone wanted to know the answer to one question. As Head of State, would Zia exercise his right of clemency and grant Bhutto a pardon? I had already heard his answer in private but, naturally, in public he played for time.

Three days later, at a ceremony to celebrate Nizam-i-

26

Mustafa, the 1407th anniversary of the Prophet's birthday, General Zia called for the strictest observance of Islamic law. What would have been, in normal circumstances, a routine announcement taken with a pinch of salt by most Pakistanis, now assumed, because of the death sentence hanging over Bhutto, a sharper significance. It imparted to Zia, at least in the eyes of his followers, an aura of retribution. To me, it merely confirmed that the outcome was a foregone conclusion. Bhutto's lawyers, however, had not given up, working furiously on an eighty-page petition for a review of the judgement.

The day before the petition was handed in, I sent a report by satellite to *News at Ten* which included an interview with Bhutto's lawyer who was perhaps for the first time, as he put it, 'not optimistic'. We also filmed the outside of Rawalpindi Jail, another relic of the Raj, a grim fortress in the Victorian manner. Somewhere behind those high stone walls a dejected Bhutto was living out his last days. His family and lawyers complained bitterly about the insanitary and unhealthy conditions he had to put up with. Government spokesmen insisted that far from being hard done by, he had been given preferential treatment, enjoying the use of two rooms instead of the usual one. His wife and lawyer were allowed to visit him regularly, but no one else. I had asked Zia after one of our many meetings if I would be allowed to interview Bhutto in prison. He said yes, in an offhand manner, without reflection. But when I brought it up again after the rejection of the appeal, he smiled ruefully and said things had changed. It would not be possible now. In a way I was glad. I could think of nothing more horrible than to interview a man in the condemned cell. Bhutto might have refused to give an interview, of course, but being a politician to his fingertips, he was much more likely to have seen it as a last, desperate chance and made an impassioned appeal for his life. Undoubtedly, Zia saw the danger. It is the only occasion I can remember him going back on his word to me.

The Supreme Court met on 14 February to receive the petition, which in effect was asking for a retrial. More than five weeks later, on 24 March, the judges unanimously rejected it but, in a remarkable admission of their doubts about the case, implicitly recommended that the sentence should not be carried out. In the past, such a recommendation had always been accepted. But Zia had made up his mind, remaining deaf to all pleas, even those from President Carter, James Callaghan and King Feisal of Saudi Arabia, his closest ally in the Moslem world. Eleven days later, at 2 a.m. in the morning of Wednesday 4 April, Zulfikar Ali Bhutto, the former prime minister of Pakistan, was hanged in Rawalpindi Jail. Thousands of his supporters went on the rampage, organising violent demonstrations across the country, notably in Rawalpindi itself and Karachi, the capital of Sind, Bhutto's home province. The police were well prepared, breaking up the angry crowds with tear gas and baton charges. The army waited in the wings but was not required. Zia had ridden out the storm.

When I talked to him on the phone the next day, he said, 'I have tried to show that nobody, whether high or low, is above the law.'

Chapter
3

In the late summer of 1978, I called on the Vietnamese Ambassador at his modest establishment in Victoria Road, Kensington, with the purpose of applying for a visa. He was small and extremely friendly and, like most old Vietnamese Communists, spoke good French. We talked about the war, which he had fought in as a fairly senior officer, serving for a time in the deep tunnels at Cu Chi which enabled the Vietnamese to survive endless American offensives and still come out fighting. Like so many other North Vietnamese he had made the long and dangerous trek south via the Ho Chi Minh Trail, the main supply route for the North Vietnamese divisions and the Vietcong in the south. Over the years, thousands of men and tens of thousands of tons of arms had come down this jungle highway in a steady stream which even the onslaughts of the B-52 bombers could not stop. But what impressed me most about him was that in 1954, as a young man, he had fought at Dien Bien Phu, the famous battle which drove the French from Indo-China – as great a victory for the Vietnamese as Waterloo for the British.

Over small cups of tea, the affable ambassador quizzed me as to what exactly my purpose would be in visiting Vietnam. I said that having reported the war for a number of years, I would like to return to see what had happened to the country since I was last there, and more specifically, to make a series of television reports for *News at Ten* to coincide with the fourth anniversary of the fall of Saigon in March 1975. I was curious to discover the fate of the once beautiful, exciting and corrupt city which used to be known as the Pearl of the Orient, a city in which European and oriental culture had blended so happily. In 1975, there were 40,000 French citizens of Vietnamese origin in Saigon – many of them the offspring of French fathers and Vietnamese mothers. The ethnic blending had worked well: many of the women were extremely good-looking. There was also a huge ethnic Chinese population of about half a million in its own vast Chinatown of Cholon. And, of course, I wanted to pay my first visit to Hanoi, the capital, which in almost every way was the exact opposite of Saigon.

Since the end of the war the Hanoi government had been actively ostracised by the Americans and largely ignored by the rest of the world. Understandably, it felt increasingly isolated and desperate for Western technology and investment. This encouraged me to believe that my request would find favour, although I knew the Vietnamese were far too proud, and too tough negotiators, to admit to any weakness. The nuances of this poker game were subtle enough for me to feel I had scored a minor victory when the ambassaor said my request seemed to be a reasonable one and, although he could make no promises, agreed to pass it on to Hanoi.

Weeks went by and I had almost forgotten about the visa application when in late November I received a message at ITN asking me to call at the embassy to see a first secretary called Nguyen: such are the vagaries of Vietnamese pronunciation that the closest most Westerners can get to it is 'nwin'. Mr Nguyen was less jolly than the ambassador who, he said, had gone on leave to Vietnam, which made me wonder if he really had gone on leave or if he had been recalled for some political peccadillo. Then, after explaining

30

how extremely fortunate ITN and I both were, he announced with a toothy smile that my visa application had been granted. We discussed at length the sort of reports I would make – he made it plain that anything that could be construed as 'unfriendly' would not be acceptable.

Finally, he asked, in his high-pitched, nasal twang rather like a power saw cutting through hardwood, 'When can you go? We need to know approximate date, because Hanoi has to make arrangements. You know we do not have many qualified, er, guides, so they need a little notice.' His request was eminently reasonable, yet somehow the slightly hectoring tone grated.

'I don't know,' I said rather casually. 'I shall have to talk to the Foreign Editor and let you know.'

Mr Nguyen saw me out with another display of sharp teeth and a parting shot. 'Don't forget,' he sawed. 'Lots of other organisations, including the BBC, want to go Vietnam too.'

The threat accompanied me back to the office and I immediately sought out the deputy editor, Don Horobin, who had a special role as Output Editor. This put him, in certain ways, above the Foreign Editor. He was also, by temperament, an enthusiast for anything that might remotely be considered a scoop.

'Would we be the only crew to be invited?' he enquired carefully.

'Oh, yes. We are top of the list and have first refusal.' As soon as the words left my mouth, I regretted them. The last thing I wanted to do was to put the idea of refusal into Don's mind, even for a moment.

But he brightened. 'Let's have this bloke, what's his name?'

'Nguyen.'

'Right, let's have him in to the office for lunch. I'll get David [the Editor] and the Foreign Editor and we'll see what he's got to say for himself.'

Feeling confident that the trip was in the bag, I withdrew to make the arrangements. Mr Nguyen was happy to come to lunch the following week. There was little news coming out of Vietnam, apart from the perennial border disputes: either with the Chinese in the north, or the Cambodians in the south-west. The Vietnamese are disputatious by nature and have a particular chip on their shoulder about the Chinese, who occupied their country for centuries, and left behind an indelible cultural imprint. I decided I would have to sell the trip on the strength of what the tough new Communist bosses had done to a country that had once been so tolerant and so close to the West. I also felt, in a not very precisely defined way, that I wanted to capture something of the continuing tragedy of Vietnam, which had been so brutally left in the lurch by the Americans. I would never forget the agony on people's faces on that last day in Saigon, before the arrival of the Communist North Vietnamese army, when thousands of Saigonese desperately, and vainly, tried to flee the dying city. But this was more difficult to sell to my editors because, although I sensed it was there, I did not know in exactly what form the tragedy would present itself.

We lunched in the boardroom at the top of ITN, the view from the picture windows being mainly a close-up of the Post Office Tower, a thing of no great beauty, and the rather indifferent skyline of the Tottenham Court Road area. Mr Nguyen, however, seemed to be pleased to be in such elevated company, sitting opposite the Editor, David Nicholas, and Don Horobin, and next to me. Mr Nguyen ate, as some Vietnamese do, with his mouth open, displaying his teeth a good deal and clearing his throat loudly and thoroughly, which made him less than ideal as a lunch companion. We ran through the various filming options and soon came up against his ingrained reluctance, typical of a middle-grade, totalitarian functionary, to give anything like carte blanche to a Western television news team.

'Mr Nguyen, we all know how well-trained and efficient the North Vietnamese, that's to say the Vietnamese, army is. Will it be possible for us to spend some time with them, filming them on manoeuvres, say?'

Mr Nguyen opened his mouth wide to remove a chicken bone and masticated in full view of his fellow lunchers. 'Difficult, Mr Horobin. Taking pictures of Vietnamese army always very difficult.' He smirked with apparent satisfaction. 'But you can take pictures lots of other things. We have built many many schools, hospitals, children's creches . . .' I tried to steer him away from this minefield, not altogether successfully.

At the end of lunch, Mr Nguyen delivered his ultimatum. 'We like very much to have ITN visit our country to see for themselves our great achievements. But you know there lot more journalists wanting to visit Vietnam. We need to know soon, very soon, if you are serious. Otherwise . . . .' He smiled broadly – luckily he had stopped eating – but his meaning was clear. He cleared his throat one last time, which brought Don to the edge of his seat in alarm, but he mercifully stopped short of actually expectorating, and then rose to go. After we had seen him into the lift, we went back to the table. I knew I would now hear the decision.

David always had the knack of putting his finger on the weak spot, although in this case it was not very difficult. 'Sandy, I'm a bit worried about what exactly we're going to get, in terms of stories. We've just heard they won't let us near their army. Are we going to get a load of propaganda footage, schools, hospitals and so on? Are we going to be able to film enough other things to make it worthwhile, or are the bureaucrats going to give us the bum's rush every time we want to do something that's politically sensitive?'

We both knew there was no easy answer and I resented being put on the spot. Either we thought the story was exciting and unusual enough to take the risk, which was largely financial, or we did not. I thought we had all agreed that, four years after the Communist take-over, the plight of South Vietnam, which had fought so long to preserve its independence, was eminently worth examining. Perhaps in the meantime the budget had shrunk. I made one last try.

'You know, with a bit of ingenuity you can always get round the bureaucratic obstructions. And I think we all agree it will be fascinating to see what the Communists have done to Saigon. What's happened to all the girlie bars, the brothels, the restaurants, all that huge private sector that used to cater for the animal appetites of the GIs? And the black market? I bet that's still going strong. The political re-education of the old guard, and so on.' Don entered the argument.

'I know, I know Sandy, and if anyone is going to get the stories, it'll be you. I have no doubts about that, whatsoever. But seriously, and I hate to bring it down to this, but we are way over budget at the moment, as you probably know . . .'

I did not, specifically, but being over budget was a recurring fact of life, like getting a common cold. At the end of every financial year, and often half-way through it, we would be over budget and the order would go out, 'Hold everything. No more foreign trips until further notice.'

I knew the budget argument was as unbeatable as a Capablanca opening. 'All right,' I said getting up. 'I'll have to tell him we've decided we don't want the visas. They'll probably give them to the BBC.' I could not repress a note of bitterness.

I went to my office and called the Vietnamese Embassy. 'Mr Nguyen, bad news, I'm afraid. ITN has decided, reluctantly, that it is not able to go ahead just at the moment, but I wonder if we could hold the visas in reserve . . .'

With what sounded like pleasure, but may have been anger, Mr Nguyen said, 'That is quite impossible, Mr Sandy. If you do not take the visas now, we will give them to someone else. Maybe the BBC. I am very sorry, Mr Sandy!'

'So am I, especially for all the trouble . . .' But he had already put the phone down.

Two weeks later, on Christmas Day 1978, Vietnam invaded Cambodia in a blitzkrieg that took the world by surprise. Infuriated by constant Cambodian raids across the border, causing many civilian casualties, Hanoi launched a full-scale attack with an army of 100,000 battle-hardened troops. The Cambodians, heavily outnumbered and out-gunned, fell back in disarray and, within a matter of days, half the country was in Vietnamese hands. On 7 January, two weeks after the start of their offensive, the Vietnamese marched into the capital, Phnom Penh, forcing the fanatical Pol Pot and the rest of the equally murderous Khmer Rouge government to flee to the remote mountains on the Thai border. Not surprisingly, the Vietnamese were hailed by most Cambodians as liberators. The Khmer Rouge had been in power for five terrible years, in which they had destroyed the economy and put to death possibly as many as a million of their fellow citizens. A few accounts of the Khmer Rouge terror had been smuggled out but it was only now the full horror began to emerge.

Soon after the first Reuter flash landed in the ITN news-room in Wells Street, Don Horobin was on the phone. He was at his most persuasive. 'Sandy, can you get on to the Vietnamese Embassy right away and ask them if there's a possibility, any possibility at all, of issuing us with those visas?' My first reaction was anger that we had, out of meanness, I felt, thrown away such a wonderful oppor-tunity. We would have been in Vietnam now, probably the only foreign journalists in the whole country and with a unique opportunity to be the first into Cambodia. All of that flashed through my mind in two seconds, but I tried to keep my tongue under control. 'Yes, Don, I'll try, but you know what they're going to say. We turned down the facility and they've got someone else lined up for those visas.' It would be ironic, and extremely painful, if that someone else was going to get the scoop that might have been ours.

'I know, mate, but I'd appreciate it very much indeed if you'd do all you can.'

Don, at least, was always polite, a rare quality in the newsrooms of this world. I rang Mr Nguyen immediately.

'Ah, Mr Sandy, how are you today?' He sounded extremely pleased with himself.

'Very exciting news, Mr Nguyen. You've taken us all by surprise.'

Nguyen laughed excitedly. 'You are surprised, are you, Mr Sandy?'

'Well, I knew you were having some border problems, but I did not realise things had become so tense.'

Nguyen laughed again. 'They are less tense now, Mr Sandy.'

'Mr Nguyen, I have something to ask you, on behalf of ITN. Something very important. They want me and an ITN crew to fly out as soon as possible to report on this situation. We'd be tremendously grateful if you could issue us with visas.'

There was a long sigh at the other end of the line. 'I am sorry, Mr Sandy, very sorry but that is now not possible. We offered you the visa, but you turned it down and we have now given the visas to someone else.'

'Who?' I asked ungramatically.

'I cannot tell you that. But, Mr Sandy, I am really very sorry. You see, when you turned down the offer of the visas, you went to the bottom of the list. There are many people in front of you. So you will have to wait your turn, now, Mr Sandy, until you get to the top of the list again.' Then Mr Nguyen giggled. Giggling, like eating with the mouth open and hawking, is another potentially irritating Vietnamese habit. But I knew it was done probably more out of embarrassment than spite.

I was so taken aback that I weakly repeated. 'Gone to the bottom of the list?'

'I afraid so. Sorry, Mr Sandy.'

36

Bastard, I thought, as I rang off.

Don was upset at the news, although he had been well warned, but refused to take no for an answer. That was his great asset as a news editor. He would never admit defeat, even when it sat on his desk and stared him right in the face. Over the next few weeks, he urged me, begged me, pleaded with me, cajoled me, flattered me, in short did everything except suggest I offer money to Mr Nguyen to persuade him to issue the visas. To no avail. Mr Nguyen was implacable, and eventually we gave up.

Eight months later, when we had nearly forgotten about the whole thing, the visas finally did come through. Although the initial excitement had gone, and a few other journalists had beaten us to it, Cambodia was still a rare enough dateline to make the offer irresistible. Of course, there was no formal guarantee we would be able to enter Cambodia, now completely under Vietnamese control, but Mr Nguyen smiled and winked encouragingly. First, however, we would have to go to Hanoi, where we would get the necessary clearance and pick up an 'interpreter'. So, making a virtue out of a necessity, we decided to spend two weeks filming first in Vietnam, north and south, starting in Hanoi and finishing in Saigon, now called Ho Chi Minh City, from where we would drive to Phnom Penh for our real assignment in Cambodia. If everything went according to plan, we would produce eight or ten special reports for News at Ten, with the Cambodian 'specials' as the climax.

Mr Nguyen, whom I had not seen since our disastrous lunch, was on his best behaviour, dishing out the visas with hardly a cough or a giggle. But he had one last request, which he delivered with so many teeth showing it obviously had the weight of an instruction. 'Mr Sandy, ugh, we in embassy here, and Foreign Ministry in Hanoi, would like copies of all your reports. For archives, you understand!' He giggled loudly.

'It will be my pleasure, Mr Nguyen. I will send you two

video cassettes when we have edited everything, one for you, one for the Foreign Ministry in Hanoi.'

Mr Nguyen came close to bowing. We then formally shook hands and I walked out, only eight months late.

On Sunday 31 August, my crew and I left London for Bangkok by PanAm, when it was still one of the great airlines of the world. Aboard the 747 Jumbo I had with me Charles Morgan, a bright young ITN cameraman who had studied design at Sussex University and was the son of the maker of the Morgan sports car, and Hugh Thomson, an experienced sound recordist with whom I had worked on many assignments, including Vietnam in 1975. We refuelled at Frankfurt and Delhi, finally reaching Bangkok early next morning, coming in to land over the green rice paddies and *klongs*, the canals which intersect the countryside like a patchwork of silver. The office had told us we would have a five or six hour wait before the flight to Hanoi, via Vientiane, the capital of Laos, so I had planned to take a taxi to the Oriental, one of my favourite hotels, and have breakfast on the terrace watching the sampans go by on the great, chocolate brown Chao Phraya River. But when we went to check the time of the Hanoi flight, eventually finding the Air Vietnam office hidden away on the second floor, they told us the flight left at 10.30, not 13.30 as we had been advised. I had a nasty moment, thinking we would have looked bloody silly sitting admiring the view from the Oriental while the once-weekly flight to Hanoi took off without us.

In fact, ITN had not been so far out after all; the plane, a twin-engined Russian Antonov, took off two hours late. In considerable discomfort – I have very long legs and there was practically no leg-room – we bumbled our way north-east across the peaceful plains of Thailand until, a couple of hours later, we dropped down towards the imposing expanse of the Mekong River which makes the border between Thailand and Laos, and landed at Vientiane to refuel. Glad to stretch our legs, we strolled over to the terminal building which seemed little changed since my last visit in 1975, when with a planeload of other journalists I had been flown out of Saigon by the Vietnamese army, after being virtual prisoners for three weeks. As we entered the transit lounge a remarkable sight greeted us. More than a hundred young men, aged about fifteen or sixteen, all dressed in identical light grey pinstripe suits, white shirts, red ties and polished black shoes, sat in neat rows awaiting their flight.

'Where are they going?' I enquired in French of a pretty Air Lao ground hostess. 'À Moscou,' she said. 'They are all going to school in the Soviet Union.'

'Really. Going back after the holidays?'

'Ah, non. They are going for the first time.'

'How long will they be there for?'

'Five years.'

'And how often will they be allowed home to see their families?'

'Jamais!' she said. 'They do not come home at all, not until the end of the five years.'

Poor kids, I thought. I wanted to ask her what she, as a Laotian, thought of her fellow-countrymen being hijacked to the Soviet Union for five years to be brought up as little Communists, but she had more urgent business to attend to and I found myself addressing her shapely back.

After waiting for two hours, we were told that due to bad weather over Hanoi we would be spending the night in Vientiane and continuing the journey next day. Our luggage was brought and loaded into an old rattletrap of a bus which was to take us to our hotel. As we trundled down the wide boulevards, I noticed with relief that the city, although even more down-at-heel, had retained much of its old charm. Vientiane is really two cities, and although the French colonial town is superimposed on the old Buddhist city, the marriage is quite a happy one.

The French contribution to Indo-China is, on the whole, stylish, although sometimes the desire to export *la gloire*

39

goes a bit far. In Saigon, for example, they built an imitation Champs-Elysées as well as a copy of the Paris Opera. In Vientiane, they went one better, leaving behind on the banks of the Mekong not only a Champs-Elysées, but a smaller version of the Arc de Triomphe as well. As we drove on, my eye was constantly captured by the graceful silhouettes of countless *wats*, Buddhist monasteries, although there were few *bonzes* to be seen in their saffron robes. Unlike the Chinese in Tibet, the Pathet Lao had not destroyed the outward symbols of religion, the temples and monasteries, but were relying on neglect and decay to do the job for them.

Our destination was not, alas, the dignified old French hotel on the banks of the river, but another, lesser establishment called the Apollo, a misnomer if ever there was one. Apollo, if I remembered correctly, was the god of light, poetry and music, and there was little of that in evidence. This Apollo was shabby and run-down, its ochre paint peeling and once-white walls blackened by rain, just the sort of place Air Vietnam would consign its passengers to. Since the day was still comparatively young, I rang the British chargé d'affaires, Bernard Dobbs, who invited us to his house for a drink that evening. Over a welcome Scotch and water, I told him about the young Laotians we had seen at the airport, in their pinstripe suits and red ties, en route for Moscow.

'Oh, yes,' he said, 'the Russians run Laos. There are a hell of a lot of them around, about 1500 in Vientiane alone, at the last count. The place is completely under the thumb of Moscow.'

Later, he dropped us off at Chez Marcelle, one of the few places in Vientiane which catered for foreigners. It sounded like a left-bank bistro but in fact was the kind of poky little dark dive to which Communist countries used to relegate anyone as suspect as a Western businessman or journalist. Things looked up, however, when two nice, smiling Lao girls advanced to welcome us and sat us down in solitary splendour at a corner table.

'What you like drink?' they asked, giggling. Unlike male Oriental giggling, which is frankly embarrassing, female Oriental giggling is delightful.

'What have you got?' asked Charles.

'We 'ave beer,' giggled one, and then added what sounded like 'and we 'ave a honded pee-ers.'

'A hundred pee-ers?' I asked, baffled.

'A honded pee-ers! Sco' wikky!' Their smiles never wavered.

Light dawned. 'Oh, A Hundred Pipers Scotch whisky!'

'Yes, a honded pee-ers Sco' wikky!' They both giggled.

'For a nasty moment,' said Hugh, 'I thought you said something rather different.' We ordered three doubles. Choosing dinner was easier.

'What have you got tonight?'

'Chik-ken.' Giggle.

'Anything else?'

'Jus' chik-ken.'

'Okay, three chicken, please.'

It was undoubtedly free-range, rather stringy and tough, but tasty. At the end of the evening, which grew progressively more convivial, thanks to the giggling and the Hundred Pipers, we asked for the bill.

It was not cheap but on the other hand not outrageous. The only surprise was that it was presented in US dollars. Then I remembered Bernard Dobbs saying earlier, 'You can live in Vientiane for a long time and never use a single kip.'

As we drove to the airport early next morning, we caught sight of the Mekong, its mile-wide, rich tea-coloured expanse dwarfing the sampans and ferries plying across it. One of Asia's most majestic rivers, the Mekong rises in the mountains of Qinghai Province in south-west China, not far from Tibet, at the start of a 2500-mile journey; flows south-east into Laos, where it makes the border first with Burma, then with Thailand, sweeps into Cambodia which it divides and enriches, debouches into Vietnam where, after a mighty meander through its own vast, rich and mysterious delta, one of the great rice-growing areas of the world, it finally discharges itself in a red-brown flood heavy with silt into the South China Sea. I thought it was the most impressive thing I saw in Vientiane.

The airport was almost empty, the pin-striped students had departed for their five years' hard labour and we boarded our flight for Hanoi without any more delay. From Vientiane we flew north-east again over the high jungle-clad mountains of central Laos, passing on our left the Plain of Jars where the French fought the Pathet Lao in the early days of the Communist insurrection, crossed the Vietnamese border and descended over the Red River Delta towards Hanoi, the craters left behind by the American bombing pockmarking the flooded plain. As we walked to the terminal building, I noticed a line of MiG fighters on the tarmac, shrouded in protective covers, and a number of anti-aircraft gun emplacements dotted round the perimeter, as if they were expecting an attack at any moment. Inside, waiting beyond the immigration counter was a small, smiling, bright-eyed Vietnamese of indeterminate age who now advanced, like a stoat on three rabbits, displaying a mouthful of gold teeth.

'Welcome to Hanoi,' he said giving a slight bow and extending a small, sinewy hand. 'My name is Kanh [he pronounced it Kang] and I am official guide and interpreter for you' trip.' He flashed gold teeth at each of us in turn and led the way to an old Russian-made Volga saloon into which he and the porters, exhorting one another in explosive sibilants, somehow managed to cram all our camera equipment and personal luggage, more than twenty pieces in all.

I felt tremendously excited. I had been trying to get to Hanoi for more than ten years, and now, after many setbacks, here we were. When I first tried, in 1967 or 1968, at the height of the Vietnam War, I consulted James Cameron, doyen of foreign correspondents in his day and one of the few Western journalists who held the open sesame to North Vietnam. Over a glass or two of whisky in the bar of the Waldorf Hotel in the Aldwych, a stone's throw from the old ITN building in Kingsway, he said in that self-deprecatory, gentle Dundee accent, 'You just have to keep trying. Whenever I was somewhere that had a Vietnamese embassy, I used to trot along and apply for a visa, on the basis that one day I might be lucky. When I was in Paris, for example, or in Prague, I'd go along and fill in another form and hope for the best. And then one day, out of the blue, it worked. I got the visa. That's what happened to me. I just kept applying and applying and one day, up it came. I was just as surprised as anyone else.'

The handful of Western journalists who did manage to breach Hanoi's propaganda defences – James Cameron and Harrison Salisbury of the *New York Times* were two of the very few – got their scoops, but at a price. Most of their reports were heavily in favour of Hanoi and critical of, if not downright hostile to Washington.

'Where are we staying, Mr Kanh?' I asked as we drove out of the airport.

'Very nice, modern hotel, call Thanh Loi. All foreigners stay Thanh Loi.'

Kanh said it would take an hour to reach the hotel, but it seemed much less, because we passed so many landmarks which had become household names to those of us who had reported the Vietnam War in the 1960s and 1970s. We crossed the Duong and Red Rivers, both very high, their waters red with silt, and the most famous landmark of all, the Paul Doumer Bridge, the target of so many American bombing raids. Although it was repeatedly damaged, the North Vietnamese repaired it so quickly and efficiently that it began to seem indestructible. It still looked massively strong, dwarfing the stream of bicycles ridden by peasants

43

in conical straw hats moving slowly along its two, narrow, single lanes. Between them, somewhat incongruously, ran a railway line.

I was quite unprepared for the beauty of Hanoi. Broad boulevards criss-crossed the centre of the city and swept round a large lake with an island in the middle. On the island, to which you could walk by a chain bridge, stood an old temple and another edifice called the Turtle Tower. Magnificent trees lined the boulevards, soaring up into the late summer sky, and at one point a huge banyan burst forth between two houses. The handsome, nineteenth-century French colonial buildings still wore their original green and white paint, and in the absence of any high-rise buildings to spoil the skyline, the city had kept its looks, like a dowager duchess who has aged but is still beautiful. The general air of harmony was reinforced by the lack of noise and pollution and although there always seemed to be thousands of Vietnamese on the streets, they moved almost silently on their bicycles, of which there were perhaps a million in the city. Almost everyone had one, but there were virtually no private cars in the whole of Hanoi.

We had to drive out of the city to reach the hotel, past a whole series of small lakes, on the last of which stood the Cuban-built Thanh Loi. It looked precisely what it was; an ugly, shoddy, Stalinist monstrosity, which exactly reflected in architectural terms the ugly, shoddy political system that gave birth to it. At a guess it was only half full and, apart from ourselves, was inhabited exclusively by large, over-weight Russian technicians and their wives, who looked unhappy and out of place in this seedy backwater miles away from the rest of the city. Our rooms were as depressing as the rest of the hotel – the curtain in mine sagging disconsolately where it had come away from its hooks – and although the windows looked out on the lake, the water, on closer inspection, turned out to be stagnant and smelly.

44

Having installed ourselves, we wanted to discuss our programme with Mr Kanh and in the process discover what he was like. In Saigon, after the Communist take-over I had found the new Communist bosses to be cautious but inflexible. Now that they had had five years to consolidate their rule, and we were on their home ground of Hanoi, I expected Mr Kanh and his fellow officials to be equally inflexible, although, I hoped, more confident. But there was no harm in explaining exactly what we wanted.

'Mr Kanh, first of all, tomorrow we want to film in Hanoi, the city, the people, the bicycles . . .'

'Yeah, yeah,' he nodded, 'no problem!'

'Good . . . the bridges, the . . .'

Kanh winced. 'Which bridge?'

'The Paul Doumer.'

Kanh looked serious. 'The Paul Doumer is very sensitive, we have to see . . . Very sensitive, Mr Gull . . .' He sucked his teeth, letting the enormity of our request hang for a moment in the stagnant air of my room.

I decided not to press the point. 'Then, the next day, Thursday, we'd like to go up north, to the border, as we discussed with the embassy in London. Is that all right?'

'Lang Son, on border with China. No problem. But it long way, so we must leave early.'

'Of course. What do you call early?'

'Seven. Leave hotel at seven.'

'Okay. And then, possibly, on Friday or Saturday, Ho Chi Minh's house and tomb? Which day is best, to get the crowds?'

'It doesn't matter. You get crowds every day.' But Kanh did not want to make it sound too easy. 'Mr Gull, Paul Doumel Bridge very difficult. I go now talk to important official. Maybe he say yes, maybe no. Not so easy.' He got up to go, then dropped his voice conspiratorially.

'Mr Gull, you need change into dong?' Dong was the local currency.

45

'Yes. Perhaps we can go to the bank tomorrow?'

Kanh was helpfulness itself. 'Mr Gull, no need go to bank. I change for you. I give you better rate, Mr Gull.' He permitted himself a small giggle.

'Oh, really? What rate do you give, Mr Kanh?'

'You have US dollar? Okay. Bank of Vietnam give one point two dong for US dollar. I give you one point five.'

Charles, Hugh and I looked at one another, the same thought in each of our minds, but no one said anything. Kanh hovered, expectantly.

'What's the black market rate?' Charles asked.

'Same. One point five dong for one US dollar. I give you best rate!' Kanh was all injured innocence, but it did not sound right. We knew the real black market rate must be much higher than that, and that he was blackmailing us.

'Okay, Mr Kanh, we'll each give you a hundred dollars. You can bring the dong tomorrow.'

The dollars disappeared into his pocket so quickly I wondered for a moment if we had actually handed them over. He gave us a full mouth of gold teeth and was gone through the door, like a genie escaping from a bottle.

Charles exploded. 'I'll bet you anything he's ripping us off, the crooked little bastard. One and a half rotten bloody dong to the dollar. The real rate must be ten or more. He's making a packet, the crooked little sod!'

'I couldn't agree more. But the little sod does have us over a barrel and he knows it. If we go somewhere else and get a better rate, he could turn nasty. Report us for changing money illegally on the black market – that's a serious offence in a country like this. The last thing we want is to be thrown out of Vietnam on a currency fiddle, it's just not worth it. And look at it this way. It doesn't make much difference to us, and it also gives us a hold over him. If he delivers on the filming, then it's worth it. But if he's obstructive, you know, we can change all we need at the bank and tell him, sorry, if you want our dollars you've got to deliver the permissions.

'What they call performance-related,' Charles said.

'Exactly.'

Chapter
4

When Kanh arrived next day, he was all smiles. 'Mr Gull, I have your dong, and I also have nice surprise fo' you.'

'Oh, good, what's that?'

'I have special permission fo' you take pikcha Paul Doumel Bridge!'

'Great,' said Charles, raising his eyebrows and nodding, as if to say, you were right, the little so-and-so has got the message.

'How did you manage that, Mr Kanh?' I asked.

He giggled happily. 'I talk very important official in Ministry Information. He said this request very, very, difficult, and he not suya. Maybe take one week, two week, get permission. So then I talk some moah. I say you only stayed Hanoi one week, and that you very good people. So after we talk some moah, he say, okay. As very special favour, you can take pikcha Paul Doumel Bridge.'

'Let's go and do it now,' Charles said, 'before he changes his mind.'

The Ministry had supplied us with a large, black, Russian limousine, with driver. Kanh sat in front beside the driver, enjoying the importance of his role. We three sat rather squashed up in the back, but the fascination of the world outside the car windows more than made up for the slight

48

discomfort within. As we cruised along, the morning sun gilded the straw-hatted tide of silently pedalling Vietnamese men and women, riding their bicycles as if in limbo, with no expression on their faces. The comparatively few vehicles we saw were nearly all military; anything civilian tended to be old and battered.

Observing the North Vietnamese en masse from the comfort of our limousine encouraged an exaggerated sense of superiority, but it also confirmed what I had always known; that here was an exceptionally ordered and disciplined society which did exactly as it was told by a small, ruthless oligarchy – the Vietnamese Communist Party. All of us who knew the country at all had always taken for granted the apparently infinite stoicism which the Vietnamese had demonstrated all through the long wars of liberation, first against the French and then against the Americans. But now, in the middle of Hanoi, I found myself wondering if it was not all too good to be true. Five years after the end of the war, they appeared just as regimented and poor as ever. Did they still worship the shade of Uncle Ho, or did their deadpan expressions as they rode past hide some dissentient thoughts? Perhaps it was impossible for a foreigner to find the answer; perhaps the answer did not matter very much. Like Alexander the Great's Greeks or the early Romans, the capacity of the Vietnamese to endure hardship and suffering was in the classical mould.

These thoughts lingered in my mind as I watched Charles filming the Paul Doumer Bridge. From where we stood, below it and off to one side, it looked more vulnerable. Its continued survival, despite American bombing, must have seemed to the man in the street little short of miraculous. It is, after all, to the Vietnamese what Westminster Bridge is to Londoners, or the Golden Gate to San Franciscans. Kanh stood just behind the camera, muttering from time to time. 'You see, Mr Gull, this permission not easy! Very difficult!

No permission, no pikcha Paul Doumel Bridge! Hee, hee, hee,' he giggled embarrassingly.

By now, Charles had taken the bridge from every conceivable angle and was ready to move on. We drove back to the city, where the cyclists still swept in an unending stream past the lake in the centre. As we glided down the boulevard, Charles suddenly said to Kanh, 'Stop here, can we?' He turned to me, excitedly. 'I've got an idea. We'll put you on a bicycle, I'll be in the boot of the car, and we'll shoot you doing your piece to camera with all the cyclists riding along behind you. It'll look great.' He rubbed his hands gleefully.

The idea appealed to me. Charles was nothing if not original. That's why I had lobbied hard to have him come on the trip. I wanted someone with imagination who would make the story as exciting pictorially as I hoped to make it journalistically.

Kanh, entering into the spirit of the thing, went off to get a bicycle, while Charles wedged the boot open and installed himself and the camera. Kanh reappeared soon afterwards with my bicycle, a typically sturdy Chinese 'sit up and beg' model, and we were ready. The car pulled slowly out into the traffic and, wobbling slightly, I set off in pursuit, my fellow cyclists staring in some amazement as this 'big nose', as the Vietnamese pejoratively call Westerners, intruded into their orderly ranks. But no one dared to laugh; they knew, after all, that the car was official.

I had my piece to camera all prepared and, although the words seemed to go quite well, it was not always easy to keep exactly the same distance behind the car as it manoeuvred through the throng of cyclists. By the time we had done it three times we had made a complete tour of the lake and were back at our starting point. Being a perfectionist, Charles insisted on doing it again and again and again, until I estimated I had made four or five circuits of the lake, and had delivered the same 'take' to Charles's indifferent black lens twenty-odd times. By the time he was satisfied, my legs were heavy with the unaccustomed exercise and he must have been stiff from crouching in the boot of the car.

To celebrate the completion of our first report from Hanoi, we stopped for a drink at the elegant old French hotel in the centre, where James Cameron told me he had stayed, long before they built the Thanh Loi. I immediately liked its old-fashioned, high-ceilinged colonial atmosphere and asked Kanh if we could move there from the dreary and incon-venient Cuban pile, where, among other things, it was almost impossible to get a taxi in the evenings. Firmly, Kanh shook his head. 'Sorry, Mr Gull. Not possible stay in National Hotel.'

'Why not? There are other journalists staying here. I've just seen someone I know.'

'Some friendly journalists, maybe.' He gave a smug smile. 'Friendly' meant Communist or fellow-travelling. 'But all other journalists from capitalist countries must stay in Thanh Loi.' Not even dollars, it seemed, could alter this rule.

We finished our beers and drove back to the Thanh Loi, passing the chain of lakes which make Hanoi such an enchanting city. It was almost dusk and the setting sun had turned them into sheets of silver. Along the paths beside the lakes young Vietnamese lovers cycled slowly, the girl usually riding pillion and holding her boyfriend round the waist, or even lower. In their long, white *ao dhais*, the traditional, sheathlike dress with a slit up one side, they looked ethereal, almost pre-Raphaelite. Other couples strolled among the trees, or sat on the grass in the parks, where apparently the police did not bother them, a rare sign of relaxation in such a regimented society.

Kanh dropped us at the hotel, reminding us that we would have an early start next morning. I fortified myself with a large glass of Scotch before walking down the corridor to the dining-room where, as we already knew, the

51

food, a poor imitation of Western cuisine, would be pretty disgusting. No wonder the Russian technicians and their enormous wives, who had had to suffer the shortcomings of the Thanh Loi kitchen much longer than us, looked so miserable. Back at my room, as I put the key in the door I looked down the dimly-lit corridor to where, at the far end, it broadened out into a kind of lobby. At that precise moment, a small, four-legged animal shot across the empty space, heading for the lake. At first I thought it was a cat. But the movement was unmistakable. It was not a cat: it was a rat.

To reach Lang Son, near the Chinest border one hundred miles north-east of Hanoi, took us four hours, largely because we had to keep slowing down for all the cyclists. Inevitably, whenever we met a lorry or, very occasionally, a car coming the other way, there would be half a dozen cyclists in front of us, forcing the driver to slow right down. The first half of the journey took us through the vivid green rice paddies of the Red River Delta, almost as rich a rice-growing area as the Mekong Delta in the south. At one point we had a vivid example of how manpower, or rather womanpower, was an essential ingredient of the Vietnamese economy. A long line of women dressed in black pyjamas and straw hats, possibly as many as a hundred of them, were scooping water out of a flooded rice paddy with a wicker basket, attached to a rope, which was passed from hand to hand to the end of a line, where the last woman tipped it into a canal. It was a hugely laborious and labour intensive operation, but with a population of 64 million labour was one thing the Vietnamese did have plenty of; and it was the way they built the Paul Doumer Bridge and the Ho Chi Minh Trail.

After the Delta, the country became more rugged until, as we neared Lang Son, steep-sided, sugar loaf mountains rose high above the road. The Chinese had invaded the year before in retaliation for what they claimed were unprovoked

52

Vietnamese incursions into their territory, occupying Lang Son for several weeks. When they left, they blew up all the public buildings; we were shown shattered schools and government offices which looked as if they had been demolished by an earthquake. Opposite the market, a Chinese-style Hoa temple, all ferocious dragons and upturned eaves, lay in ruins; only a large Buddha had survived more or less intact, whether by accident or design it was impossible to tell. We drove on towards the border town of Dong Da, which the Chinese had also demolished, but were stopped in our tracks by the absence of a road bridge, according to Kanh also blown up by the departing Chinese.

But the violence was all in the past. A group of friendly Vietnamese soldiers were hoeing happily in a field beside the road, their AK47 rifles stacked casually in a corner. One was washing his boots in the river. A sense of desolation hung over the countryside, however: perhaps because there seemed to be so few civilians about. A few hundred yards away the rusting shell of a burnt-out steam locomotive and several coaches stood forlornly on the railway line which had once run to the border. The Chinese must have caught the Lang Son to Hanoi express by surprise. Strangely, nothing was being done to get rid of the wreckage. Perhaps the Vietnamese government was too poor to rebuild Lang Son, but I also got the impression that it was in no hurry to do so. In the propaganda war which the Vietnamese waged non-stop with the Chinese, the ruins of Lang Son were potent ammunition, a constant reminder of just how 'treacherous' and 'aggressive' the Chinese were.

We arrived back in Hanoi late and rather tired, but with something to look forward to. We had been invited to dinner by the British Consul, John Ramsden, and a young colleague, Mark Whynbourne. They lived in a charming old house and gave us a glass of Scotch and a dinner that was doubly delicious after the squalors of the Thanh Loi. Ramsden was a mine of information about Hanoi and the North

53

Vietnamese, although the Hanoi government did its best to pretend he was not there. He never saw the Foreign Minister, for example, or any other senior official; in fact, they treated him as if he were a non-person. Although accredited to Hanoi, his real job lay in the South, in Saigon, where thousands of the million or so ethnic Chinese were Hong Kong citizens. Most of them wanted to leave the sinking ship of Vietnam – these were the days before the great exodus of the 'boat people' – and for the same reasons. There was no work, no money and no prospects, and as ethnic Chinese they felt discriminated against. John Ramsden and his colleague did not seem to mind being ostracised, being quite happy to go their own way, usually by bicycle, and observe the local scene with a practised, diplomatic eye.

Over dinner, John explained that housing conditions were appalling by Western standards. Most Vietnamese families lived in one room, nine or ten of them all crowded together. Often they lived not above, but behind the shop. In many cases, the acute shortage of space forced families to take it in turns to sleep, adopting a rota system, and using the beds twenty-four hours a day. Sometimes they lived, literally, on the street. In the summer months the whole family would work, eat and sleep on the pavement, rather as in Calcutta; in the winter, which can be cold in Hanoi, they somehow had to find shelter or freeze. While the parks were the preserve of young lovers, less romantically inclined Vietnamese would congregate of an evening opposite Ho Chi Minh's tomb, strolling up and down to take the air or just sitting on the pavement and chatting.

The tomb, which we filmed next day, is the main tourist attraction of the country, something which every visitor is expected to pay his or her reverential respects to. It stands on one of the main boulevards, an imposing red marble edifice, a copy no doubt of Lenin's Tomb in Red Square. Here lies the Father of the Nation, it proclaims, to whom every citizen, at some point in his life, must make obeisance. It reminded me in that sense of Tienanmen, the Square of Heavenly Peace in Peking, which every Chinese had to see once in his lifetime, not I suspect because of the square itself but because of the huge portrait of Mao Tse-tung which dominates it.

We climbed up the steps to Ho's last resting place, following a long line of peasants and their wives, all dressed in their Sunday best. At the top of the steps, we filed into a large, air-conditioned chamber in the centre of which, under a brightly-lit glass case, Uncle Ho lay peacefully, a small smile on his lips, wispy beard neatly combed, his frail body clad in an immaculate Mao suit. I only had time to reflect momentarily on his remarkable career as a revolutionary; the little *plongeur* in Paris who became a founder-member of the French Communist Party, started the war of independence against the French and went on to inspire the war against the South and the Americans, although he did not live to see the final victory, dying in 1969. Then we were hustled on by the gentle tide of adoring peasants, as devout as any churchgoers. Perhaps they saw in Ho not just the liberator he undoubtedly was, but a god as well, a worthy addition to the Buddhist pantheon to which all good Vietnamese, before Communism, had always prayed. No doubt, as in Russia, once you stripped away the Communist trappings, the Vietnamese would turn out to be just as loyal to their ancestral faith. We left as we had entered, under the watchful eye of the ramrod-stiff, white-gloved guards who stood at attention, bayonets fixed, at each corner of the chamber.

After the tomb, a subdued Kanh led us to Ho's house, a beautifully simple wooden bungalow in the grounds of the old, ochre Governor's palace, once occupied by General de Lattre de Tassigny, the last French Governor in Indo-China. Ho was too modest to occupy the big house and deliberately chose to live in the small two-up and one down – bedroom and study upstairs and meeting room downstairs – with a carp pond in front. He fed the carp every morning, the legend has it – they still floated fatly in the greenish water –

and planted the grapefuit trees which shaded the small garden.

That evening, we went at Kanh's invitation to the nearest thing to a night-club Hanoi could boast. Like Chez Marcelle in Phnom Penh, it was dark and dingy, but unlike Chez Marcelle it could offer no Hundred Pipers; only lukewarm beer and coffee, which seemed to be the favourite tipple. Kanh explained that people had so little money that even if more exotic drinks had been on offer, no one would have been able to buy them; and customers like ourselves were so rare they did not really count.

'This is not for Westerners. This special place for Vietnamese!' he said proudly. It was the most bohemian hang-out in Hanoi, a favourite haunt of poets and artists – although there did not seem to be any there that night. Kanh even hinted, inscrutably, that if dissidence was to be found anywhere, it was here. As we drank the imported beer, I asked him how he had come to acquire his present job. Like every able-bodied Vietnamese I had met, he had fought in the war. Then he manged to get a job in the Foreign Ministry, serving abroad in various 'friendly' countries. At some point he had been transferred to the Committee for Cultural Relations with Foreign Countries. I wondered later if his liking for the bottle and generally louche behaviour had brought about this apparent demotion. Or had his Communist bosses decided that, being a bit of a fly boy himself, Kanh was the right man to keep an eye on the unreliable cadres of the capitalist media? But if he had come down in the world, Kanh gave no sign of being a disappointed man: quite the opposite. Accepting another beer, he turned to me as if in great confidence.

'Mr Gull, I want to ask you something very important.' He took a swig of beer and wiped his mouth with the back of his hand. 'After we finish here in Hanoi, we go Saigon, yes?'

'That's what we agreed, isn't it?'

He nodded. 'Then, after one week Saigon, we go Cambodia, yes?'

'That's what we proposed to the Ministry, Mr Kanh. I didn't know you were coming with us, so I suppose it depends . . .'

'On what, Mr Gull?' The beady eyes did not blink.

'Well, this is really a decision for the Cambodian authorities, is it not?' I knew, of course, that although Cambodia was nominally run by a Cambodian government under Heng Samrin, a pro-Vietnamese puppet, it was really under the control of the Vietnamese and their 150,000 strong army of occupation.

Kanh showed signs of considerable agitation. 'Mr Gull, I talk Ministry. They say not safe you go alone in Cambodia. You must have escort. Cambodians bad peoples.'

'Not all, surely, Mr Kanh.'

'No, not alls, Mr Gull. But somes. Ministry say me I must go with you to see you safe.' He took another gulp of beer while he marshalled his clinching argument. 'You mus' have Vietnamese person, like me, who speak English and know army peoples. Else, Mr Gull . . .' He looked extremely serious. 'Else, Mr Gull, they not let you go Cambodia!'

'Oh, but they've agreed we can go to Cambodia. We've already got our visas, as you know.' I chose my words with care. 'You see, Mr Kanh, I thought they might give us a Cambodian escorting officer?'

The thought was so loathsome that Kanh merely shook his head in disbelief. 'Cambodian escort, Mr Gull? You no understand! You *must* have Vietnamese person who can arrange everything with army peoples. Otherwise, you not able go any place outside Phnom Penh.' There was a note of desperation in Kanh's voice. I wondered why he was so determined to come with us. Was it to keep an eye on our movements in Cambodia, on behalf of Vietnamese intelligence? Was he worried by the thought that the goose that laid the golden eggs, in the shape of Charles, Hugh and

57

myself, was about to fly away? Or was there some other, personal motive, which remained hidden? Kanh remained inscrutable.

Perhaps it was the strain of pulling all these complicated strings to produce exactly the desired effect which caused Kanh to reveal a very different side to his character the next evening. We were bidden to dinner by his boss, Mr Vu Quoc Uy, acting chairman of the Committee for Cultural Relations with Foreign Countries. Being capitalist roaders, we were not to be dignified by direct association with the Foreign Ministry, but kept at arm's length via Mr Uy's committee. He himself was small, like most Vietnamese, with glasses and lots of teeth, clearly a hardened apparatchik of the old school. Mr Uy's hospitality was lavish, with dish following dish relentlessly, and although the snails were quite good, I began to find the surfeit of food boring and exhausting. Although not exactly a stranger to Vietnamese table manners, I also found the combination of Mr Uy's masticatory processes and the lecture he delivered about the iniquities of the West in general and of the Western media in particular extremely tiresome.

We drank some foul-tasting alcohol like Chinese mao-tai, and after several toasts, which I tried to avoid by sipping rather than swallowing, I noticed that Kanh, at the end of the table, was steadily getting more and more drunk. Not only did his table manners become increasingly unpleasant, but with every succeeding toast, his normally sallow complexion became noticeably redder and his giggle louder. At one point Mr Uy glanced venomously in his direction and spat out what sounded like a sharp rebuff. But Kanh was too far gone to care, leaning sideways out of his chair to make what I assumed were lewd suggestions to the extremely pretty waitress. His disgraceful behaviour did have one good result, however; it brought the festivities to an abrupt end, Mr Uy rising to his feet with an angry glare

58

in the direction of an unrepentant Kanh and stalking off with a curt farewell.

The following day Kanh arrived late at the Thanh Loi, obviously nursing a nasty hangover. I decided to attack. I wanted one shot in particular before we left Hanoi; a group picture of all the members of the Politburo, which was to all intents and purposes the government of Vietnam. I had asked Kanh several times if he could arrange it and he had been evasive; I suspected it was too difficult, even for his powers of persuasion. But I decided to make one last attempt; only one thing, I knew, would influence him.

'You know, Mr Kanh, we may not need to change any more money.'

Kanh stuttered in pain and surprise. 'You not need change any more money? I not understand, Mr Gull. How you pay hotel bill when you leave Hanoi?' He licked his lips hungrily to see how I would get out of that one.

I decided to lie outrageously. 'My office in London has sent a message to the British Consul in Hanoi, asking him to lend us money if we are short.'

Kanh spluttered in consternation. 'Short. But you not short of dollars, Mr Gull!'

'No,' I agreed. 'But London does not know that. You see, if we don't spend our dollars here, we'll have more to spend in Hong Kong.'

Kanh's eyes glistened at the mention of Eldorado. 'Hong Kong? You go Hong Kong after Cambodia? You not say this befo'.'

I shrugged. 'I did not think you would be interested, Mr Kanh.'

There was a pause, while Kanh sucked his teeth in reflection. 'Mr Gull, you know you want take pikcha of Politburo leaders at meeting?'

'Yes, Mr Kanh, but I had rather given up. I thought it wasn't going to be possible.'

He turned on his most ingratiating smile. 'Now is possible. I talk big official in cabinet yesterday and he say, in yo' case, okay! We can take pikcha tomorrow.'

'Tomorrow's our last day. Are you sure, now, Mr Kanh?'

'Sure, sure, Mr Gull. I promise.' His smile grew even wider and less sincere.

'Right, that's very good news. London will be very pleased.' The picture was a specific request from the ITN Foreign Desk. 'Oh, by the way, Mr Kanh.' I gave a discreet cough.

'Yes, Mr Gull.' He was all ears.

'I'm, er, we're getting a little low on . . . local money. Do you think you could . . . ?'

'Of course, Mr Gull, first thing tomorrow. How much you like?'

'Oh, a couple of hundred each? That be all right?'

Kanh's smile revealed all his teeth, especially the gold ones, his hangover cured.

We got the picture of the Politburo because, as I had suspected, they were already having one taken for domestic publicity purposes. Vietnamese Television and several photographers were at the offices of the Socialist Workers' and Peasants' Party, to give the Vietnamese Communist Party its official name, when we arrived.

The assembled party leaders made a fascinating study; the picture before it was retouched. They were nearly all in their seventies, many of them red-faced, notably Pham Van Dong, the Prime Minister, who looked as if he might be a candidate for a heart attack at any moment. His highly-coloured complexion, I was told later but possibly apocryphally, was due to his consumption of a bottle of Scotch a day. Then there was the small, chunky figure of General Giap, Vietnam's most famous soldier who defeated the French so devastatingly at Dien Bien Phu in 1954 that it brought down the government and led to France's withdrawal from Indo-China. Giap was a military genius, trained in France, but most of his colleagues looked like the peasants they were; shrewd, no doubt, and tough, but hardly capable, one would have thought, of getting the better of the French and then, even more surprisingly, forcing the Americans to abandon what had become a hopeless war. Yet that is exactly what they had done; thanks to that remarkable tenacity which Ho Chi Minh knew he could count on.

Years later, I was fascinated to see recognition of the Vietnamese capacity to endure from no less a person than General Norman Schwarzkopf, of Gulf War fame, who served two tours in Vietnam, one as an adviser attached to the South Vietnamese Airborne. In his autobiography, *It Doesn't Take a Hero*, he recalls how, in 1965, his unit had overrun a Vietcong headquarters and captured a directive from Ho Chi Minh. This said in effect that, despite the increasing number of American troops being sent to Vietnam, 'We're going to win the war against America the same way we won the war against the French: not on the battlefield, but in the enemy's homeland. All you have to do is hang on. The American people are not tough enough to see this war through and we are. We have fought for twenty years; we can fight another twenty years; before then, they will give up and not support their troops any more and we will claim victory.' Schwarzkopf says he and his fellow officers dismissed the claim as a joke, adding: 'But Uncle Ho had known what he was talking about – he was an astute student of the western mind and understood his enemy better than we understood ourselves.'

In the afternoon, we visited the war museum in Hanoi where the American bombing raids were re-enacted in graphic detail with the aid of film and sound track shot at the time. Naturally, the presentation emphasised the courage and skill of the Vietnamese anti-aircraft gunners who brought down considerable numbers of American jets using Russian and Chinese guns and SAM ground-to-air missiles. Outside, we inspected some of their handiwork, the remains of a B-52 claimed to have been shot down over Hanoi – a remarkable feat since it normally bombs from a height of 40,000 feet – and wreckage from other American jets, some of which had taken part in the raids on the Paul Doumer Bridge. Groups of Vietnamese schoolchildren were being taken round and lectured by their teachers about the great victory of the heroic workers' and peasants' army.

Indoctrination was always a favourite tool of Communist ideologues and the Vietnamese Communists were past masters. At one school we visited the pupils were not only taught Russian and politics, but had to attend military classes as well. The headmaster proudly led us to a playing field where boys and girls were practising throwing dummy wooden grenades with a zest that is normally reserved for more congenial sports. But then militarism is the national sport of Vietnam.

On Tuesday 9 September my alarm call woke me at four and we left the hotel half an hour later, checked in at the airport at five – Kanh was at his most officious – ready to depart at six. But unlike Mussolini, the Vietnamese Polit-buro was apparently unable to make the trains and planes run on time, and we did not take off until seven. Our route took us down the coast, with its miles and miles of unspoiled white beaches on our left, the rich, green coastal plain below us and the jungle-clad mountains to our right. The coastal plain is narrow, often only ten or twenty miles wide, and the rest is mountain, so thickly wooded that concealment is easy. This thick jungle canopy covers most of Vietnam and was one of the main reasons the Americans found it impossible to land a knock-out punch on the Communist armies. Ten years later the Russians found the Afghan mountains, although bare, almost as intractable.

After an hour we swung inland, over the Central High-lands, dropping towards the startling green of the Mekong Delta, and cradled in it, the great sprawl of Saigon. I felt excited, and rather tense to be landing again at Tan Son

Nhut, the airport which I had flown into so many times and which was, to me, almost synonomous with the Vietnam war. It looked startlingly familiar; the battered terminal buildings, the pockmarked runways, the bullet and rocket holes in the aircraft hangars and dozens of C130 Hercules transport planes and DC3s, better known as Dakotas. They had been handed over by the Americans to the South Vietnamese Air Force, only to be captured by the North in 1975. Many were now engineless, but the ranks of Huey gunships seemed to be in better working order; it was strange to hear the brittle 'phut-phut-phut' of their rotor blades again, a sound as reminiscent of wartime Saigon as the racket of the Honda scooters and the throb of pop music from the girlie bars in Tu Do.

Chapter
5

Superficially, Saigon seemed to have changed very little. The treacle-coloured, rubbish-filled creek, lined with rickety houses on stilts, which lay halfway between the airport and the city centre, was as evil-smelling as ever. I wondered, once again, how anyone could bear to live beside it. Farther on, the broad, tree-lined streets laid out by the French were just as handsome, and the Avenue Pasteur still as elegant. The Roman Catholic cathedral, one of the most imposing monuments of French colonial rule, glowed warm pink in the sunshine, and the Presidential Palace, which the North Vietnamese army had smashed its way into five years before, still looked vice-regally down the wide sweep of Thong Nhut. But even if the facade had scarcely altered, the life of the city was clearly different; the army of Honda motor scooters which had once clogged Saigon's streets and poisoned its atmosphere with blue petrol fumes had all but disappeared; and there was hardly a car to be seen. Tu Do Street, the once busy heart of Saigon, fashionable in the days of the French but increasingly sleazy towards the end of the American era, was half empty and half dead; the girlie bars and GI hotels closed, the pimps and hangers-on dispersed.

We drove down Tu Do towards Lam Son Square, with its rococo Opera House which the Vietnamese had converted

64

into the National Assembly standing forlornly in the middle. Beside it, the Caravelle Hotel, patronised by most British and American journalists during the war, famous for its hectically busy bar and execrable food, had lost what little character it once possessed and was now some sort of party stronghold. On the opposite side of the square, where little Vietnamese girls with bare feet and dirty but angelic faces used to waylay you on your way to dinner to sell you a wreath of scented jasmine for a few piastres, the Continental was an even sadder sight. The famous terrace known as 'the beach' where, in the evening over a glass of whisky you could observe *le tout Saigon*, pressmen and prostitutes, intellectuals and Vietcong agents, ebb and flow like flotsam on the tide, had simply been torn down and removed, the victim of Communist paranoia. It was too much of a symbol of the old, French, civilised Saigon to be tolerated any longer; who knows, the chance to sit and argue and watch the world go by might have corrupted the youth of what was now called Ho Chi Minh City.

I had stayed in the Continental once, in 1967 – it was always difficult to get a room, unless you were French – and found it wonderfully nostalgic. Graham Greene had been there in the late 1940s and 1950s, when he was reporting the first Indo-China War for the *Sunday Times* and gathering material for *The Quiet American*, which I had read and admired long before I ever saw Vietnam. I read it again while I was staying in the Continental and found it even more poignant, and also surprisingly relevant to the new conflict, fifteen years later. We were not permitted to stay in the Continental either, but instead continued down Tu Do to the old Majestic Hotel, overlooking the Saigon River. I remembered, when it was hit in 1968 by a Vietcong rocket attack launched from the swamps of Gia Dinh across the river, going to call on Mark Frankland of the *Observer* who was staying there. One rocket had landed near his room, making a big hole in the outside wall and giving him a nasty fright, although he was delightfully sanguine about it all.

After settling us in, Kanh, who was obviously itching to start wheeling and dealing, disappeared. We decided to have a drink in the hotel bar – we were the only clients – and afterwards to walk up Tu Do. As we stepped out into the afternoon heat, I suddenly realised I had been in this very spot nearly five and a half years before, the day Saigon fell. Relatively few Western journalists were left in the city, most of the press corps having been flown out in a mad scramble by helicopter from the roof of the American Embassy the day before. A small number of British journalists including myself and a French ITN camera crew had stayed behind. On the morning of Wednesday 30 April 1975, Lucien Bottras, the cameraman, and I had found ourselves outside the Majestic, watching and filming hundreds of desperate Vietnamese trying to escape on two ships tied up at the quayside. There were no gangways and the sides of the ships were so high that people had to climb up on one another's shoulders to reach the decks. The only way to get the old men and women and the babies on board was to pass them up bodily, from hand to hand, like so many parcels. On one of the ships, a small group of heavily armed soldiers had taken over the bridge. They were paratroopers, from the Airborne Division, once the elite of the South Vietnamese army. Now they looked dejected and lost, and small wonder; they were witnessing the collapse of their world, betrayed by their own leaders and their allies, the Americans.

As we walked up Tu Do now, a middle-aged woman, her face deeply sad, shuffled forward and held out a ragged sheaf of papers in cellophane. 'Please,' she said, 'you buy Vietnamese stamps.' It was not a request but a desperate appeal, and as we walked away, I realised that we had added a few more ounces of despair to the burden which was already too much for her. Five years before, Tu Do had exuded vitality, even if it was a corrupt vitality, now it simply seemed sad.

The feeling of a once vibrant city that had been brought to its knees and was now awaiting the *coup de grâce* was reinforced that evening. We took a taxi to one of the only two or three private restaurants left in Saigon, run by a remarkable lady called Madame Dai. John Ramsden, the British Consul in Hanoi, had recommended her warmly, both for her cooking and her interesting political background. Madame Dai had been deputy speaker of the National Assembly in the days of President Thieu, and spoke excellent French. But as a member of the old establishment, she had fallen on hard times. Out of desperation, she had converted part of her own house into a restaurant. It was small, only four or five tables, and deliberately modest, probably because, if not illegal, it was privately-owned and therefore out of tune with the times. When we arrived, she greeted us rather nervously, ushering us to a table in the corner. 'What would you like to drink?' she asked.

'What have you got?'

'Oh, everything, beer, whisky, brandy . . .'

'Scotch?'

'Bien sûr!'

Then, lowering her voice, she indicated three or four Vietnamese men dressed in rough working clothes at a table by the door. 'You see those men over there?' she asked in French. 'Well, they are important party members from Cholon [the Chinese quarter]. They come here almost every night. So you see, we never have any trouble from the police!' She gave a brave smile, but it was a sad smile, almost as sad as the lady selling stamps.

When the waiter brought me a large glass of Ballantine's, I knew that, whatever else had happened to Saigon, the black market at least must still be thriving. Half an hour later, the men from Cholon left and Madame Dai became more relaxed, joining us at our table and showing us photographs of her daughter and grandchildren in Canada. Somehow, the daughter had managed to escape, but like the majority of anti-Communist Vietnamese, Madame Dai had been left behind in 1975, trapped by the speed of the North's victory. Her husband, a well-known surgeon trained in London, had been arrested and imprisoned, had a stroke and although later released was now unable to practise. After five years of occupation by the Communists – that is how she saw it – Madame Dai was desperate to leave the country. As she talked about the difficulties of life in Saigon and the need to accumulate enough dollars, or gold, to 'buy' an exit visa, I suddenly understood the significance of her art collection – a number of bronze heads, including a small bronze Buddha which I admired and for which she wanted 400 dollars, and a collection of Bleu de Chine porcelain from the old Imperial city of Hue.

To make good their escape, Madame Dai and her husband would need Western visas and here she asked for our help. Would I take a letter with me when we left and post it to her daughter in Canada? I said I would. We parted on the warmest of terms, having clinched our friendship in the time-honoured way.

'Mr Sandy,' Madame Dai smiled her sweetest smile. 'You know, to get an exit visa in Saigon costs a lot of money. *Beaucoup, beaucoup d'argent*! Dollars! So, if you need local money, I will change for you, at a good rate.'

'Of course, we'd like to help you and your husband, Madame Dai. What is a good rate these days?'

'Ten, Mr Sandy. Ten dong to one dollar.' Kanh, the robber, had been giving us only one and a half. Ten, we had discovered, was about the going rate.

'All right, Madame Dai. Two hundred dollars' worth?'

She nodded happily. '*Un moment*.' She disappeared into the kitchen and was back almost immediately, pressing a small bundle wrapped in newspaper into my hand. Stepping out into the warm darkness, half blinded for a moment from the lights within, we were accosted by a sinister figure who towered over us, chattering incomprehensibly. Suddenly, I realised the man was speaking English, or at any rate American English with a Vietnamese accent.

'Hey there, let's go check it out! You wanna go check it out?' The cyclo-pousse driver manoeuvred adroitly towards us, his face invisible under a baseball cap.

'How the hell did he know we were here?' I asked Charles.

'Probably saw us leave the Majestic. Anyway, his initiative deserves a reward.'

We climbed up into the rickshaw and rolled off down Tu Do, watching the dimly-lit, empty streets of the old capital unfold beyond Check It Out's muscly legs. There were certainly no temptations to lead us astray here. Apart from a few beggars and the odd rat, Ho Chi Minh City was as dead as a dodo.

The next day dawned bright and sunny, revealing Saigon in all its sleaziness, and idiosyncracy. We drove up Tu Do to the Caravelle, where I asked Kanh to tell the driver to turn right, past the old Brinks Hotel, once a club for American enlisted men, and now some sort of government office. It was here, on the last day of the war, that I watched the Vietnamese start looting with ferocious energy, one man cycling past me with a large cupboard roped to his back. Now, parked in front of the old Brinks were thirty or forty vintage American cars, their exaggerated tail fins and exuberant chrome reminiscent of some 1950s film.

'What on earth are all these American cars doing?' I asked Kanh, who in turn interrogated the driver.

'Marriage cars,' he explained triumphantly. 'When Saigon people gets married, they hire one car like this to take them to reception. If plenty people, they hire maybe two, three car.' Kanh giggled. 'American car better than Russian car.'

We made a semicircle past the old Continental and rejoined Tu Do, driving up to Thong Nhut, the main boulevard and the scene of the North Vietnamese army's victorious entry into the capital in 1975. We turned left at the cathedral and drove slowly towards the Presidential Palace, an imposing building right at the end. I was looking for the exact spot where, five years earlier, I had stood, on camera and microphone in hand, describing the arrival of the North Vietnamese while Lucien filmed the T-55 tanks and lorry loads of troops driving down the boulevard behind me. The plan was to start our first report from Saigon with Lucien's archive film, then mix to me standing on the same spot, today. We had just started filming when several hatchet-faced men, ostensibly party officials but probably secret police, arrived and immediately started interfering.

They wanted us to stop filming, insisting that everything had been arranged and we were late for our appointment. We refused and a furious argument broke out. Our new minders, whoever they might be, were interested only in their own script, and kept shouting that we should stop filming and go instead to a kindergarten and various other propaganda locations. I kept trying to get Kanh, who had been so willing and helpful in Hanoi, to intercede on our behalf, but to my fury he retreated into the background, as if it were none of his business. He was either frightened, or more likely, anxious not to compromise his real concern; his black market business.

Finally, in frustration and anger, I shouted. 'We do not want to film a kindergarten. I have not come all the way to Vietnam to film kindergartens. In fact I absolutely refuse to film any schools or kindergartens. And that's final!'

The hatchet-faced men did not like it and muttered angrily among themselves, the sibilants and plosives flying like missiles over a battleground: the Vietnamese language, when spoken in anger, sounds as if ping-pong balls are being batted viciously round your ears. But our victory was short-lived. They got their own back later when they simply drove us to the kindergarten, which had been decked with flags like a village fete, its shiny-faced staff and pupils drawn up on parade, ready to sing a Communist song of welcome. I found the propagandising of the puppet-like children nauseating, and the contrast with the depressed air of the rest of the city, obscene. We retaliated in the only way open to us; by refusing to take the camera out of its case. I wondered why Communist officials in Saigon were tougher and nastier than they had been in Hanoi, and came to the conclusion that in Hanoi, Communist rule was so firmly entrenched, it could afford to be more relaxed; here, in the south, it was comparatively new, highly unpopular, and still very unsure of itself.

Later, having got rid of the minders, we drove up the boulevard, past the red-brick cathedral which looked deserted, to the vast American Embassy building on the left, and beyond it on the right, the much humbler British Embassy. Both of them, especially the old American Embassy, evoked many ghosts. Both had been looted by the Saigonese in an orgy of resentment at their betrayal in those last hectic hours before the arrival of Hanoi's troops; I had a vivid memory of the blue surface of the swimming pool in the American compound choked with papers from the looted files. The Vietnamese government had simply expropriated the building and turned it into an oil headquarters. As befitted its lesser standing, the British building had become a sports centre.

From there we went to see how the new Vietnam was dealing with its thousands of drug addicts, seen as a heritage from the evil, imperialist past. The answer was: ferociously. On the parade ground of the correction house were about 150 drug addicts, at various stages of rehabilitation, undergoing a punishing course in physical jerks. The instructors made our minders look like wimps, and it was not difficult to guess what happened to inmates who failed to meet the exacting standard demanded of them. The men on the parade ground were mostly in their late teens or early twenties, young Vietnamese who had been uprooted by the war, drifted into the Saigon underworld of drugs and petty crime, and become hooked. I felt sorry for them, not least because of the ruthless-looking martinet in charge, who had the hardest black eyes I have ever seen. We had another row about what we were going to film, and to get my way I had to thump the table in a shameful display of capitalist anger.

That afternoon, we drove to Cholon, the great sprawling Chinatown, which is really a city on its own. We might have been in Kowloon; all the street signs were written in Chinese characters; the shops were selling Chinese goods; and the cinemas showing bloodthirsty Chinese films. As soon as Charles got the camera out, we were surrounded by a crowd of dirty, aggressive-looking teenagers. Kanh shrank even further into his shell. I could not make out if the teenagers, all ethnic Chinese, were hostile, or simply curious. We were still debating the point when a downpour started. It was like a monsoon squall, the rain lashing down so hard we had to stop filming and take cover. The teenagers pressed even closer round us. Suddenly the police, who presumably had been warned that we were coming, moved in and started dispersing the crowd. The noise level rose, like a flock of angry starlings. Kanh appeared at my elbow. 'Police say we must go now.'

'But we've only just arrived,' I said, conscious I was being awkward.

Kanh became agitated. 'They say must go now.' He looked like a drowned rat, the rain glistening on his black hair and yellow skin. The police hovered, impatiently. I wondered if they were afraid we would provoke a riot. The crowd of youths had grown bigger if anything, apparently oblivious of the pelting rain, their black eyes hard as stones.

'We can't film in this,' Charles said, 'so we might as well bugger off.'

A curtain of rain drummed on the roof of the car as we

drove away through the now deserted streets, leaving the strange phenomenon of the young Chinese behind us. I decided that they had been drawn towards us, like a herd of young bullocks in a field, by intense physical curiosity. As Westerners we represented a link, however tenuous, with the outside world from which they were so agonisingly cut off.

After an exhausting day arguing with the bloody-minded Saigon bureaucracy, I had been looking forward to a large Ballantine's at Madame Dai's and a quiet dinner. But her husband, the surgeon, was already in the restaurant, anxious to reminisce about his days as a student in London. His English was still quite good, although the effects of his stroke were obvious. He said he had stayed on largely because of his mother, who he felt he could not leave behind. Now that the old lady was dead, there was no longer any reason for them to stay.

'There is nothing here in Vietnam any longer, for people like us. It is finished.' His nephew, who spoke very good English, agreed. 'It is like living in a morgue,' he said. 'You know, we have lived for five years now under Communist rule, and it is impossible to have any illusions any more. There is simply no future here. The people who've taken over, the people from the north: they don't want Saigon to have any future. They want to make us pay for the past.' Madame Dai flitted about busily, happy that her husband, for once, had a sympathetic audience. When I told her we would be leaving in a couple of days' time, her face fell, but brightened again when I said we would come for dinner on our return, and collect the letter for her daughter.

I also made another inspection of the bronze Buddha, with which I had fallen in love. 'You know, Madame Dai, I do like your Buddha. Since we have been such good customers, will you give me a special price?'

She turned on all her charm. 'Monsieur, I am already

giving you a very special price. Believe me. Four hundred dollars for a piece like that is nothing.'

'One thing worries me. Are you sure it wasn't looted from Cambodia?' I knew there was plenty of evidence that when the Vietnamese invaded at the end of 1978, they had helped themselves to whatever they could lay their hands on.

'No, no,' Madame Dai protested. 'It comes from the south-west corner of Vietnam, where there has always been a strong Khmer influence. It did not come from *le Camboge*. It was not looted, I can assure you.' I was only too pleased to be persuaded that I would not be buying stolen property. I promised to close the deal when we came back from Cambodia.

Outside the restaurant, it was a clear, starry night, warm and not too humid. We were debating whether to walk back to the Majestic when, silently, out of the darkness, a tall figure glided into the light.

'Hey, let's go check it out! You wanna go check it out?' Like some character from a traditional play, momentarily terrifying, Check It Out loomed above us, waiting for us to climb into his cyclo. It had become a nightly ritual: he would wait outside the Majestic, ready to take us to Madame Dai's, or if he missed us there, he would turn up later, like tonight. On the rare occasions we did not go to Madame Dai's, Check It Out would find us unerringly. We used to joke that he must be working for the secret police, keeping us under surveillance and reporting on our nightly movements.

Charles decided to hire Check It Out and his trishaw for our next report, an impressionistic account of what sort of city Saigon had become five years after the end of the war. For an hour or so they stole the show, gliding up and down Tu Do, as, with Charles filming alongside, I sat in the back and tried to recapture the flavour of the old Saigon. To us it worked wonderfully well, but some unimaginative dolt in London cut it out of the package. News can be intensely frustrating: there is nearly always pressure on space and very often a report that has taken hours to set up and shoot is hacked to ribbons, or dropped altogether, because of some late-breaking story.

By now we had accumulated a large amount of film, 3400 feet to be exact, and the three of us with Kanh in attendance drove to Tan Son Nhut airport to ship it to London. The amount of paperwork was almost unbelievable, and we were there for several hours. Tan Son Nhut had been given a face lift, but behind the new facade little had changed. The old buildings were, literally, falling to bits and desperately in need of a coat of paint. Long queues of people waited patiently outside customs for parcels from relatives abroad; not that you could not obtain just about everything in Saigon's famous black market – but at a price.

While we waited for the paperwork to be completed and the numerous obligatory stamps to be affixed, Kanh broached a subject that had been worrying him for several days: the question of dollars. He looked around to make sure no one was listening. 'Mister Gull, you have to pay hotel bill tomorrow. How much dollars you like change?'

'Why, Mr Kanh, that's very kind of you, but we're all right for dollars at the moment, thank you very much.'

Kanh could hardly believe his ears. 'But you no change since we come to Saigon,' he spluttered.

'Oh, yes we have.'

Kanh became almost apoplectic. 'You change on . . . black market?'

'Tut, tut, Mr Kanh. What makes you think we'd do an awful thing like that?'

His voice rose in anger. 'That is forbidden, Mister Gull, change dollars on black market is very serious.'

'Shhhhh. Keep your voice down, Mr Kanh. Everyone's listening.'

One clerk had in fact looked up when he heard the magic word, dollars; it was a subject of universal interest in Vietnam. But my remark had the desired effect. Kanh shut

75

up, although he looked poisonously bad-tempered. Later, driving back into town, he brought up the subject again, but this time he tried a more subtle approach. 'Mister Gull. You my friend. I not want you get into trouble. You see, if authorities find out you not change dollars in official place, they get very angry! They expel you from Vietnam and then you not able go Cambodia!'

I was fed up with being conned and decided it was time to get tough. I also thought a little bluffing would do no harm. 'Look here, Mr Kanh, I have a lot of contacts in Saigon, and we know the score as well as you do.' He looked puzzled.

'The score . . . ?'

'We know perfectly well that on the black market you can get ten dong to the dollar, not one and a half as you've been giving us. I'm sorry, Mr Kanh, but if we have any more trouble, we will go straight to Mr Uy and tell him exactly what has been going on.'

There was a long silence, broken only by the noise of traffic. Finally, Kanh said, 'Mister Gull, I only trying to be helpful. If you not need change dollars, then it okay by me.' He smiled, showing all his gold teeth and, leaning over the back seat, shook hands solemnly. Reflecting later on the remarkably calm way Kanh had accepted the rebuff, we came to the conclusion he was making such a killing on the black market – or would be as soon as he got home – that our petty deals were of no more consequence.

In the afternoon, we visited the orphanage for half-caste children, most of them GI babies, the offspring of American servicemen, black and white, and Vietnamese mothers, a doomed category in the new Vietnam. There were forty-nine children there, some very white-looking, and although it seemed a happy enough place, there was a deep, under-lying sadness. These children, innocent victims of the war, had probably never seen their fathers and had been abandoned by their mothers, who were either unable, or unwilling, to look after them. In all of these cases, the traditional Vietnamese safety-net of the extended family, a product of the old Buddhist system, simply had not worked, either because the family had been destroyed in the war, or because the mothers were too ashamed to take the child home. None of them, without exception, can ever have known what it was like to belong to a family, even a poor family; and they can never have experienced what most of us take for granted: the benison of parental love. But perhaps the saddest thing of all is that these Americo-Vietnamese children belonged nowhere: forgotten by America, and rejected by the Vietnamese. Not only were they different-looking but they were tainted with the blood of the hated, erstwhile occupier. They had no place in Vietnamese society, except as pawns in the game of diplomatic recognition and financial reparation which the Vietnamese played so determinedly for so long.

That night, since Madame Dai was having a night off, we dined in what seemed to be the only other private restaurant in Saigon, the Thai Nam, which, despite its name, was Chinese-owned. There were no other customers, and despite the freshness of the crab claws – the seafood in Saigon was always excellent – it lacked the familial warmth of Madame Dai's. The waiter, who spoke good English and was extremely forthright, tried to describe the despair which affected most of his fellow-Chinese, which made me think of the strange behaviour of the crowd of teenagers in Cholon. We asked him how many of the two million or so ethnic Chinese who lived in Vietnam, North and South, would leave the country if given the opportunity.

'Everyone would leave, if they had the chance,' he said with a dramatic wave of his arms. Then pointing out of the window to the street outside, he added, 'Only the trees would stay behind!'

Kanh was negotiating to hire, for dollars, of course, a battered old Volkswagen Kombi to take us to Cambodia, and we spent our last day in Saigon organising our departure and doing some last-minute shopping. I strolled up Tu Do to one of the antique shops where my eye had been taken by some pieces of Bleu de Hue; I particularly liked two small, blue and white opium pillows, used by opium smokers as headrests when they passed out after a hefty pipe. The shop was owned by a niece of Madame Dai, a handsome woman in her thirties, bigger than most Vietnamese women, who tend to be small and slender. She still had some nice pieces, but no customers. 'No one comes to Vietnam any more,' she said with a shrug of her shapely shoulders, 'no tourists, nobody.' We haggled amiably for a few minutes over the Bleu de Hue, which I eventually bought, quite cheaply but for dollars, of course: she was as desperate as her aunt to leave the sinking ship.

Chapter
6

The road to Cambodia runs north-west from Saigon through the territory of the old Cao Dai sect, with its curious hodgepodge of religions and saints, who included Joan of Arc, Victor Hugo and Sun Yat-sen, the first president of the Chinese Republic. We crossed the border just north of the Parrot's Beak, a Communist stronghold during the war, and the reputed site of their headquarters in the south, COSVN. In the 1960s and early 1970s, the Americans launched several ponderous operations to find it and wipe it out, but never succeeded. As on so many other occasions, they and their equally road-bound South Vietnamese allies were beaten as much by the jungle as by their more mobile enemy, who slipped skilfully through their fingers.

The Vietnamese frontier post bore signs of more recent fighting, the bullet scars of the persistent Khmer Rouge cross-border raids of 1978 which finally drove the Vietnamese to invade. After the border, the road suddenly deteriorated, becoming more like an obstacle course than a highway. Every twenty or thirty yards, the Khmer Rouge had dug trenches in the tarmac six inches deep and eighteen inches wide. Our speed was suddenly cut to ten or fifteen miles an hour, and our progress became a succession of jarring crashes. These Khmer Rouge equivalents of sleeping policemen cannot have presented much of a challenge to the Vietnamese tanks, but they were hell for an ordinary motorist.

After the deserted border region, the country became more populated. Men and women dressed in the traditional black pyjamas were hard at work in the rice paddies, looking like so many dark triangles as they bent over industriously, legs apart, and ramrod straight, their conical straw hats making smaller, paler triangles against the verdant green. At one point, we came on a crowd of people congregated beside the road; there must have been a couple of hundred of them. We told Kanh to stop and went to investigate. It turned out that Oxfam was distributing rice seed to local farmers. There was almost a carnival atmosphere as they queued up for their ration, a sackful per family, which the men then shouldered and carried off in triumph to their bullock carts. The general impression of vitality was astonishing. Not only had these people risen, to all practical purposes, from the dead, but they were full of life and energy. As we drove away, we passed a long line of bullock carts making the return journey to their villages, wooden axles creaking, the whole cart swaying rhythmically to the stately stride of the water buffaloes.

The country became increasingly lush and fertile as we approached the Mekong, a mile wide at this stage in its journey, moving majestically on its appointed way. We had to cross by ferry, sharing the wooden deck with dozens of women who were going home from market laden with wicker baskets holding all manner of treasures; chickens and ducks, and even the occasional pig. The ferry took half an hour and when we landed on the other side, I felt we had done more than cross the river, however vast. We had, it seemed, penetrated to the very heart of Cambodia, lying between the arms of the Mekong and the Tonle Sap, a watery embrace which makes it the most fertile country in Asia and one of the richest rice-growing areas in the world.

We now followed the south bank of the Mekong for fifty

miles or so, our progress still painfully slow, reaching Phnom Penh as the sun was setting in front of us, the half light lending a curious quality of mystery, and perhaps apprehension, to our arrival. I remembered how the first thing the Khmer Rouge did after marching into the city in 1975 was to give the population, then about half a million, twenty-four hours to leave. Instead of liberation, they were faced with a ruthless evacuation, a forerunner of the terror to come. In the weeks and months that followed, the whole country was forced to submit to Pol Pot's crazed vision of the New Kampuchea, his attempt to go back to the origins of Khmer society, eradicating everything and everyone that stood for a modern, civilised society – a vision that was summed up in the chilling phrase, Year Zero. All this went through my mind as we drove along the wide, main boulevard which leads to the centre of the city and the Hotel Monorom, where I had stayed in 1968. It looked run down but clean, and the staff were friendly. The famous Khmer smile of welcome was still in evidence, despite the recent past.

Our first stop next morning was the Foreign Ministry where we explained that we had been filming in Vietnam and wanted permission, and assistance, to spend ten days doing the same thing in Cambodia. We all knew this was really a formality, since the presence of Kanh meant we had the approval of Hanoi, but at least we were observing the courtesies. I could sense immediately that Kanh's presence was not popular. He was seen, rightly, as a Vietnamese government stooge, who had no business to be there. But the realities of power were such that no Cambodian official could afford to upset the Vietnamese, however much he disliked them. Their army controlled the country, and the Heng Samrin government was their puppet. After some discussion, it was decided that a young man called Tuy would be our guide and interpreter on our tour of the country.

81

But first we wanted to look round Phnom Penh. I remembered it as an enchanting backwater, washed by the Mekong, full of palaces and pretty girls. Prince Sihanouk was still on the throne then, his beautiful, eldest daughter was the star of the Royal Ballet, and all was well with the world. In comparison with Vietnam, where the war had just erupted in the Tet Offensive, Cambodia was at peace, an idyllic lotus land. But, between then and now lay a bloody revolution. The charm, surely, must have vanished.

We walked along streets that were full of people; few cars but hundreds of bicycles. To my surprise, the place was alive, busy, and the market in full swing. We stopped at the stalls selling gold. 'Stall' is too much. The merchant simply sat on a chair with gold chains hanging up in a wooden case beside him, and small pieces of jewellery on a box that served as a table in front of him. I was surprised at first to see so much gold, until I reflected that in a country like Cambodia, where the infrastructure of everyday life had been almost totally destroyed, it was the one commodity that retained universal value. The food stalls were a marvel in another way. Piles of fruit and vegetables rose in exotic pyramids, but prices were, inevitably, high for the ordinary Cambodian. Bales of brightly-coloured cloth, brilliant blues and greens and dazzling reds, beckoned seductively, and Kanh was beside himself with excitement. After the cornucopia of the Saigon black market, here was another, perhaps unexpected, gold mine. I could see his business antennae twitching and his eyes shining beadily behind his spectacles. What puzzled me was the source of much of this merchandise; where did this cloth, these Western cigarettes, these watches come from? It was not until a few days later that we discovered the answer, and it proved one thing. The Khmer Rouge murdered possibly a million of their fellow citizens; but they were unable to kill off the country's entrepreneurial spirit.

Next day, 14 September, we visited Tuol Sleng, on the

outskirts of Phnom Penh. It had been a secondary school, but when the Khmer Rouge drove everyone out of the capital, they turned it into an 'interrogation centre'. At first glance, it looked ordinary enough, a modern school building on two floors; until you noticed the barbed wire, which not only surrounded the building but also sealed off various parts of it, like the upstairs balconies. For this was not only an interrogation centre, it was an extermination camp, a death house.

The night before, we had met a gentle young Australian historian called Ben Kiernan, and his Cambodian wife, Chanthou. Ben said that to understand the Khmer Rouge, we must see Tuol Sleng. Indeed he offered to take us.

'Twenty thousand people came in here between 1975 and 1979,' Ben said, as we stood at the bottom of the stairs in the main building, 'and none came out.' We were alone in the building. Yet in my imagination, I heard a scream.

'They were very bureaucratic, the Khmer Rouge,' Ben continued. 'They kept extensive records. Upstairs, there are 150,000 pages of documents. I'm trying to read them, but it will take a long time.'

We walked up the stairs to the first floor. 'These are the cells, where they kept the most important prisoners. They had to write their confessions here.' He waved a hand at the cramped, squalid cells where even one man would scarcely have enough room to lie full-length on the floor. 'They had to sleep on the floor, they had no beds, and were chained up.' We walked down the central corridor; the iron cell doors stood open on each side, revealing the chains which attached each prisoner to a ring in the wall.

'They often spent weeks writing their confessions. A lot of them have corrections, made in red ink, in the margin. Those were written by Deuch, the head of the Nokorbal, Pol Pot's secret police. There is one very interesting confession, made by Hu Nim. He was one of Pol Pot's closest colleagues until they fell out.'

83

I asked what had happened.

'Pol Pot was crazy. He was completely paranoiac. For some reason he took against Hu Nim, accusing him of secretly working for the CIA. He had him arrested and brought in here. Can you imagine? That hoary old chestnut: working for the CIA. The system was that a prisoner had to write and rewrite his confession until it was acceptable to Deuch. It had to be a fair copy, with no mistakes, and no crossings out. Then, when it was perfect . . .' Ben paused. I could hear that scream again, in my imagination. 'When it was perfect, they killed you.'

In one room there was a huge pile of dead men's clothes, twenty feet high and as much again across. They were torn and dirty, like beggars' rags. One wondered why the Khmer Rouge had not burnt them. Or did they store them up and then give them away, to the needy? Finally, we went to the other wing. It was like a hospital: rows and rows of bare, iron beds, on both floors. 'This is where they did their interrogations,' Ben explained. 'The suspects were brought in here and tortured on the beds. If you look closely, you can see blood on the floor, under the beds, and sometimes the victims' hair still on the springs.' I looked, while Charles filmed. He was right.

'They were chained to the beds, and whipped and beaten, until they were ready to make a confession. Sometimes they never got that far. Sometimes they died under interrogation, beaten to death. Or they were taken out and shot, at the back of the school.' We went outside with the caretaker, a Cambodian who had been a prisoner in Tuol Sleng. 'He was one of the few who survived,' Ben said. 'He was here when the Vietnamese arrived in Phnom Penh. They came soon afterwards and freed the prisoners.'

I asked the curator, through Ben, what he remembered most about being in Tuol Sleng. 'The screaming. When the prisoners were being tortured, and beaten. In the daytime, and also at night. But it was worst at night.'

What happened when the Vietnamese arrived?

'Everyone ran away. When they heard that the Vietnamese were coming, they ran like rabbits.' The curator laughed, showing broken teeth. 'Pol Pot and the rest of the Politburo were the first to go. Deuch and the guards left soon after.' The curator laughed again. 'Then the Vietnamese soldiers came and released all the prisoners. I did not think I would ever see my family again.' Before we left I stood for a moment on a first floor balcony in the cell block, looking through the barbed wire. Even eighteen months after liberation, the horror of the place was still palpable, the sense of dread still overpowering.

The effects of the Khmer Rouge terror, which had covered Cambodia like a glacier, were at last beginning to recede, and a few hardy green shoots were starting to push up through the ice. Among them was a textile project financed by Oxfam. Bill Yates, who was the head of the Oxfam programme in Cambodia, took us to see it. It was the perfect antidote to the horrors of Tuol Sleng. The factory was not much to look at from the outside; like most things it had suffered from the excesses of Year Zero; but inside, it was humming with hard work and enthusiasm. We had to shout above the whirring din of the 350 looms to make ourselves heard. Bill Yates introduced us to the manager, a small, smiling, bespectacled man of about fifty.

'This is Mr Ky, who has been here since 1954, except for the Pol Pot period.' Mr Ky gave an apologetic grin, as if ashamed that he had not suffered the fate of so many of his less fortunate compatriots. 'I was lucky,' he said. 'I manage to escape from Khmer Rouge.' According to Bill Yates, he had done a first-class job getting the factory back into production in no time at all. 'We have five hundred workers,' Mr Ky said. 'Nearly all been in textile business before. So very experience.' He took us to a frenetically shuttling loom and showed us what they were weaving: a rather pretty dark red and green cloth with a familiar motif. Phnom

85

Penh Paisley Pattern,' I shouted above the rattle of the loom, in an attempt at a joke. Mr Ky grinned happily. Pol Pot, who hated all things Western, would not have approved.

In the afternoon, we visited a kindergarten. Unlike the one in Saigon, which we found so depressingly authoritarian, the atmosphere here was much more relaxed and friendly. About one hundred small boys and girls, the little girls with huge black eyes and pigtails, were learning the Khmer alphabet. It looked hugely difficult to a Western eye, rather like an ornate shorthand, but these tiny things were scrawling away quite happily. They were too young to understand – they had been born around the time of the Khmer Rouge takeover – how lucky they were to be able to learn to read and write. Pol Pot had destroyed all the schools, and banished education. He even carried his hatred of 'intellectuals' to such absurd lengths that the young Khmer Rouge soldiers had orders to kill anyone wearing spectacles.

The next day, Kanh having completed the arrangements for our trip round Cambodia, we set off for Kampong Cham, a once prosperous market town on the Mekong, about sixty miles north-east of Phnom Penh. From there we would make a great loop, following the northern shore of the Tonle Sap, Cambodia's inland sea, to Siem Reap and, I hoped, the great temples of Angkor Wat; to Sisophon in the west, near the Thai border; and then back to Phnom Penh by the road which runs south of the Tonle Sap. It was a journey of about four hundred miles and under normal conditions, would have been an easy enough drive. But with the roads in such a deplorable state, it promised to be anything but a picnic. Kanh drove, with our guide Tuy beside him, hardly bothering to conceal his dislike of the trip in general and of Kanh in particular. Charles, Hugh and I sat in the back, being thrown up and down by the potholes and the Khmer Rouge trenching. But the discomfort was outweighed by the exciting prospect of seeing Cambodia, which had been a closed society for so long, and especially Angkor, which virtually no outsider had visited since the Khmer Rouge had seized power. We had heard conflicting reports about the damage they had done to it, and we were anxious to see for ourselves. But we had been warned it was going to be difficult if not impossible to get there. Tuy was especially pessimistic, saying it was 'too dangerous'. The Khmer Rouge, he claimed, were still active in the area, and foreigners were advised not to go there.

We crossed the Mekong in an ancient but surprisingly efficient ferry, the slow haul across the huge river having an almost ritual, healing quality: it was easy to see why the Cambodians thought of the Mekong as an all-providing, beneficent goddess. As we drove north, we soon forgot the discomforts of the journey in admiration of the beauty of the landscape, which even the Khmer Rouge had been unable to destroy, and which now began to unfold before us in mile after mile of emerald green rice fields, symmetrically planted with tall, graceful palm trees. Ridiculously, it made me think of a well-manicured, exclusive and extremely expensive golf and country club in Florida. The effect was spoiled only by the villages, which although charmingly rustic with their thatched roofs, were not particularly tidy. Pigs rootled under the trees and chickens scurried frantically on the verges. But the sense of an orderly and ageless culture was soon restored by the sight of the bullock carts pacing serenely through the fields, their pointed, centre shafts curving upwards in exactly the same way as in the frieze carvings at Angkor.

Suddenly Kanh swore and gesticulated at the road ahead. Half a dozen lorries and a jeep were immobilised along a sort of embankment and as we got out to inspect more closely, we found ourselves staring down at a swirling spate of angry brown water. Torrential rain had swollen the river to flood proportions, sweeping away a bridge. Tuy, who had gone off to talk to a man in what looked like a

87

doorman's uniform and who was presumably a local official, came back with a long face. 'This man says it will take two, three days to mend the bridge. We cannot go any farther. We must go back to Phnom Penh.'

'That's the last thing we want to do,' I said, looking firmly at Tuy. 'Mr Kanh, surely there must be another road we can take to Kampong Cham?' Kanh, who obviously wanted to see Cambodia as much as we did, rounded on the luckless Tuy. An intense and acrimonious argument took place. At the end of it, Kanh emerged looking triumphant while Tuy subsided into a sulk. 'We go other way,' Kanh declared, turning the Kombi with much clashing of gears and driving back the way we had come. The detour turned out to be lengthy and we did not reach Kampong Cham until early afternoon. We drove slowly through the town which had been badly damaged in the fighting between the Lon Nol Government and the Khmer Rouge in the mid-1970s. After asking directions, Kanh drew up with a flourish outside a ramshackle villa which, he said, used to be a guest house belonging to Prince Sihanouk. It had clearly come a long way down in the world since then, helped no doubt by the Khmer Rouge, and could only offer a minimum of amenities. But it did have beds, and you could get food, of a kind.

After lunch some local officials took us to see the town's orphanage. In nearly thirty years of being a roving reporter, I have seen many depressing sights, but this was one of the most moving; not so much because of the grinding poverty of the place – they did not even have enough money to buy the children pencils – but because nearly all of them were orphans of the terror. The Khmer Rouge had murdered their parents, and they too were victims of Pol Pot's policy of mass extermination. We returned to our guest house feeling depressed and angry, having promised to help. Writing those words today, I feel a stab of guilt that, apart from publicising the children's plight on television, our good intentions came to naught.

Next morning we rose early, Charles being determined to film the town from the river, a branch of the Mekong. It would, he said, make a wonderful shot. To do this we needed a boat, a sampan. You would have thought this would be easy, since once thing the Cambodians were not short of was sampans, the traditional mode of transport in a country where life revolves around the waterways. But Tuy, still smarting from his failure to make us return to Phnom Penh, now raised a series of objections. There was no suitable sampan available; the owners did not wish us to take pictures from their boat; it was forbidden to film, anyway; we had an appointment with the chairman of the local council; and so on. Finally, we ignored him and Charles simply accosted a boatman and made his own arrangement. Having filmed the sequence he wanted, he returned to dry land, paid off the smiling boatman, and turned his attention to the examples of Khmer Rouge wrecking we had seen the day before: a broken, orange tractor which lay upside down like a dead praying mantis; a gutted and wheel-less Land Rover. Tuy kept interfering, constantly trying to hurry us up, giving all sorts of specious reasons. Finally, I lost my temper and shouted at him. His face grew white, his eyes glittered angrily behind his spectacles, and he withdrew into an icy silence. I knew I had probably alienated him for good, and that we were now at the mercy of Kanh, which was not a position I would have chosen to be in, but at least he was a businessman; he had his price.

Having finished filming in Kampong Cham, we drove to Two Hills, just outside the town, where we were told there were a number of mass graves. Leaving the Kombi at the side of a wooded valley, we walked down through the trees to a flat area where a series of ditches, stretching into the distance, had been dug in the dark red earth. These were the mass graves where the bodies of Khmer Rouge victims had been thrown and then lightly covered over with soil.

89

The sun was high, the day a hot one, and the stench appalling. As we gazed at these at first innocent-looking pits of red earth, my first reaction was one of anticlimax. Then, as we looked closer, we saw bits of white bone protruding from the earth, and here and there a skull. A Cambodian dressed in an old army jacket had drifted up and began explaining to Tuy, who reluctantly translated.

'You see how all the bones are lying separate? One by one, you see?'

'Yes.'

'That is because the farmers who live here come and dig up the bodies.'

'Why?'

'They look for gold. The gold from the teeth of the people the Khmer Rouge killed. So they dig up the bodies, all the time.'

We started to film, the sun beating down, the smell of rotted flesh hanging round us in a miasma of horror, investing the nostrils, the lungs, every part of one's body. We walked down the line of pits. In some, the earth had either been dug out, or had subsided, leaving visible whole layers of bones; in others, the skulls lay exposed, having been examined for the sought-after gold fillings and then cast aside. It reminded me of the way the Nazis had collected the gold from the teeth of the Jews they exterminated. The Khmer Rouge had not bothered to exploit their victims in the same systematic way. They were only interested in the killing, the actual elimination of the enemy. As for the Cambodian farmers, if you are that poor and that hardened by privation and terror, I told myself, perhaps such heartlessness was understandable.

The man in the old army tunic said there was a place we must see, where there were many bodies. How far? we asked. He pointed a skinny arm that protruded from the sleeve of his tunic. 'Not far. Maybe one kilometre.' As we walked across the fields, I began to count the number of graves and tried to calculate the number of people whose bodies had been hurled, like so much rubbish, into the red earth. Our self-appointed guide said the whole plain was full of graves, sweeping his arm in a semi-circle. In the end I calculated there might be about fifty graves, but it was more difficult to estimate the number of bodies to a grave: I thought possibly one hundred. So, if there were fifty graves, each containing one hundred bodies, that meant five thousand people were buried in this one area. Each town and village in Cambodia had its own 'killing fields', so there could be as many as one hundred mass grave sites across the whole country, giving the staggering total of half a million dead. One ambassador I met subsequently in Phnom Penh told me that was the estimate he found most credible, and not the commonly accepted figure of one million.

The guide was stopping and pointing. 'This is the place he told you about,' Tuy translated. 'You see the well? After they killed the people they threw their bodies into the well. He says come and look.'

Holding handkerchiefs to our noses and avoiding some very unpleasant-looking substances on the ground around the well, we leaned over the parapet and looked down. It was wide and deep, and more or less empty. The guide, apparently impervious to the stench of death, launched into his explanation. 'This well was full of bodies, right to the brim. But now as you see, it is empty.'

Removing the handkerchief from my nose and mouth for a second, I asked, 'How did they empty the well?'

'Workmen go down into the well, and start lifting out the bodies with their hands. Then they put ladder down and pull out rest of the bodies. Sometimes not complete bodies, just arms and legs.' For a moment Mr Tuy's icy disdain unfroze. 'It was very bad job. The men had to wear a towel round their faces, but they still got sick.'

We backed away, feeling sick ourselves from the smell and the hideous sense of death, but I forced myself to squat down beside the well and describe, on camera, what had happened at Two Hills. Afterwards, our guide took us to see a memorial made of thousands of skulls which had been collected from the mass graves, and arranged as a macabre mural. It was a grim reminder of the insane terror which had destroyed so many innocent and helpless Cambodians.

Chapter
7

Leaving the mass graves of Kampong Cham behind us, we drove west to a small town called Skun, on a crossroads at the eastern end of the Tonle Sap, where we planned to spend the night. Kanh went in search of accommodation, and as we were stretching our legs at the side of the road, a man approached with a six-foot python draped round his neck. He stopped in front of us and struck up a conversation, the python dangling limply, as if drugged. Tuy, who was always more amenable when Kanh was absent, said, 'This man wants to sell you his snake.'

'But we don't want to buy his snake.'

'He say very good snake, very cheap.'

We inspected the reptile from a safe distance. 'Thank you, but no.'

'He ask how much you want to pay?'

'Tell him, we don't actually want a snake, nice snake though it may be.'

The snake seller thrust a gold-mottled coil towards us. 'He say, snake very fat and good to eat. How much you give him?'

'Tell him, sorry. But we don't eat snake in our country.'

With a grin that seemed to suggest that foreigners must be completely mad, but with no sign of disappointment, the man hitched the python more comfortably round his neck, and strolled off down the road. Soon afterwards, Kanh returned, looking pleased with himself. 'Mr Sandy Gull, I have good news. We stay tonight in Skun, with the Vietnamese army. I find one friend from Hanoi, who is commander here. He invite us to eat dinner and sleep in his house.'

'That is good news, Mr Kanh, and very kind of your friend to invite us.' We all got back in the Kombi, except for Tuy, to whom the thought of spending the night with the Vietnamese army clearly did not appeal. He said he would stay with friends and meet us in the morning. We drove a short distance out of the little town and down a sandy track to a fairly large house which was Kanh's friend's headquarters. The major, a small, neat figure in his light-coloured uniform, wearing the pith helmet which is the curiously colonial trademark of the North Vietnamese army, came out to greet us. The sun was setting beyond the great lake, but it was dark in the house and we had to grope our way forward with only an oil lamp to guide us; there seemed to be no electricity in Skun. Sitting, sipping tea in the semi-darkness, idly listening to the verbal ping-pong of the conversation as Kanh and his friend caught up with one another's lives, induced a curious feeling of disembodiment. When the rapid-fire chatter slowed down eventually, I said I would like to ask the major a question. How was it, I asked through Kanh, now in his element, that despite the Vietnamese having 150,000 men in Cambodia, the Khmer Rouge were still able to launch guerrilla attacks in the west of the country?

As befitted an officer in the army that had seen off the Americans in such spectacular fashion, the major brushed the threat aside. 'When the dry season comes, we will launch a big offensive against them. Then you will see that the Khmer Rouge are only a paper tiger.' He laughed at his own joke. Dinner, served by a couple of young Vietnamese batmen, cut short further conversation. It also made me

94

think of the La Fontaine fable of the Fox who is invited to dine with the Stork. Having a short muzzle instead of a long bill, the Fox finds itself unable to get at the food, which is deliberately served in a long-necked dish. The test in our case was how, while sitting on the floor in semi-darkness, to convey rice to the mouth with chopsticks, without spilling most of it; and also, more importantly, how to cope with the invisible main course. Having only chopsticks as a guide, I established that it was slippery, cut in longish pieces, tasted a bit like chicken, and had a bone, like a backbone.

In an aside to Hugh, who was also struggling in the dark beside me, I hissed, 'What do you think this is? Chicken?'

'Dunno,' he whispered back. 'Could be that snake the man tried to sell us in the street.'

I thought at first this was a fairly typical Hugh joke, but as I took another mouthful, it did seem possible. The pieces were rounded, like eel, only bigger, and had the same sort of fibrous backbone. I felt it would be impolite to ask, so we chewed away doggedly in the darkness, pretending to be enjoying it. I knew the Chinese considered snake a delicacy, so I presumed the Vietnamese, much of whose culture derives from China, although they are loath to admit it, would also enjoy it. The Chinese eat snake mainly in winter, because it heats the blood, and it was still high summer, but an army in the field cannot be too choosy. I asked Kanh later if it really had been snake. He denied it, insisting it was chicken, but none of us believed him, perhaps because of the way in which he sniggered. We all remained firmly convinced that the snake seller had got us to eat his python, after all.

We left next morning, feeling none the worse for whatever we had eaten, and looking forward to what, for me, was the most exciting part of our journey, the visit to Angkor, the great twelfth-century Khmer city half lost in the jungle. On the only occasion I met Lord Clark, whose brilliant *Civilisation* programmes made a lasting impression on television viewers of my generation, he said it was one of the main regrets of his life that he had never been there. The stretch of road running along the north side of the Tonle Sap was one of the worst we had experienced, with a bone-shaking series of trenches dug close together for mile after mile. It was almost inevitable that one of our balding tyres should have a puncture, leaving us without a spare, and it was late afternoon by the time we reached Siem Reap, the little town which, in the days when there were tourists, served as the jumping-off point for visits to the ruins. The hotel where I remembered staying twelve years before was empty. The friendly woman who ran it apologised for its run-down condition, explaining that the Khmer Rouge had used it as a 'honeymoon hotel' for their soldiers, and that there was no money to do it up.

But the state of the hotel was the least of our worries. Tuy, who had said little since Kampong Cham, showed himself determined to stop us visiting Angkor. In an attempt to persuade him otherwise, I suggested the five of us discuss the matter over a drink. 'Mr Tuy,' I began, 'we have come a very long way to tell the world what is happening in your country. Angkor is a very important part of it. Everyone in the West has heard of Angkor. If we don't go there, people will think there is something wrong. You want tourists to come back again to Cambodia, don't you?'

His thin face was taut with obstinacy. 'It is not allowed to go to Angkor. You were told that in Phnom Penh. It is forbidden. You have deliberately come here, to Siem Reap, although you know it is not possible. You are disobeying the instructions of the Foreign Ministry. If you go to Angkor now, it will make big trouble for you, and for me.'

'But why?' Charles asked. 'What is the objection to us filming the most famous historical site in the country?'

'It is too dangerous. The Khmer Rouge kill some people near Angkor, and the Foreign Ministry has forbidden all foreigners to go there.' At that point Charles lost his temper

96

and a furious argument ensued. But Tuy, pale and trembling with rage, had left himself no room for manoeuvre. To give in now would mean a serious loss of face. In the end he rose stiffly and left the room.

'Well, Mr Kanh, what are we going to do now?' I asked.

To my surprise, Kanh gave a little giggle. 'Mr Tuy very angry. I think only one way you can go to Angkor.' He paused and gave us a cunning look. 'Tomorrow morning I take car to garage to have puncture mended. Maybe not easy to find right garage to fix tyre. Maybe I have to try two, three garage, before I find right one.'

'I see. How long do you think it will take?'

Kanh shrugged. 'Maybe one half day, I think.'

We looked at one another. Kanh, whose deviousness we had come to know well, was clearly offering us a way out of the impasse. 'Okay,' Charles said, 'while Mr Kanh takes the Kombi to get the puncture mended, we will have a look round Siem Reap. We can meet back here about lunchtime.'

'Will you take Mr Tuy with you?' I asked.

Kanh got up. 'I will try. Excuse me, I have to go now. I have appointment with mayor of Siem Reap.' As we left the room, Kanh to keep his grand appointment, we to have dinner on our own, I said, 'If you help us tomorrow, Mr Kanh, we will know how to show our appreciation.' Kanh grinned. 'I hope so, Mr Sandy.'

Over dinner in the cavernous dining-room, peopled with the ghosts of the Khmer Rouge honeymooners, we made our plans for the next day. We would make sure we did not have Tuy on our tail, and try to hire a taxi outside the hotel. It would be better, we decided, not to let the hotel know what we were doing. They might, after all, have picked up bad habits from the Khmer Rouge.

Next morning, looking conspiratorial, Kanh left in the Kombi shortly after breakfast to have the puncture mended. A few minutes later, Charles, Hugh and I walked out of the hotel, carrying the camera gear as unostentatiously as possible, and keeping an eye open for Tuy in case he appeared at the last moment with a posse of police. Within five minutes we had flagged down a passing taxi. It was old and extremely decrepit and the young Cambodian behind the wheel spoke very little English.

'Angkor?'

'Huh?'

'Angkor Wat. You take us, in taxi, to Angkor Wat?'

'Angkor Wat?'

'Yes. We go. With you. In taxi. To Angkor Wat. Now. Yes?'

'Ha. Ha.' The taxi driver nodded his head furiously up and down, then reaching round the seat beside him to unlock the back door, said, 'Come on, please.' We looked around before getting in, just in case we had been spotted, but no one seemed to be taking the slightest interest in us. I had a delicious, schoolboyish feeling of doing something naughty, for which we might be punished, but not too severely. The road at first was busy with bicycles and bullock carts which swayed slowly out of our path in response to frequent and noisy applications of the horn. But gradually the traffic grew lighter, and the surrounding country emptier. As we approached our destination, I felt excited, and slightly nervous.

Angkor Wat emerges out of the jungle suddenly, like a thunderclap turned to stone. A dark red temple, three storeys high, terraced and turreted, silhouetted against a hot blue sky, and standing majestically at the end of a stone causeway. Once the shallow waters of an ornamental lake reflected its glory; now the incomparable causeway, adorned with stone dragons, traverses a dry meadow. But the impact is still superb, and as we walked across its century-smooth paving stones, through the mighty gateway and to the steps of the temple, I experienced the same thrill and the same feeling of awe as twelve years before. The great frieze which runs round the whole temple and is one

98

of its chief glories was as magnificent as I remembered it; a sandstone masterpiece depicting the battles which made the Khmers rulers of Indo-China from AD 800 to nearly 1400; men in armour ferociously hacking at one another with swords and spears, horse-drawn chariots galloping furiously in headlong charges, and mighty war elephants, trumpeting in rage as they crushed everything in their path. But the sensuous side of life was also here, the sinuous figures of the scantily-clad temple dancers as wonderfully erotic as the day they were carved.

Inside, however, the Khmer Rouge had wreaked their usual destruction; almost every one of the long line of statues, known as the Hundred Buddhas, had been beheaded. Only one of the four guides who had been here in 1975 had survived the terror, and only one of the original two at the neighbouring, equally splendid temple of Angkor Thom. The guide led us up the main stairway of Angkor Wat, but would not let us climb to the highest, and holiest tower, where a great statue of the Buddha, surrounded by hundreds of bats, gazes out over the countryside. The building was unsafe, he said, although whether because of the Khmer Rouge or from natural causes was not clear. When we descended to the courtyard, he showed us a small statue with its head missing, chopped off with an axe, he said, by looters. Gangs of Thais and Vietnamese came and looted the temples at night, when the demoralised-looking soldiers supposed to be guarding Angkor against the Khmer Rouge were asleep.

Angkor is a city comprising dozens of temples, and it would take a month to do them real justice. We had time for only one more, Angkor Thom. It has a superb approach, the paved road leading up to it lined with magnificent carvings of elephants, tigers, gods and devils. Fortunately, they were unharmed, presumably because they were considered by Pol Pot to be the untainted expression of Khmer civilisation. Angkor Thom is a Hindu temple. Angkor Wat is Buddhist, and therefore in the eyes of the Khmer Rouge, I supposed, foreign. In the autumn of 1980, no conservation was being done in Angkor. The great restorations begun by Henri Groslier, the French archaeologist who rediscovered Angkor and reclaimed it from the jungle, had been halted. Inevitably, the jungle was encroaching again, but when, eighteen months later in Paris I saw Groslier *fils*, who had carried on his father's work until shortly before the arrival of the Khmer Rouge, he assured me things were not quite as disastrous as they might seem. Before he left Cambodia in the early 1970s, he said, he had removed all the most valuable statues from Angkor, replacing them with copies, and stored the originals, with a quantity of gold from the base of one temple, in the vaults of the National Museum in Phnom Penh. The beheaded Buddhas we had seen in Angkor Wat were fakes. The originals, Groslier insisted, were safe.

We filmed for four hours, thanked and paid the lonely guide, and drove back to the hotel. Tuy was waiting for us, in a temper.

'I know where you have been,' he began, eyes shining angrily.

'Really, Mr Tuy. Where?'

'You have been to Angkor, although you were told it was forbidden.'

'What makes you think that?'

He almost stamped his foot in rage. 'I know you have been to Angkor. It is no use lying. I know.'

'Well, if you know best, Mr Tuy, there's nothing more to be said.'

Bypassing him, we headed for the dining-room where Kanh was having lunch. Kanh beamed. He had heard the row with Tuy. Yes, the puncture had been repaired, he said, and the Kombi was ready for the next stage of the journey. We joined him, and while Tuy fretted outside, discussed our itinerary.

Our next stop was Sisophon, near the extreme north-west tip of Cambodia, only a few miles from the Thai border. It is less than eighty miles from Siem Reap, but because of the appalling conditions of the roads we arrived only at dusk, having spent four uncomfortable hours getting there. The following morning, we strolled round after breakfast, and found that Sisophon, although small and dirty, was extremely animated. Here, in fact, lay the answer to the great black market mystery. Sisophon was the first stop inside Cambodia on the smuggling route which ran from the Thai border all the way to Phnom Penh, and then on to Saigon.

Later that same morning, we watched hundreds of oxcarts loaded with sacks of rice distributed by Western relief agencies at the border arriving in the town. The rice was free, but according to one of the local chief's men, much of it was intercepted at the border by the Khmer Rouge, who then sold it to the peasants. What did get through was loaded on to lorries in Sisophon and trucked east to Battambang and Phnom Penh. Battambang was the nerve centre of the smuggling operation, and the base for many of the new-style smugglers, dressed in jeans and dark glasses, mounted not on oxcarts but on Honda motor cycles. We saw hundreds of these entrepreneurs in Battambang, and talked to some of them. One young man said he crossed the border not at the official frontier post but on jungle trails, which was easy on a Honda. He would meet a supplier at a prearranged spot in one of the villages near the border, load up his Honda with cigarettes, sandals, or cloth, and drive back to Battambang, or Phnom Penh. But the ultimate destination was farther afield. 'It all goes to Vietnam,' he said. Business was obviously good; a new Honda cost US$1000, an unimaginable fortune to most Cambodians in 1980.

We spent the night in the old Bishop's Palace, once a handsome French colonial mansion, now sadly neglected.

The caretaker who, like so many Cambodians looked battered and shocked by the trauma from which he had just emerged, told us the story of the palace. It was, alas, not untypical.

'When the Khmer Rouge came, they killed the Bishop, four of the French priests and seven hundred Catholics.'

I asked how many were left.

'Three hundred are still here, all Cambodians, including the head catechist. But no French.'

How had they escaped?

'They were lucky. They managed to run away to their villages where they hid until the Vietnamese came.'

At eight next morning, we watched the departure of the train to Phnom Penh. It was an amazing sight, with every carriage packed to the windows with travellers clutching bags and bundles, babies and livestock. Hundreds more sat on the roofs of the carriages, straddled the buffers and even squatted on the flatcar which preceded the engine as a kind of decoy to set off any mines the Khmer Rouge had planted on the track. A few months previously, we were told, 150 passengers had been killed when the train was blown up, and more recently, fifty more had died. Yet, remarkably, as the train pulled out everyone seemed to be happy, and every face was radiant with a smile.

It was time to start our own bumpy journey back along the southern half of the loop road, through Pursat and Krakor, where they catch and dry huge quantities of fish from the Tonle Sap, to Kompong Chang, at the eastern end of the great lake, finally reaching Phnom Penh just as the light was fading. After the relative hardships of the journey, Phnom Penh seemed a haven of delight. This may sound strange, but the experienced traveller is one who has learned to profit where he can, and to enjoy where he may. The Monorom may not merit a place in a list of the world's great hotels, but I gave it full marks that night for simple pleasures: a restful night without any mosquito bites; a

102

shower with hot water – what luxury; and delicious, fresh pineapple juice for breakfast.

We lunched with Ben Kiernan, the young historian, and his wife Chanthou, telling them about our trip and in particular about the mass graves at Kampong Cham. Ben explained that the people in that area, the eastern zone, near the Vietnamese border, had been the main sufferers in 1978, when the Khmer Rouge terror was at its height. This was surprising, because initially people in the east had been relatively privileged, presumably because they were regarded as a buffer against the Vietnamese. 'But in the end,' Ben said, 'even the old people suffered and many peasants were killed.'

I was determined to spend my last day in Phnom Penh seeing some of the sights which, so often, a busy journalist has to forgo. Accordingly, after breakfast, the three of us set off for the Royal Palace, once the home of Prince Sihanouk, who had become first a puppet and then a virtual prisoner of the Khmer Rouge, and was still in exile in Peking. Happily, if somewhat surprisingly, the magnificent ensemble of palaces and temples appeared to be in superb condition, especially the Throne Room with its golden, high-backed chairs and the throne itself, shaped like a howdah, from which lofty eminence the God King would lord it over the assembled throng. The Queen, significantly, was relegated to another, lesser throne placed well behind. The Silver Pagoda was equally impressive, with a floor of silver tiles each weighing a kilo, a Golden Buddha encrusted with diamonds, weighing two hundred kilos, and an Emerald Buddha.

'It looks like green glass, to me,' I said, but the guide contradicted me. 'No, sir, it is not glass. It is pure emerald. It came from Nepal.'

We moved on to the museum, which had been partly damaged by Pol Pot's troops, who had painted one Buddha black. But it contained some fine pre-Angkor statues, one of which looked, to my inexpert eye, strikingly Egyptian. There were also some statues from the Angkor period: possibly some of the originals the younger Groslier had removed and sent for safekeeping to Phnom Penh. There was one other institution I wanted to see: the ballet school. This had been closed down by the Khmer Rouge, and a number of its teachers, and pupils, murdered. It had recently re-opened in an old building near the Palace. There, in a couple of bare, upstairs rooms, we found several classes being taught. One was for tiny children of five or six; another for pupils of ten or twelve; and finally, a class for teenagers. The beauty of some of the girls, with their oval faces and perfect features, was breathtaking. Khmer dancing is religious in origin, stylised and, by Western standards, almost static. But what it lacks in movement it more than makes up for in sophistication. The hands are particularly important, the dancer's long, supple fingers conjuring up a series of infinitely subtle movements, and sometimes bending back in an almost complete semicircle. The body movements are limited, but sensuous, and the feet, bare and high-arched, grasp the ground like a warrior's.

Closing my eyes, I imagined I was back in Angkor Wat, watching the same dances being performed by identical dancers in a tradition which, despite wars and revolutions, has endured for over a thousand years. I asked how the students were enrolled, where did they come from? Mostly, I was told, they came from families of dancers, often going back several generations. Through it all, then, the Khmer genius had survived, and re-emerged. There was something enormously encouraging, triumphant even, in the way this expression of the national spirit had pushed its way out of the cold earth into the sunlight, like the first primrose of spring.

We had two more things to film; the first was an interview with Ben's wife, Chanthou. As a Cambodian, Chanthou was not at all pro-Vietnamese. But, she said, the great majority of Cambodians agreed about one thing. They might not like the Vietnamese very much, but they welcomed them as liberators. 'If it wasn't for the Vietnamese, the Khmer Rouge would still be in power in Phnom Penh. Nobody wants that. And I'll tell you something else. No Cambodian in his or her right mind wants the Vietnamese to leave. Because they know that if the Vietnamese leave Cambodia tomorrow, the Khmer Rouge will come straight back. And certainly nobody wants that. Nobody.'

The last piece of filming we did was on the ferry over the Mekong. I cannot remember the precise words I addressed to the camera, standing on the deck of that antique ferry, but I know my own hope was that a new, happier Cambodia would rise from the nightmare of the old, that Tuol Sleng would be forgotten, and that Angkor would continue to enchant the world.

We arrived in Saigon after dark, to find the streets full of children carrying lanterns, celebrating a mid-autumn festival. After Phnom Penh, the city looked marvellously festive, the night cloaking the daytime dreariness of Communist rule. After a quick shower and change of clothes, we emerged from the Majestic, expecting to find Check It Out waiting, face expressionless under his baseball cap. To our surprise, he was not at his usual stand. Perhaps, for once, we had caught him off guard. I was glad, in one way, that he was not there. To ignore him would have been unthinkable, and yet I very much wanted to walk up Tu Do for the last time, and try to imprint its ravaged charm on my memory for ever. It would be impossible, I knew, but I wanted to try. It meant as much to me, after all, as any street in Berlin, Nairobi, Bonn, Budapest, Johannesburg – all cities I had lived in – or even London. I had walked up and down it several times a day for weeks on end; had my 'correspondent's suits' made there by Mr Minh, a refugee from Hanoi; changed my dollars at the 'Indian bank' up a back stairs; drunk in one or other of the dozens of girlie bars, where you paid as much for a glass of 'Saigon tea' – all that the bar girls were allowed to drink – as you did for a Scotch; and booked my tickets home in the Air France office next to the Caravelle.

We did not linger in any of the old, hardly recognisable girlie bars, now converted into dull little cafes, although a spurt of two of pop music was still allowed to leak out. We bestowed barely a glance on the renamed and completely uninteresting Caravelle Hotel – I could think of it only as the Caravelle – and crossed the square with the old Opera House in the middle to the derelict Continental on the far side, so completely robbed of all its old magic. Then we gained the upper reaches of Tu Do, still looking remarkably French. Some of the French journalists used to stay in the flats there, including the Vietnam war's most famous woman photographer, Cathy Leroy. From there, it was only a few steps to the cathedral, in what was once Kennedy Square, and then to Madame Dai's, discreet in its side street.

The former deputy speaker of the National Assembly of the Republic of Vietnam (South Vietnam) had prepared well for this, our last night. The menu was remarkably good for a city as impoverished as Saigon, and although dollars could buy almost anything, except perhaps a good bottle of claret, she had quite clearly taken a lot of trouble. Most importantly for her, she had written a long letter to her daughter in Canada, which I promised to post in London. She clearly set great store by this, not having heard from her daughter and grandchildren for a long time. At the end of dinner, everything else having been disposed of, I said I would like to buy the Buddha we had seen on our first night, partly because it was so beautiful and partly because of the profound influence Vietnam had had on me. It was a country that had been torn apart by war, almost obliterated. The Americans' huge military presence, like some runaway bulldozer, had crushed the landscape, the cities, the people and finally their whole way of life with a careless brutality

106

that in the end turned even anti-Communist Vietnamese against them. And yet, despite the horror, the destruction and the death, the Vietnamese spirit, like the spirit of the Cambodians, had somehow survived.

Madame Dai fetched down the Buddha from its high shelf and placed it on the table. It had a small flaw, the pointed top of the headdress having been broken off, but the serenity of the figure, seated in the traditional lotus position, was unimpaired. I took it, at the agreed dollar price, we said our fond farewells to Madame Dai and walked out into the night. Inevitably, and happily, Check It Out was waiting for us, his silent entry on stage still slightly sinister, his first line still immensely evocative.

'Hey, let's go check it out . . .' We climbed into the flimsy back seat and watched the dark, empty city glide past us for the last time. With virtually no tourists, how did he make a living, I wondered for the umpteenth time. Our linguistic incompatability was such that we were unable to discover, but at least we could give him a large tip: in 'green', of course.

Next day, Kanh drove us to the airport from where we were to catch the flight to Paris. The tattered terminal building, and the lines of Huey helicopters on the tarmac conjured up a last flock of memories. Kanh brought me back to reality, and the present, in his own resourceful way. He was at his most assiduous and attentive, overseeing the handling of our vast quantity of baggage, and personally supervising all the details of our check-in. When all the formalities had been completed we gravitated to the duty-free shop, Kanh manoeuvring us expertly like a good sheepdog.

He had already dropped a number of hints about 'presents', building up to it over the last few days, and we all knew the argument had been conceded. It was only a question of what, and how much.

107

'Right, Mr Kanh,' I said firmly. 'We have promised you a present. What do you want?'

Eyes glistening, Kanh, who was not allowed to cross the threshold of the duty-free shop, pointed. The shop was full of the usual offerings of alcohol and tobacco: outsize bottles of whisky, gin, vodka and brandy, and cartons of American cigarettes. But Kanh ignored all these. His gaze and out-stretched arm were directed at a large cardboard box high up on a shelf. Looking closer, I saw that a picture of the contents adorned the side facing us.

'Is that what you really want, Mr Kanh?' I asked, rather surprised.

'Yes, yes, Mr Sandy,' he said, his voice low and intense. His eyes shone damply through tears of desire.

'Are you sure, Mr Kanh?'

He nodded dumbly, for once bereft of words.

I motioned to the expectantly hovering salesman. 'Give me that electric fan, would you? The one on the top shelf. The big one.'

Chapter
8

While General Zia and the former prime minister, Zulfikar Ali Bhutto, were fighting their duel to the death, a less dramatic but potentially more explosive situation was developing across the border of Pakistan to the north. In April 1978, nine months after Zia's takeover, another coup had taken place, this time in Kabul, the capital of Afghanistan. Unlike Zia, who was staunchly pro-Western, the new men in Kabul were Marxists, protégés of Moscow and determined to hoist the red flag of communism over the still essentially feudal society of Afghanistan. To students of the Great Game, the coup gave a fascinating new twist to the old rivalry between Imperial Britain and Tsarist Russia which had lasted for more than a century, led to three Anglo-Afghan wars, all of them in their different ways unmitigated disasters, and brought about the deaths of thousands of British soldiers in what Kipling called 'that mysterious land beyond the Passes of the North.'

Throughout the nineteenth century, successive British governments had been alarmed by the apparently unstoppable Russian drive south, which added millions of square miles to the Tsar's dominions, swallowed up the ancient khanates of Samarkand, Bokhara, Khiva and Merv, and in the 1870s finally brought the Russians to the Oxus, the present Afghan border. Where would the insatiable Russian appetite for territory end? The British feared their ultimate goal, like that of so many conquerors from Alexander the Great onwards, was India itself, a nightmare that was not finally dispelled until we left India for ever in 1947.

Britain's last adventure in Afghanistan, the month-long third Anglo-Afghan War of 1919, had a happier ending, at least for the Afghans who emerged for the first time as an internationally-recognised, independent, non-aligned nation. That state of affairs lasted for sixty years, until the 1978 coup. Although the West was unable to deny that Afghanistan was within the Soviet sphere of influence, it was concerned that a Communist government in Kabul might destabilise Pakistan, Afghanistan's neighbour to the south. Pakistan had been the linchpin of American military planning in the area since the 1950s, forming an essential part of the South-East Asia Treaty Organisation (SEATO), the Asian equivalent of NATO, and a counterweight to Moscow's close alliance with India.

The alarm bells really rang, however, twenty months later when on Christmas Eve 1979, in an attempt by the half-senile Brezhnev to prop up a regime that was on the point of collapse, the Soviet Union invaded Afghanistan. The speed and efficiency of the attack staggered the West: Kabul itself and all the other major cities were occupied in a lightning operation which moved 80,000 Soviet troops and hundreds of tanks into Afghanistan by air and road in forty-eight hours. Next day, Christmas Day, a shocked and worried President Carter rang Mrs Thatcher in Downing Street. The British Prime Minister, as she then was, told me later the President seemed to be taken completely by surprise – although the Americans must have known from spy-in-the-sky intelligence that the Russians had been massing troops in the Tashkent area for months. Even ordinary mortals knew that; tourists who visited Tashkent that summer reported seeing tanks and troops in large numbers in the back streets of the town. The only possible explanation is that the President did not believe the Russians would actually invade, rather as, eleven years later, no one thought Saddam Hussein would march into Kuwait.

Jimmy Carter's telephone call to Mrs Thatcher was an appeal for help to which, as one would expect, the Iron Lady responded immediately and positively. The resources of both countries, mainly political and diplomatic, were rapidly mobilised to arm and support the Afghan resistance, then in its infancy. President Sadat, a staunch anti-Communist, promised to help his fellow Moslems by making available the output of a Russian-built arms factory in Egypt producing Kalashnikov assault rifles (AK47) and other Soviet weapons. The Chinese, who as neighbours both of the Soviet Union and Afghanistan were equally taken aback by the Russian intervention, also responded quickly, agreeing to supply – at a price – the products of their own extensive arms industry, which was based almost entirely on the Soviet model.

The idea from the start was to provide the Afghans not with Western arms but with Soviet-style weaponry. This was done primarily to protect Pakistan, which was able to deny giving the Afghans any military help. No one believed it, of course, least of all the Russians, but it was precisely the Big Lie technique they themselves had used to successfully in Vietnam. Sticking to Soviet weaponry made sense in other directions too. It meant that anything the mujahideen captured – mainly small arms and ammunition, but considerable numbers of heavy machine-guns as well – could be put to immediate use: even damaged weapons were valuable as a source of spare parts. In fact, most mujahideen commanders preferred the Soviet-manufactured originals to the various Egyptian, Chinese or even Pakistani copies which the CIA bought for distribution to the resistance. One well-known commander, Abdul Haq, was convinced the Soviet-made weapons were superior. 'The steel is better in the Soviet AKs,' he once told

111

me and it was the ambition of every self-respecting mujahid to acquire one, preferably by killing its Russian owner in battle.

Apart from appearing to signal a return to the smash-and-grab style of Soviet foreign policy in the 1940s and 1950s as perfected by Stalin, the invasion raised fears in the West not only about the security of Pakistan, but even more of that of the Gulf, the source of most of the West's oil. Soviet jets based at Shindand, in south-west Afghanistan, would be only 300 miles and a few minutes' flying time from the oil fields of Saudi Arabia, Kuwait and all the other rich but vulnerable Gulf states. For no one were the consequences more spectacular than for General Zia who, nine months after the opprobrium of the Bhutto hanging, found himself being courted by Washington as a key ally against the suddenly real threat of Soviet expansionism. Not only was Pakistan and its large army the only thing that stood between the Soviets and any designs they might have on the Gulf, but its mountainous border with Afghanistan provided the only practical route by which arms could be supplied to the Afghans.

Early in the New Year of 1980, President Carter sent his National Security adviser, Zbigniew Brzezinski, a tough-minded professor of politics of Polish origin, with no illusions about the real motives of the Kremlin, to Islamabad to confer with General Zia. The agreement reached by Brzezinski and Zia was to be the foundation, over the next twelve years, of Pakistan's crucial role as the middleman in the Afghan war. Under this agreement, the United States undertook to provide the cash – $150 million in 1980, rising to $650 million in 1989 – to buy the arms which Pakistan, under General Zia, would channel to the mujahideen. The CIA, as the arm of the Administration responsible for carrying out the clandestine side of American foreign policy, was put in charge of the operation, running the war from its offices in the American Embassy in Islamabad and the

Consulate in Peshawar, the capital of the North-West Frontier Province.

This colourful, noisy, romantic frontier town, once the winter capital of the Afghan kings, was to become the headquarters of most of the Afghan mujahideen parties and the refugee centre for thousands of homeless Afghans, driven out of their own country by the Red Army. In the words of the Austrian judge, Felix Ermacora, the United Nations Special Rapporteur for Afghanistan, Soviet bombing and 'search and destroy' operations in which villages were razed to the ground and the male population deported or shot out of hand, were fast assuming the proportions of 'genocide'. All across the North-West Frontier Province, hundreds of refugee camps sprang up, some the size of small cities, housing 100,000 people. Soon there were three million Afghan refugees in Pakistan alone, with another two million in Iran; it was by far the biggest refugee problem in the world.

On the diplomatic front, Washington and London did their best to isolate Moscow. The most striking rebuff came when the Americans refused to attend the 1980 Olympic Games; but in lots of other ways the West applied the pinpricks of diplomatic displeasure. Western ambassadors in Moscow, for example, boycotted all official functions including the annual parade to mark the anniversary of the October Revolution, the most hallowed date in the Soviet calendar. In the United States, opposition to the invasion and support for the mujahideen united Congress in a way that few issues have done before or since. This remarkable unanimity was partly due to admiration for the Afghans' courage in standing up to a Communist aggressor which happened to be their own principal adversary, but there was an even stronger motive. From the very beginning, the Afghan war had all the makings of Vietnam in reverse, as the hawks in Washington were quick to realise. Here was a golden opportunity to avenge the ignominy of that defeat

113

and make the Kremlin pay dear for its support of the Vietnamese Communists. The failure in Vietnam remained a bitter experience, but it would be slightly less bitter if the Soviet Union could be humbled in Afghanistan.

Unlike Vietnam, of course, there was no overt American presence in Afghanistan: although American influence was enormous, thanks to the long arm of the CIA, there were no American troops and no American advisers 'in-country'. In Vietnam, the Americans had insisted on 'micro-management', by which they attempted to orchestrate and control every aspect of the war, from major policy decisions taken on a national plane, down to the details of command at company or village level. To do that competently would have meant acquiring an intimate knowledge of the country and the people who ran it, something the Americans never aspired to. Indeed one of the commonest criticisms of their conduct of the war was the almost complete ignorance of the Vietnamese mind, character and psyche displayed by the decision makers from the President down. With staggering arrogance, the lessons of France's defeat in Indo-China were ignored and relegated to the dustbin of history.

Determined to avoid the mistakes they had made in Vietnam, the Americans went to the other extreme; instead of micro-management, the watchword was now macro-management. Instead of supervising every aspect of the war down to the last detail, they would hand over its day-to-day running to their good friends and allies, the Pakistanis, restricting their own involvement to the most important decisions. It was known as an 'arm's length' policy. More than that: they would take the Pakistanis' word for who was who in Afghanistan, who was worth supporting and who was not, and how the arms should be allocated. It must have been an enormous comfort to Brzezinski and all the National Security and CIA officials who followed in his footsteps to Pakistan when they first met Zia and were confronted by his film-star smile and impeccable military appearance. He fairly exuded self-confidence and charm and was clearly in complete control of the army and, indeed, the country. If you had to delegate, who better to delegate to than this British-trained soldier who spoke good English and as Bhutto's former Chief of Army Staff knew his way round Washington and other Western capitals. On top of all this, those from the Pentagon and the CIA found that Zia, both as a politician and a devout Moslem, was if anything even more dedicated to driving the Russians out of Afghanistan than they were themselves. As he said to me one day: 'Quite apart from my commitment to the Jehad [Holy War], I have a duty to Pakistan. I cannot ignore the fact that one hundred thousand Soviet troops are sitting on the other side of the border. It may be Afghanistan today, but it could be Pakistan tomorrow – even if tomorrow is in fifty years' time.'

To their surprise, the first Soviets to arrive in Afghanistan found themselves being if not exactly welcomed, at least met by Western reporters and television crews who either hapened to be in Kabul at the time or who were able to fly in soon afterwards from Moscow or Delhi, only a short hop away. The *Times* correspondent was enterprising enough to make his way up the Salang Highway and meet the Soviet tanks on their way south, and one tank commander was even relaxed enough to give him an interview. But after a few weeks the Russians put up the shutters, expelling all Western correspondents and imposing a complete news blackout. Early in 1980, Afghanistan became forbidden territory to all but a handful of Communist or fellow-travelling journalists. The only way to penetrate this new extension of the Iron Curtain was to cross the border illegally in the company of the mujahideen. It was risky and extremely arduous. Because of the threat of attack by Soviet helicopter gunships and jets, the mujahideen kept well away from the roads, which, in any case, were few and far between, and

115

moved along mountain trails on foot. The only means of transport available to heavily-laden television crews, more at home in a Volvo Estate, was the pack horse. Small wonder that the long trek through the mountains, taking weeks rather than days, and the uncertainty of what would materialise at the end, discouraged virtually all the big television companies and all but the hardiest of film makers. Nick Downey was a notable example of the latter, although Thames Television had to fight a running battle with the film and television union, the ACTT, to be able to show his material at all. But films like Downey's, including his remarkable pictures of a mujahideen attack in the middle of Kandahar, were the exception, and the silence surrounding the war in Afghanistan descended like a fog.

This worried the British Government in general and Lord Carrington, the Foreign Secretary, in particular. In 1980, he went to Moscow to try and persuade Brezhnev to withdraw his troops from Afghanistan, arguing that the British had made the same mistake three times in the past 140 years and had lived to regret it. The Russians, he warned, would find themselves in the same mess. Brezhnev did not take kindly to this lecture, riposting that there was no comparison between British and Soviet intentions: the British had been imperialists, the Russians on the other hand were engaged in a civilising mission. Lord Carrington departed empty-handed.

Not very long after that I received a call from a friend in British Intelligence telling me that the Foreign Secretary remained particularly concerned about Afghanistan and was anxious to keep the war 'in front of the British public'; how could that be done? Would I talk to someone from his office and give him, and Lord Carrington, the benefit of my advice? Feeling flattered, I agreed, although making the proviso that I might not be able to contribute anything very significant. That was all right, my friend said, at least they would have tried to meet the request.

116

We met for lunch at Stone's Chop House in Piccadilly, an old-fashioned eating-house in the English style, and over roast beef and Yorkshire pudding I said that television could not report a war or anything else unless it had pictures. The trouble with the Afghan war, I lectured my bespectacled and earnest interlocutor, was that hardly any pictures were coming out of the country and unless that could be changed, television would continue to ignore it in favour of more visual subjects. My host asked me how the situation could be changed and I said, with difficulty. The mujahideen did not come from an urban, television-watching, PR-conscious society, but were simple, rural souls brought up in villages where there was no running water, electricity or telephone. Their idea of good communications was knowing which pass to take into the next valley. Most of them had never seen a television camera in their lives, let alone knew how to use it. The only way, in my opinion, the British Government could keep the Afghan war in front of the British people was by getting freelance cameramen to go there and take pictures of the fighting which, if exciting enough, the television companies might buy and put on the screen. Since no freelance would go there unless he was guaranteed a financial return, they might have to provide some inducement, in the shape of money.

The man from the ministry listened carefully. Would television companies like ITN be prepared to buy such material, he asked. I said if the material was genuine and good enough, I was sure they would. If ITN did not buy it, the BBC might. This was how the freelance market worked: like any other system of supply and demand. It was quite a good lunch but I was not sure, as I said goodbye to my new friend, that my advice would be acted upon and there the matter rested until 1982 when, deciding it was time the world should be told just what was going on behind the official Soviet smokescreen, I decided to see for myself what was happening in Afghanistan. I rang the same friend in

117

Intelligence, told him my plan and he said, 'Oh, I'll send you the same chap that you talked to before.'

'Fine,' I said, 'the lunch is on me, this time.' We met, again, in Stone's and had a very similar sort of lunch. The menu had not changed but our roles were now reversed. I was the one seeking advice and he was the expert, although a modest one. 'We really know very little of what is happening in Afghanistan,' he said, 'although the French are for historical and cultural reasons better informed, and my advice is, go to Paris and talk to one or two people there.' Which people? Well, he said, there was a very knowledgeable and much-travelled scholar called Olivier Roy, and another man, also deeply interested in the subject and well-travelled too, called Jean-José Puig. Both were worth talking to. I wrote down their addresses and telephone numbers. He then delivered his bombshell, although I did not know it was such at the time.

'There is, however, one young Afghan guerrilla leader who we think is exceptional. He's called Masud – Ahmed Shah Masud – he's still in his twenties, and he operates from a place called the Panjsher Valley, north-east of Kabul. It's quite a long way in from the Pakistani border, and you'll have to climb several high passes to get there. But if you have the time, he might be worth it.' He paused, then looked at me very seriously. 'Because, you see, we think he has all the makings of a second Tito.'

A second Tito. The words cut through the babble in the restaurant like a sword, shimmering in the smoky haze. 'Really? That's a pretty big claim, isn't it?'

'Yes, and of course it's early days.' He shrugged. 'Only time will tell. But we think he has that sort of potential.'

As I walked back to the office I felt more excited than I had been for a very long time. It sounded like the adventure I had been looking for, without realising it. I started planning the trip to Paris, but already at the back of my mind

118

the idea was forming for a one-hour television documentary on the war, with Masud as the principal character.

Charles Morgan, who had recently left ITN and joined a small independent company, was keen to go with me. His enthusiasm was refreshing but sometimes a trifle alarming. On one occasion he went off and ordered an elaborate camera harness, based on an old British army design for pack mules. This, he assured me, would be the best way to transport the camera equipment over the mountains. Unfortunately, the Afghan horsemen who had to handle our baggage took one look at it and decided it was not for them. The last time I saw it – or part of it – was in a village which the Russians had just been bombing. When we went to inspect the damage, we found bits of the harness outside one house. It is probably still there, having been adapted to local use. I also recruited Nigel Ryan, an old friend and former editor of ITN. Nigel sold the documentary idea to Charles Denton of Central Television, who made only one proviso: Nigel would be the producer, a condition with which I was happy to agree. Preparations went ahead throughout the summer, and finally, by the end of July, our small team which, with the addition of a soundman, Tom Murphy, had now grown to four, was ready to depart.

On 1 August 1982 we caught a PIA flight to Islamabad, from where we drove to Peshawar. From there, dressed like Afghan mujahideen in baggy trousers and shirts, with flat Chitrali *pukuls* on our heads, we crossed the border heading north. Twelve days later, after what seemed incredible exertions, we reached our destination, the Panjsher Valley, Masud's base and theatre of operations. Unfortunately, the Soviets had forestalled us, and were bombarding the valley with jets and helicopters. A few days later they launched a full-scale ground offensive with tanks, armoured personnel carriers and Spetsnaz commandos. This went on for three weeks, and as the Russians advanced up the valley, we were hurried on Masud's orders from one mountain hideout

119

to another to avoid capture. During these three weeks, partly through bad luck but also partly because of bad management for which I blame myself, we were separated from our television equipment, and unable to do more than take still pictures of the bombing.

Against all the odds, however, we did succeed in making a very creditable documentary which was shown on ITV in peak time, immediately before *News at Ten*, on 23 November. It was watched by 7.6 million viewers, an exceptionally big audience for a documentary, helped no doubt by some excellent pre-publicity. The *Daily Express*, for example, ran a splendid piece in which, tongue in cheek, their correspondent drew a Hollywood parallel. Nigel Ryan and I, he said, were like Errol Flynn and Victor MacLaglen conquering the Khyber Pass. To my chagrin, I was cast in the role of Victor MacLaglen, a rugged old Scots tough, while Nigel was awarded the part of the smooth and dashing Errol.

The three-month expedition had a number of surprising consequences; for one thing, I lost a stone and a half, and came home looking like a skeleton. But much more importantly, it aroused a passionate interest in the Afghan struggle for independence, first against the Russian occupation, and secondly against the Communist regime which succeeded it. This interest has grown with the years, and among other things, led me to start a family-run charity which provides artificial limbs for Afghans disabled in the war, and also treats children suffering from polio, spina bifida, cerebral palsy and other diseases bred by overcrowding in the refugee camps.

It also prompted me to accept an invitation to go back two years later to make a second film about the war. The invitation came from General Zia, in a roundabout way. Mrs Thatcher visited Pakistan in early 1984, at Zia's invitation, to lend moral support to the man whose support for the mujahideen in the struggle against the Russians was crucial to the West. All Western aid to the mujahideen, whether

120

arms, equipment, or training, running into billions of dollars, went through Pakistan – there was no alternative. Mrs Thatcher may not have had much sympathy with General Zia, the military dictator, but she was determined to oppose the Russian invasion of Afghanistan, and she was realist enough to know that Zia was an essential ally. She also succeeded spectacularly well in grabbing the headlines, making a much-publicised trip through the Khyber Pass to the Afghan border, where she held a Kalashnikov rifle aloft for the photographers and shook hands with a bemused Afghan border guard. In private, Zia asked for her help in keeping the issue of the Afghan war before the British public, in the newspapers and especially on television. He then added, I was told later, 'We must encourage people like Sandy Gall to come out here and report what is happening in Afghanistan.'

This conversation was minuted, in the standard Whitehall manner, and eventually a copy found its way to the desk of a friend. He rang me up and asked me to lunch. It was a good lunch, but the idea he now laid out before me was so surprising that I have forgotten where we went and what we ate. But I remember the conversation vividly. After explaining the genesis of the idea, he said, 'This is really Zia's idea, so you would have his personal backing. The plan is that you would go in with a group of mujahideen who are going to carry out a number of operations against Soviet and Afghan regime targets. One operation is for an attack on a Russian convoy in a narrow gorge somewhere between Kabul and the Pakistani border. Zia wants to give you a personal protection squad of Pakistani Special Forces just in case anything goes wrong. He is very concerned about your safety.'

I laughed. I was flattered to think that a head of state should show such concern for my personal safety. But more seriously, was this a proposition that one could accept, ethically? It did not take me long to make up my mind. I

121

said my immediate reaction was yes, provided nothing was staged, and that I would be able to do my job in the normal way, on my own terms. I said I would obviously have to discuss it with ITN, but I did not foresee any great difficulty, although I would keep the Zia–Thatcher conversation to myself. My friend said he absolutely understood and we agreed to keep in touch. Over the next few months, as the project gradually took shape, and the war in Afghanistan ground on, the question that increasingly concerned me was whether the heavily-armed Soviet Mi24 helicopter gunships, in many ways the Russians' most effective weapon, were finally beginning to tip the balance against the mujahideen? There was reason to think that this could be so, but less and less news was coming out of Afghanistan, and the world's media seemed to have lost interest.

Winston Churchill MP, the grandson of Britain's great wartime prime minister, had encouraged my interest in Afghanistan in the first place. He was particularly critical of the dearth of coverage on the BBC, and when he wrote complaining, he received a dusty answer saying the BBC did not think the risk involved in sending crews to Afghanistan was acceptable. All the more reason, in my view, for us to go.

As I had hoped, my editor, David Nicholas, gave me complete support, agreeing that, with Zia smoothing the way, it was far too good a chance to be missed. He went further. He suggested that, since Central Television had entirely financed the first documentary, ITN should play a bigger role this time, providing an ITN crew and editor, while Central would partly finance and screen the one-hour documentary on ITV. Paul Carleton, one of ITN's best and toughest cameramen, and his soundman Jon Hunt, volunteered for the assignment and were immediately accepted. We sealed the deal over lunch in Bertorelli's, round the corner from ITN, over a plate of pasta and a few bottles of white wine. David Nicholas made only one condition for giving us his blessing: we must attend a briefing on gas warfare – which the Russians were rumoured to be using – and take protective clothing with us. I said I thought the risks of being subjected to a Russian gas attack were minimal, but he insisted. So shortly before our departure we visited the offices of one of the cloak-and-dagger agencies run by former members of the SAS and were given a long and extremely boring lecture about the origins of gas warfare, finishing up with a description of the various nasty gasses the Russians might use against us. We were each given a rubber suit adorned with several patches of chemically treated cloth which turned the colours of the rainbow when exposed to gas, before which, of course, you would have hoped to have donned your gas mask. A pair of rubber boots completed the ensemble. We dutifully carried the whole lot round Afghanistan with us among our many bags of equipment but never, I am happy to record, had to use it.

Soon after arriving in Islamabad, I was summoned to Zia's house. He gave me a warm greeting and then suggested we stroll in the garden among the roses and flowering shrubs, just in case the Russians had bugged his house, I presumed. After a brief discussion on the progress of the war, about which he seemed to be fairly optimistic, he asked me if there was anything I wanted.

'Yes,' I said. 'May I ask which group we're going in with?'

'Which group do you want to go in with?' he asked.

'Well, not with Hisb-i-Islami, at least not with Gulbuddin,' I said. Gulbuddin Hekmatyar, a Pashtun extremist, had founded the party, but one wing had broken away under a tough old mullah called Younis Khalis. During my trip to the Panjsher two years before, I had seen how ruthlessly Gulbuddin was seeking to extend his power: Masud claimed he spent more time killing other Afghan mujahideen than Russians. Zia simply said, 'No problem.'

'Anything else?'

'Yes. Would it be possible to have some SAM 7s with us?'

Zia laughed. 'SAM 7s? I don't see why not. But why?'

'We're likely to come under attack by Mi24 gunships, I suppose, and it would make some spectacular pictures if one of them were to be shot down.'

Zia laughed again, seeing the point. 'I'll see to it,' he promised. 'You'll get your SAMs.'

As we walked back to the house, he stopped for a moment and took my arm. 'Sandy, I'm sending my best Special Forces officer and a small team in with you. They'll look after you. I know you can look after yourself, but I want you to come back in one piece.' He laughed again, easily, to reassure me. The car was waiting by the front door, and Zia, as was his custom, opened the door for me himself. 'Come and see me when you get back,' he said with a farewell wave.

Next day I was briefed by General Akhtar, Zia's head of Intelligence, and introduced to Colonel 'Faisan', the Special Forces Officer who was going to take us into Afghanistan. He was a pleasant-looking man in his early thirties, and spoke excellent English. I had a feeling we would get on. General Akhtar, who apart from Zia himself had more influence on the day to day running of the war than anyone else, outlined the general plan of campaign. He was taller and thinner than Zia, rather pale complexioned, with blue eyes. He was a Pushtun, which may have explained why, when I mentioned that I had spent several weeks with Masud two years before, and had found him extremely impressive, he wrinkled up his brow and said, 'Masud? Masud? Oh, you mean Masud Panjsheri,' as if he were only one of many Masuds. The Pushtuns, as I was to discover, have a wonderful arrogance which leads them to believe they are superior to everyone else.

The general went on, 'You will be travelling with the Colonel here, and a group of Younis Khalis people. They are the strongest party in Nangarhar Province, the Jalalabad area. In fact, Din Mohammed, the deputy leader of the party, will be in charge of the group. They have devised, with a little assistance from us' – he permitted himself a slight smile – 'quite a full programme. First of all, they are planning to ambush a Russian convoy on the main road to Kabul. If all goes well, they will blow up a lot of tanks, and Russians.' He gave his thin smile again. 'Then they plan to return by way of a place called Hissarak, where there is a government fort. This fort sits astride one of the most important mujahideen infiltration routes, and it would be a big success if they can capture it. They have other plans as well, but those are the two most important operations.'

'If only one of those comes off, it will be worth it,' I said, rising to go.

'Good luck,' General Akhtar said. 'I can tell you one thing.' He nodded in Faisan's direction. 'You are in very good hands.'

Chapter
9

We crossed the border west of Peshawar, at Terri Mangal, named after the two tribes which live in the area, just as we had done two years before. But the place had changed out of all recognition: it was as if Hildenborough, my local railway station in Kent, had suddenly grown to the size of Charing Cross. The arms convoys were running at full spate, with hundreds of horses setting off for the interior daily, all through the summer. In 1982, we had climbed the hill that lies beyond the caravanserai into Afghanistan on foot; this time, we bounded up in a jeep, horn blaring. Five miles in, we stopped and Din Mohammed took us for a stroll to see the ruins of a government fort which, he said, the mujahideen had captured the year before. In the distance, rockets glowed against the mountain, like fireflies. The mujahideen were attacking Ali Khel, another government fort designed to block an infiltration route. These forts clearly did not stop infiltration – the mujahideen simply bypassed them – but they flew the government flag, and provided the regime with intelligence about mujahideen movements.

Next morning we broke camp before five and, faintly illuminated by a sickle moon, started walking across the plain towards the foothills of the Hindu Kush. Two hours later our horses appeared and we mounted gratefully. I

126

remembered how exhausting the climb had been two years before, in the heat of high summer, to the top of an 11,000-foot pass. I had learned my lesson and during the planning for this trip, made sure we had enough horses both to ride and to carry our equipment. Now, climbing the pass on horseback, even with unequal stirrups and uncomfortable saddles, was child's play: for one thing, we could actually enjoy the scenery, instead of plodding upwards, lungs bursting and eyes fixed on the stony path ahead. After the pass we descended by easy stages through a valley in which the colours seemed especially vivid, due to the absence of pollution in Afghanistan. Huge clumps of wild lavender, growing on the stone walls of the terraced fields, shone like stained glass with the sun behind them; and the young maize was the tenderest green. The farmers in the village of Mangal were ploughing in the ancient way with a wooden hand plough pulled by a pair of oxen; and two men in bright blue baggy trousers and shirts were reaping wheat by hand. We slept on the flat roof of a farmhouse under a sky full of stars. I lay briefly looking up at the huge expanse of the Milky Way, a great handful of silver dust thrown on the black carpet above us.

In the morning, we rode through what seemed endless dry river beds, the heat bouncing off the rocks, the horses plodding gamely up the ravines. Many of the villages were deserted, most of the inhabitants having fled across the border to Pakistan, leaving only an estimated five per cent of the population behind; mostly men who had taken their families to the refugee camps in Pakistan and then returned to fight. Every so often we would stop for a blessed rest and endless cups of green tea, without which I do not think I could have survived. On our way down the mountain, we came on a group of refugees toiling up to the pass, some carrying children in their arms. One little girl who couldn't have been more than three was perched on top of a donkey. It was a heartrending but not unusual sight. Paul had been

127

commendably quick in getting his camera off one of the pack horses and had already started filming when a middle-aged man stopped in front of us, and burst into English. A civil engineer from Kabul, the strength of his feelings made him eloquent as he explained that he and his family simply could not endure life under the Communists any more.

'We can't stand it any longer: my nephew has just been in jail for two years, in Pul-i-Charkhi, and maybe they will arrest him again. They keep telling us to join the party, and we do not want to. We are Afghans, we don't want to work for the Communists . . . So we are leaving, the whole family, to join our brothers in Pakistan.

'We are afraid. Life is dangerous in Kabul,' he said, his voice breaking with emotion. 'We can't live under the Russians any more . . . We want the Russians to leave our beautiful country.' Another splendid-looking man carrying a small boy sucking a sweet delivered an impassioned tirade in Farsi. He was from Mazar-i-Sharif, in the north. He said he was bringing his family out and would then go back to fight the Russians.

But it was only afterwards that the grimmest part of the story emerged, recounted to me by Faisan. He said that the four young women in the party had told him and the other Pakistanis that they had been repeatedly raped by Russian soldiers and were all pregnant, one being close to giving birth. Even if we had known at the time, we would have been unable to interview them, or even to film them, given Moslem susceptibilities. One wild fellow in a fur hat even stopped us filming the civil engineer's wife, despite the fact that her husband did not mind. But Fur Hat, an Islamic zealot, objected strongly. Afterwards Din Mohammed asked me not to mention the story of the raped women. He said, through Faisan, that of course this was not the first time it had happened, but that on previous occasions the women had preferred to kill themselves rather than live in dishonour. It also offended Din Mohammed's strict Pashtun

128

code of honour, the *Pashtunwali*, that Afghan women should divulge their secrets to strangers; they should never have told the Pakistanis their story in the first place. I tried to argue that if the Afghans refused to tell the world the terrible things the Russians were doing in Afghanistan, they would fail to make their case as powerfully as they might. Din Mohammed was not convinced, but I included the story in my report.

The next day saw us arrive at one of the party's main bases in the mountains, guarding an ammunition dump hidden in a narrow, rocky gorge. Another surprise awaited us: three Russian prisoners came up and introduced themselves. They did not look like prisoners, being dressed like mujahideen, and told us they had all defected, one, Vadim, the youngest, after only a week in Afghanistan. Vadim was nineteen, Vladislav, the leader of the group, twenty-one and Sergei, twenty. Over a cup of tea in a tent, they told us their story in halting English, with the help of a mujahid interpreter who had been educated in Russia. They looked so young and vulnerable, I felt paternal and concerned for them. What had made them defect?

They were opposed to the general lack of freedom at home, they said, and to the Soviet government's policy of destruction in Afghanistan. Vladislav said he had been in constant trouble with the authorities, and had spent a month in KGB custody just before he decided to make a run for it; Vadim said he simply could not take the brutality of military life and the injustice of what was being done in Afghanistan; and Sergei, who was the shyest and simplest, said he had been beaten up so much by NCOs and other soldiers – all too common, apparently, in the Soviet army – that he had decided to run away. They seemed genuinely disgusted by the brutal things that were undoubtedly happening. They had already been with the mujahideen for more than a year, and as we talked it became clear they were desperate to leave Afghanistan and somehow reach the West – although they were cautious about saying this. When they discovered that we came from Britain and worked in television news, their reaction was immediate. Would we take a letter to Mrs Thatcher? (presumably asking for asylum) I said I would and promised to have it delivered to Downing Street.

Vladislav, who appeared mature and highly intelligent, said he was writing a book about his experiences in Afghanistan. He had also, of his own accord, written open letters to Soviet soldiers serving in Afghanistan, criticising the Soviet occupation, and gave me copies of two, which he said the mujahideen had distributed secretly to Soviet barracks and outposts. They told us they were well treated by the mujahideen, and had considerable freedom of movement: they were, for example, allowed to have lunch with us alone. Afterwards, it was strange to see them praying alongside all the other mujahideen; although they were all European Russians, they had converted to Islam and adopted Moslem names. No doubt they had little option, especially in a party as strongly Islamic as Maulawi Khalis's.

Interviewing them turned out to be complicated, since their English was extremely limited, and I could not speak Russian. Eventually, with the help of the Russian-speaking Afghan, we worked out the questions and the answers in advance, so that both sides knew more or less what the other wanted to say. When the camera started rolling, I asked the questions in English, the Afghan translated into Russian, and Vladislav, the spokesman, answered in Russian. To save time, we did not translate the answers into English, which would have been beyond our translator in any case, leaving that until we got back to London. Vladislav said that as a member of an airborne assault battalion he had trained on replicas of Afghan villages built by Soviet engineers near Termesz, on the Oxus. 'That was how we were taught to fight the war in Afghanistan,' he said. It was common practice, when they came under attack, for Soviet troops to surround and search the nearest Afghan villages for mujahideen. If they suffered casualties, the Russians usually burnt down the houses and killed many or all of the inhabitants.

'The Afghans know what they're fighting for,' Vladislav said. 'They're fighting for the independence of their country. Soviet soldiers don't know why they've come here. Their attitude is unenthusiastic . . . they're afraid of death. That's why, when they carry out these operations [against Afghan villages] Soviet soldiers are usually high on drugs, which are freely available . . . They don't know what they're doing, and so they just kill everybody who gets in their way.'

Our horsemen were Persian-speaking Tajiks, from Baghlan Province in the north. Mine was an amiable simpleton, almost a village idiot, with the infuriating habit of repeating himself over and over again. Early on, I made the mistake of showing off my few words of Farsi, such as *asp*, meaning horse. As I rode his fiery little grey stallion up and down the mountains, my simple friend would walk beside me, grinning broadly and chanting '*asp . . . asp . . . asp . . . asp.*' There was nothing for it, finally, but to avert my gaze and pretend not to hear. Like most people, the Tajik horsemen delighted in the misfortunes of others, especially if they were infidel foreigners, and our poor horsemanship occasioned much mirth. One day, as we were passing through a small wood, my grey stallion, who obviously did not like me, made straight for the tree with the lowest branches. Fighting off my attempts to divert him, he swept me Absalom-like under the lowest bough, forcing me to lie along his neck and cling on desperately. I nearly lost both my hat and my seat as the low bough scraped across my back to the guffaws of the horsemen. I kicked the stallion angrily, while my idiot horseman followed me with a huge grin on his face, enjoying the fun. Later in the day, stopping for tea at some *chaikhana*, or teahouse, to my astonishment

131

and delight the horseman who had laughed loudest and longest at my discomfiture somehow contrived to fall off the back of his own horse, tumbling clumsily into a dry river bed. Furious, he got up and beat the wretched animal, while I tried to hide a smile and reflected that Allah was just.

When, after another stop, we were remounting, my stallion laid his ears back, bared his teeth and struck out with his forefeet. Luckily, I was standing beside him and not in front of him, and his driving hooves missed me. But the ferocity of the attack took me by surprise,and as I stood indecisively wondering what to do next, my horseman, who was nearby, caught the animal's head and with a few curses and mighty tugs on the bridle brought him swiftly under control. Simple he might be, but he certainly knew how to handle horses. After that, I did not mind his inane 'asp . . . asp . . . asp . . . asp.'

On Monday 30 July, our sixth day inside Afghanistan, we made a long, hot climb to the top of a mountain to inspect the position for the proposed ambush of the Russian convoy. Sitting among the rocks at the top of the escarpment, we gazed down at the Kabul River and the Kabul-Jalalabad road, shimmering in the heat two or three miles in the distance. To the west lay Kabul, hidden in its ring of mountains, and to the east, Jalalabad.

Occasionally, a lorry appeared and moved at a snail's pace across the baking landscape, its garishly painted coach-work clearly visible in the dry air. We examined the projected site for a long time. It seemed to me, scanning the area through binoculars, that there was hardly any cover at all within five hundred yards of the road, which Faisan suggested was a safe range for filming. We might have to spend all day lying in wait for the convoy, virtually in the open, and almost certainly visible from a Soviet post on the left, close to where the river issued out of a gorge. That was the main drawback; but there was another, political one. One of the local commanders explained that this was a main

132

north–south crossing point for both Jamiat and Hisb-i-Islami convoys. Our ambush would disrupt their traffic and that would cause trouble.

I turned to Faisan. 'It seems to me it's no go. What do you think?'

He pulled a face. 'You're right. We'll have to try another site, in the gorge.' Then, after an earnest conversation with Din Mohammed, he turned to announce another setback. 'You know the plan calls for mines to be planted on the road, as the trigger for the ambush? Well, they're saying now they can't do that, because the road is fully tarmaced.'

I groaned. 'You'd have thought somebody would have realised that before?' Faisan shrugged, as if to say that he was not responsible for the inefficiency of his Afghan comrades-in-arms. A new plan would have to be devised, involving a lengthy detour to the new ambush site, but the mujahideen did not seem to mind. Time is of little consequence to Afghans, and they find our Western sense of urgency incomprehensible. But if their timekeeping is deplorable, their sense of humour is altogether admirable. One mujahid told me, 'There is a Russian convoy on the road every day, except on operations day. Then,' he added with a grin, 'they don't come.' Din Mohammed, in particular, had an excellent sense of humour. He laughed a lot in a high-pitched, almost falsetto giggle, and cracked jokes at us in his curiously accented English. I noticed, too, when he was with his commanders and followers, there was a lot of laughing and joking, although they also whispered conspiratorially for hours, a common Afghan habit which probably comes from the very public kind of life the men lead. They are the opposite of the English; far from his home being his castle – except where his women are concerned – an Afghan's is open to all comers, rather like a bazaar.

Next day we were invited to lunch by a local commander. It was an invitation we could not refuse, although it meant walking about five miles through rugged country reminiscent of the approaches to the Grand Canyon; near desert, with huge boulders perched one on top of the other. Occasionally a shot would ring out from a crag as one of the sentries announced his presence. Lunch was spread in a grove of huge walnut and mulberry trees, and we lounged on rugs and cushions like travellers from the *Arabian Nights*, or characters from some Moghul miniature. A very young boy with a Kalashnikov slung over his shoulder helped with the preparations. He was only twelve, although he had been a mujahid for two years and had already taken part in the ambush of a Russian convoy. He was one of thirteen brothers, who included the commander, and all of whom were in the mujahideen. Six were in the camp, the other seven in Pakistan, and they apparently rotated so that there were always some on active service. The boy, they said, was always volunteering. We walked back with the new moon rising and the sunset painting a salmon backdrop to the sharp edge of the mountains. It was completely still, the tattered green flag of Islam hanging motionless beside the grave of a *shaheed*, a mujahid who had fallen in battle, as we walked through the old graveyard, full of ghosts in the evening light.

Next morning, things started happening. The commander in charge of the ambush, Hussein Pacha, took a roll call and distributed Kalashnikovs to a line of waiting mujahideen, throwing them down from the top of a rock for each man to catch. Ammunition followed. Everyone then gathered in a circle for prayers, and the mullah recited some verses from the Koran. This was followed by a lot of slogan-chanting: long live the Mujahideen, long live the *Holy War*, long live Afghanistan, each slogan being cheered enthusiastically. Ready for battle, we now set off to climb the hill opposite on our way to the new ambush position. It was a long hot climb and my ankle was rather painful after the trek the day before, but we were able to ride most of the way, up steep, rocky paths, and then down along dry stream beds overhung with sweet-smelling wild lavender, its blue mist softening the harshness of the rocks and sand. A huge lammergeyer sailed past, its breast strikingly yellow, like a trendy waistcoat. We had a new team of porters who had to be thoroughly briefed and told not to throw down the camera gear, as they did their own equipment: the previous team had been drafted into the front line, on ambush duty.

At midday we halted at a *chaikhana* perched among rocks by the side of a rushing torrent. Collapsing into a bright blue tent, onto Pakistani-made khaki quilts, we were served green tea, to our surprise, in cups and saucers captured from a government rest house. They were French-made and mine still bore a sticker saying 'Extra resistant', which Din Mohammed thought a good joke. Although he came from an important family and was deputy leader of the party, he was the opposite of authoritarian. If our group was anything to go by, Pashtun society was very democratic. Anyone could sit at the top table, as it were; anyone could approach the leader directly and put his case to him. My simple friend the horseman, for example, after spending the morning happily chanting 'asp . . . asp' at me, now sat grinning with inordinate pleasure next to Din Mohammed.

After some delicious *mast*, the local yoghurt, and *nan* bread, we rode up and down the mountains all afternoon, eventually halting in the evening by a stream in a small valley, just below a rocky ridge: on the other side, we knew, lay the Kabul River, and the road. As the light faded in a haze of gold and pink, we watched the mujahideen washing in the stream and then praying, facing Mecca, kneeling among the stones. It is a sight that never fails to move me, this display of a simple faith, the sort of faith we European Christians used to have. After prayers, Din Mohammed himself broke the news: the mines had still not arrived, so the operation would have to be postponed. Resisting the temptation to make a ribald comment – I could hear Paul and Jon supplying their own in the background – I urged

Din Mohammed and Faisan to go ahead with the operation, despite the lack of mines, as there was definite information that a convoy carrying ammunition was due from Kabul the next day. Din Mohammed, however, was reluctant, adding that he was also short of mortars. The mines, of course, were the most spectacular element of the whole operation, so I soon agreed that we should wait until they arrived. I had really been making a point: that we did not have unlimited time and we wanted action. We camped beside the river *à la belle étoile*. It was a lovely spot, but we were beginning to find the humidity enervating, and I longed for the invigorating air of the high Hindu Kush.

After a rather sticky night, we rose early to find that the sky had clouded over, which was a good omen for our recce of the ambush position. We climbed about 500 feet to the top of the ridge, and then scrambled down the other side until, far below, we could see the road, and just beyond it the sprawling green rush of the Kabul River. Buses and cars crawled into view intermittently, like insects. We chose a point below us and to the left for the camera position and then walked further down to a big rock from where we could look down on a Russian post. As I focused the binoculars I was unpleasantly surprised to see two heads apparently looking straight at me, and stepped back quickly. We climbed back up the hill and sat down under a rock to await developments. At about two o'clock, a couple of Mi24s appeared and circled purposefully overhead. They stayed above us for a long time, which suggested a big convoy, possibly as many as 250 vehicles.

In the afternoon, the Chinese mines finally arrived. Made of yellow plastic, they looked exactly like the sort of old-fashioned jelly moulds Mrs Bridges would have had in her *Upstairs, Downstairs* kitchen. They worked on the pressure principle, but they now had to be modified so that they could be detonated by remote control. After testing the remote control exploder, the minelaying party set off late in the afternoon, carrying their mines, long lengths of bright yellow detonator cord and the SAMs. The operators had been briefed not to open fire until the helicopters attacked, although this seemed somewhat academic since a SAM 7 cannot be fired until the operator has 'lock-on', which means the target is within range. Despite serious doubts about their professionalism, I could not help but be impressed by the mujahideen. They displayed no fear, not even nervousness, behaving almost as if they were going on a picnic. They appeared genuinely to despise the Russians as soldiers, although they did have a healthy respect for their air power.

As we watched them disappear over the skyline, Faisan explained the operational plan, which I was convinced had been drawn up by the Pakistanis, making a rough sketch as he talked. 'We expect the convoy to come from the direction of Kabul, from the west. There will almost certainly be two or three tanks at the head of the column, and then the main body of the convoy, trucks, petrol tankers and so on. Now, the mines will be planted in groups, and linked with detonator cord so as to go off in series, ten at a time. The plan is to let the lead tanks and the rest of the convoy pass in front of the ambush party and get as far as here . . .' he drew a cross on the right-hand side of the paper . . . 'before the first batch of mines is set off. That will cut the lead tanks off from the rest of the convoy which will then be stalled in front of the ambush party, here, on the hillside above the convoy. As the Soviets are recovering from the initial shock, the rest of the mines will be detonated. By that time, there will be a good deal of confusion among the convoy, we hope.'

I knew he meant the mujahideen would then open up with everything they had: AK47s, RPG7s, and recoilless rifles. Faisan gave a modest laugh. It sounded a good plan. I wondered if it was too good to be true. 'How will they plant the mines?' I asked.

'They will dig holes in the road during the night, in the darkness, lay the mines and then conceal their traces.' I imagined the road was so potholed that no one would notice another few holes. 'Afterwards, they'll take cover among the rocks above the road until the convoy comes along. *Insh'allah.*'

Insh'allah, if Allah wills, that infinitely useful word which conditions every situation in life with the factor of God's will, thus providing the perfect excuse for every inadequacy. It almost does away with personal liability, since everyone is subservient to God's will, and encourages, to use another overworked word, the attitude of *mañana*. There was nothing we could do now, except wait, and hope that someone would bring us supper, and tea, *insh'allah*. It had been an almost tea-less day, and I had come to depend heavily on the delicious, green *sabs*. At ten past seven, we heard the unmistakable heavy thud of mortar fire from the direction of the road. I hoped the ambush party, which represented 120 of our total force of 200, had not run into trouble already. Shortly afterwards, Din Mohammed left, without explanation, and we sat down with Faisan to await developments.

It was clear that we needed to move into our camera position while it was still dark, but by late evening nothing had happened so we stretched out on a flattish piece of earth, the mujahideen spreading blankets for us. I slept uneasily, conscious that time was slipping away and we were getting no closer to our ambush position. Where was Din Mohammed? Not even Faisan seemed to have any idea, but about four in the morning, he got up and said we ought to move closer to the scene of the action. We trudged down the slope with our porters but by the time we had reached the chosen rock, which was clearly in view of the right-hand Russian post, it was light. Our porters tramped happily along the skyline and any Russian lookout must have seen

138

them. When I questioned if this was wise, Faisan gave a little laugh.

'The mujahideen don't bother about being seen. They say the Russians are frightened of them, and simply turn their backs, pretending the Afghans are not there.' This sounded like Pashtun bravado to me, and a small seed of doubt began to grow in my mind. Paul and Jon set up the camera behind the rock, draping a blanket over it and we sat there, on the bare mountainside, as the sun rose. By eight it was already hot and Faisan suggested we retire to the shade, which we did, leaving the camera in position. Then, without warning, the Russians started shelling the hillside with their tanks; we had seen three or four T-55s by the post beside the river. Between the metallic sound of the explosions, Faisan explained that tank rounds had a solid steel core and a very flat trajectory. A ricochet, he said, sounding like a lecturer at staff college, can fly as far as fifteen kilometres. Not long afterwards, heavy, 122-millimetre mortar rounds began to land on the rocky hillside, about 200 yards away. I began to worry about having no camera, so I went to inspect between rounds, and saw it sitting disconsolately behind its rock, the blanket stirring in the breeze. Whether the Russians had seen it, which was doubtful, or had spotted us and our porters, which was more likely, they certainly had the camera position bracketed. Finally, Faisan, Paul and two porters went to retrieve it. Paul took a couple of excellent shots of the road, where all traffic had been stopped, and queues of civilian lorries and cars stretched on either side of the post.

'So much for the element of surprise,' I said facetiously, wondering what on earth we were going to do now.

'The mujahideen made so much noise laying the mines the Russians heard them,' Faisan said. 'They even went and washed in the river.' He gave a shrug of disbelief.

With the mortars still coming in quite close every few minutes, Faisan suggested moving higher up to a narrow gully which would give us more protection. We had just completed the exhausting move when a messenger arrived to say that two Soviet tanks were on fire below us, hit by mujahideen rockets. We were wrestling with the decision whether we should go all the way down again – no one was particularly eager – when Faisan, generously, said he would go. He reappeared ten minutes later to report that he couldn't see the road because of an overhang but he did see smoke from the two stricken tanks: three others and at least one APC were still firing away. We crouched in the gully as the mortars kept coming over – first the bloodcurdling screech, then the nerve-wracking *crump* as it landed. Then, around midday, came the sound everyone had been expecting, the low rumble of two Mi24 helicopters. The beat of their rotors came closer and they began to circle.

None of us doubted that they were going to attack, but they took their time, circling the hillside several times and then lining up, one behind the other. There was a long moment as the lead gunship hovered in the strike position; then in rapid succession came the flash of the multi-barrelled machine-gun mounted in the nose, accompanied by an obscene, deep growl; then twin double streaks of rocket smoke and a second or two later the sharp crack of the rockets being fired. They went over our heads with the whoosh of a diving aircraft and exploded on the hillside above us with a terrifying roar. This was repeated half a dozen times, the target varying. Each time, the mujahideen fire came back, in short bursts, but the Mi24s were too high for the SAMs. After about an hour, the gunships wheeled away and we went back to the more mundane business of being mortared.

At this point Din Mohammed decided it was time to pull out. Obviously, no convoy would enter the gorge now and obligingly blow itself up on our mines; and by staying we only invited more air strikes and mortaring. I fully expected the jets to be sent in, but for some reason they were not: perhaps they were considered too inaccurate, as likely to

140

bomb their own troops as the mujahideen. We moved up the hill and came across Din Mohammed observing operations from the shelter of a large rock. Although Faisan had said he was not well, he seemed perfectly healthy, giving a recoilless rifle team orders to attack a Soviet post that had been mortaring us all day. High time, I thought. The excuse was that they had been conserving ammunition. The recoilless rifle, a long tube held balanced on the shoulder, and fired by pulling a trigger just in front of the point of balance, went into action with a terrific whoosh. After several rounds, the Russians retaliated with airburst shells from artillery about seven or eight miles away on the plain beyond the gorge: Faisan said he saw the muzzle flash. The mujahideen let go with their own mortar and more recoilless rifle fire.

At the end of the day, as we climbed back up the mountain, Faisan reported that all the mines had been detonated just before the mujahideen withdrew, blowing up a third tank and an APC. The recoilless rifle had also severaly damaged the main Russian post and the smaller one had been totally destroyed. Russian casualties were not known. We came down the mountain to have our first tea of the day. It tasted wonderful. I drank about a dozen cups. We then walked to the river where we had camped two nights before, taking the opportunity to wash while the mujahideen prayed. Afterwards, we walked to another sandy spot where we spread blankets and ate a meal of mutton and bread, which was very good. Tea appeared again, magically refreshing. One thing slightly worried me. We were still close to the battlefield, yet there seemed to be no sense of urgency about moving on. At the risk of being what they call in Scotland 'a fear't sheep', I put a question to Din Mohammed through Faisan.

'The Russians must know we've withdrawn. Does he think they might move a blocking force ahead of us and try

141

to ambush us? If so, would it be a good idea to get a move on?'

After consulting Din Mohammed, Faisan said, 'Yes, he thinks it's a good idea. We will be leaving soon, in any case.'

It was two hours later, about eleven, when we started off, the moon having set. Luckily, the horses appeared which was a godsend because they could see in the dark much better than I could. We rode for about three hours, passing at one point through a narrow, twisting pass over a steep mountain range. The track, mostly a dry river bed, wound round and round like a corkscrew and after a fierce scramble to the top, during which Paul's saddle slipped and he crashed to the ground, we came to our destination, a large village. There, gratefully, we collapsed onto our sleeping bags. It had been a very long day.

Over breakfast next morning, I asked Faisan for his professional view of the operation. 'I think the Russians reacted in a very unprofessional way, making no attempt to come out of their positions and carry the fight to the mujahideen.' He laughed. 'They walk even less than American GIs, and apart from the Spetsnaz, hardly ever leave their vehicles.'

My own view was that the Pashtuns were brave, but poorly trained. Their noisiness and indiscipline had thrown away the chance of turning the ambush into a big victory. But then, to be fair, it was a mistake to try to lay mines so near a Russian position. Whose idea was that? Almost certainly, Zia's ISI, the Pakistani intelligence planners. Far better, in my view, to have let the Afghans stage the ambush in their own way, by lying in wait and then shooting up the convoy with RPG7s, recoilless rifles and AK47s. The results would almost certainly have been better.

Luckily for them, their incompetence was more than matched by the poor performance of the ordinary Russian troops, most of whom were conscripts and had no stomach for the fight. The Russians were able to hold the cities and keep their lines of communication open – although with difficulty, as we had seen from the ambush – by relying on firepower and air power. The crucial question was: would their technological superiority, especially their Mi24 gunships, give the Russians eventual victory, by wearing down the courageous but ill-equipped and ill-trained mujahideen? The next stage of the journey might tell us.

Chapter
10

We now turned south and east, away from Kabul, across the bare uplands of western Nangarhar towards Tizeen and Hissarak, where Din Mohammed intended to lay siege to an important government fort. Everywhere, wild lavender laid a blue wash over the harsh landscape, softening the contours and bringing a touch of romantic innocence to the heartlessness of the scene. Wild thyme imparted a delicate perfume to the stoniest of defiles. In the evening, the scents grew richer, the light faded and we blundered up a long river bed, accompanied by two mujahideen who seemed as lost as ourselves. 'Where are our bloody companions?' we grumbled to ourselves. 'Why haven't they left someone to guide us?' Our escort enquired the way by firing his Kalashnikov in the air and waiting until someone shouted from what seemed a mile away. Eventually, about ten o'clock, fourteen hours after departing, we stumbled up a slope, across a stream and into a tent where Din Mohammed sat smiling, a touch smugly, I thought. Despite his portly build, he had survived the long day rather better than us.

We had our first view of Hissarak on 10 August, not that there was much to see: a mud fort with a tower and a flag on top, and a few long low buildings half hidden among trees. A group of mujahideen were getting ready to mortar

144

the fort. There was the by now familiar discussion about range and direction, and then the firing started. The first three rounds were more or less on target but the actual dropping of the mortar round into the barrel, performed by one of the SAM operators, was done in such a lackadaisical, amateurish manner, that we were almost embarrassed to record it. Paul then moved the camera high to film the rounds landing, but not having a base plate, the mortar dug itself into the sand, and they started dropping wide of the mark. At the same time, the recorder started tearing the cassette and we had to switch off the camera. Jon tried to carry out running repairs in the full glare of the midday sun, slipping and stumbling on the shale, but without success and we had to abandon the expedition. Frustratingly, just as we left, the mujahideen were getting into their stride, dropping several rounds fair and square on the little red fort – with some help from Muslim, one of Faisan's NCOs. At dusk, a duel started between a machine gunner on a nearby mountain and mortars from the fort. White phosphorus rounds, which give off a lot of smoke and burn relentlessly, landed very close but the machine gunner kept firing, his tracer making red streaks in the dark. The fort shot back, its tracer bouncing off the rocks near the Dashaka position and flying up the hillside. Faisan said they had been trying to knock out the position for two years, a good example of Pashtun tribal warfare: much noise and bravado, but very often no positive result.

Paul, who never complained, had now been suffering from diarrhoea for days, if not weeks, and was looking very weak and emaciated. He ate hardly anything, and stead-fastly refused my advice that the local yoghurt was the best thing he could take for his stomach. In an effort to be helpful, Din Mohammed suggested we have our meals on our own, and with their limited resources the mujahideen tried to produce dishes which would tempt the patient, but to no avail. To make matters worse, none of our drugs

145

seemed to work. So it was in a mood of some desperation that I suggested he should escape from the claustrophobic atmosphere of our room, always crowded with curious Afghans, and do some filming. We walked a couple of miles to the mortar position and found a more efficient team in action. Almost immediately, they lobbed three rounds straight on to the fort, and having filmed that we scrambled to the top of the ridge of loose shale to watch the next salvo landing. Again, there was a long pause until the defenders reacted, when a few bullets swished over our heads like angry bees.

Having finished with the mortar, we set off to find one of the machine gun posts that ringed the fort. After a hour's walk which brought Paul to the point of collapse, we climbed to the top of another thin, sandstone ridge where three wild-looking mujahideen were dug in with their heavy, Russian-made 12.7 mm. DshK, which the Afghans call a Dashaka. They invited us to peer through the sights, which were lined up on the fort's tower, and watch them fire off a series of deafeningly-loud short bursts, kicking up clouds of dust. After about five minutes there came the vicious whine of returned fire, which made us quickly duck for cover.

On the way back, we stopped in the village of the local mujahideen commander, called Naeem. An old man brought carpets out beneath the trees and served us with green tea. Other men appeared with handfuls of eggs for Paul's supper. Small children herded their animals back from the hills, or played in the dust, all apparently oblivious of the explosions which echoed round the hills every few minutes. We walked back to our own village following irrigation channels brimming with red spate water, John and I to dine off a good omelette, while Paul ate two not very hard boiled eggs.

The next day was the Twelfth of August which, having been brought up on the Scottish moors, I think of automati-

146

cally as the Glorious Twelfth. It was not so glorious here, I reflected, trudging up and down the sandy hills with Paul and Jon in the laborious task of translating the siege of the fort on to video. Making a film about this sort of warfare is both difficult and time consuming, and we had to walk several miles to and from the location, carrying the camera equipment, to record what was at best desultory action. We had already filmed mortar and machine-gun attacks, for what they were worth, and we were now hoping to see a recoilless rifle in action. Accompanied by Muslim and several mujahideen, including a two-man recoilless rifle team, we walked across the dusty fields to a stony ridge from which the attack was to be launched. The two men crawled up the slope, which was as bare as a billiard table, until they could see the target, and fired. There was a lot of dust and noise, but reloading took a long time, with considerable prompting from Muslim.

'Bloody amateurs,' I muttered to Paul.

He took the camera off the tripod and lugged it to the top of the ridge for the next shot, which he hoped would be the puff of smoke made by the round when it struck the fort. Lying full length with the camera pointing at the target, Paul switched on and then started cursing.

'What's wrong?' I called, from halfway down the slope.

'Camera jam,' Jon answered, climbing up the shale to assist Paul. This was the second time in almost identical circumstances. As they worked on the recalcitrant piece of machinery, we came under unpleasantly accurate mortar fire, the first round landing quite close. I listened for the next one. There it was, a dull *thump* in the distance. Muslim placed his hands over his ears and said, 'Coming here!' We all crouched down. I started counting seconds, and had nearly reached twenty when a sound between a whistle and a scream announced the projectile's imminent arrival, accompanied by an ear-splitting *cccrrrump!* Five or six more

147

followed in rapid succession, and then Muslim, who had his orders to bring us back in one piece, said, 'Mr Sandy! I think better go now.'

'I think you're right, Muslim. They seem to have got our range pretty accurately, and there's no point staying here with a useless camera.'

We walked back to the village, arriving tired and hot to find the three young Russian defectors had arrived and were having lunch. They said they had come to give a hand in the siege of the fort and were anxious to show off their prowess with a machine-gun.

'Would you mind if we filmed that,' I asked, 'providing we can get the damned camera to work.'

'You're welcome,' Vladislav grinned.

Surprisingly, when Paul and Jon switched on the camera and recorder again, they both worked. Infuriated by the morning's failure, I asked for an explanation. 'Probably the heat, and the humidity,' Jon said. 'Makes the equipment temperamental.'

'Or the dust,' Paul said. 'There's so much sand and dust in this godforsaken country it's surprising the bloody thing works at all.'

After lunch, we went to another hilltop with a good view of the fort, the Russians bringing a Grunov light machine-gun with them. Vladislav sat on a rock, lined up the gun and blasted away happily at the fort. Unlike most of Din Mohammed's mujahideen, he looked as if he had fired a machine-gun before. Vadim and Sergei then each had a turn, laughing and joking and obviously enjoying them-selves. Eventually, we discovered why they were in such good spirits: they had been told that they were going to Pakistan soon, and then to America in a couple of months' time. They had been promised visas, they said, unable to hide huge grins. Vadim said he had an uncle in Washington and they talked of having sponsors at Freedom House, an anti-Communist organisation in New York. (I heard much

148

later that after endless delays they were finally allowed into Canada, where there is a big Russian émigré population.) We said goodbye, and watched them depart with some sadness, on my part at least. Meeting them had been extremely lucky from our point of view. It had given the film a lift, and a different flavour; and I found their rejection of the Soviet system and desire for freedom brave and moving.

By a curious coincidence I had brought with me and was reading *Hope against Hope*, the story of the Russian poetess, Nadezhda Mandelstam, and her husband, Osip, also a poet. I found its description, in minute detail and without the slightest hint of self-pity, of day to day life in Russia at the height of Stalin's terror, absolutely compelling. There were striking parallels with the contemporary scene: the same devotion to mass extermination and the mass movement of population – the six or seven million dispossessed Afghans immediately came to mind; and the same lying propaganda about democracy and the interests of the people that, then as now, characterised every Soviet official utterance.

A day or two later, Din Mohammed suddenly announced there was a battle going on: would we like to go and film it?

'Yes, all right. We'll get ready,' I told Faisan. 'Why didn't he warn us this was going to happen before?' I grumbled. We set off at about ten thirty to walk the two or three miles to a small village near the fort, where we arrived at midday. Faisan chose a vantage point, a deserted house set in trees overlooking the battlefield, where we installed the camera. Unfortunately, it did not have a view of the fort, but was in a reasonably safe position and gave us some protection from the midday sun. War in Afghanistan, or rather tribal warfare in the Pashtun tradition, now showed its gentler face. Local farmers appeared carrying carpets, which they spread under the trees, and dishes loaded with fried eggs, spinach, yoghurt, fresh *nan* and *halwa*, a dessert which tastes like not

149

very sweet brown sugar. Having served us, they sat and watched us eat, urging us to finish every dish. Afghan hospitality is truly remarkable.

Peace now reigned, while everyone had a siesta, the garrison of the fort, the mujahideen and ourselves. Then, at about four, the shooting started again, mainly mortars, and at five we heard the sound of helicopters approaching, four Mi8s in line astern. They circled once, dropping anti-SAM flares and then came round a second time and rocketed the hillside opposite. Disappointingly, from the filming point of view, they then flew off home and we followed, stopping on the way to see a peasant who had been wounded by a mortar while having his frugal lunch in the fields. He had an ugly black hole in his side and a damaged ear. There was nothing we could do. A woman had been killed in the same attack.

That night, Faisan, who knew we were becoming impatient at the apparent lack of action, said he thought the next day would be 'a big day'. We went to bed early, rose at five thirty, left our base at a quarter to six, and arrived at our vantage point in the deserted house at seven. But the promised action did not materialise and the day passed uneventfully except for an unpleasant incident when a local lout shot a beautiful grey and white Saker falcon in the trees near us, a piece of wanton killing which made me angry and sad. We waited until six when, no helicopters having appeared, we tramped home in the dark along the now familiar stony wadi, over the bare sandstone hills, through the villages sunk in rural squalor among their walnut and apricot trees. At the camp, two wounded mujahideen on saline drips were lying in obvious pain, on blood-soaked sheets: so far ten had been wounded, Faisan reported.

Next day brought worse news. Din Mohammed, looking serious, said that he had run out of recoilless rifle ammunition and it would take 'several days' to get fresh supplies

150

from Peshawar. Knowing that several days in Afghan terms could mean anything up to a month, we concluded that the long-heralded attack on Hissarak Fort would now not take place. That would mean no air strikes, and a correspondingly less exciting and informative film. This presented us with the familiar dilemma: should we wait, and if so how long, and what would be the outcome? I asked myself why I became involved in this endless game of oriental patience, having very little patience in any case? After another fruitless day, Faisan and I decided we must tell Din Mohammed that we could not afford to stay here any longer, simply awaiting developments. It seemed clear that there would be no frontal attack on Hissarak for a week at the earliest. The recoilless rifle expert, who had fired off eighty rounds during what was almost a single-handed assault on the fort, and had his own sight shot off, had already left for the Kabul area. He allegedly told Din Mohammed, in the Churchillian manner, 'Give me the ammunition and I'll finish the job.'

Knowing how anxious I was to see the SAMs in action, Faisan now made a suggestion. 'You remember Engineer Mahmoud, the commander from Jalalabad, the one you called the barbecue specialist?'

'Yes, I do.' I laughed. He had indeed cooked us a very good dinner one night, grilling goats' kidneys expertly over an open fire.

'Well, he says he will barbecue a transport plane for you, taking off from Jalalabad airport.'

'Really? That sounds exciting.'

Faisan got out his notebook and drew a sketch of the airport, elaborating in detail how the commander saw the operation. 'They take off very slowly, so if you are here, at this end of the runway, it's easy to shoot them down. The only trouble is the escape route. He says there's a canal here and usually several T-55s near the runway which will react as soon as they know what's happened. Now to get round the canal . . .' I looked up to see Jon, who was sitting only a few yards away, listening open-mouthed to what must have sounded like a suicide mission.

I gave Faisan a meaningful look. 'I think we should drop the subject for the time being,' I said as calmly as possible. On reflection I realised I had been rather undiplomatic. After a month of strenuous activity in hot, humid and generally trying conditions, we were all exhausted. The thought of spending another week trekking through the mountains to Jalalabad, on what might well turn out to be a wild-goose chase, was probably the last straw, as far as my companions were concerned. Paul especially looked at the end of his strength, and I suddenly realised we should get him to a doctor as soon as possible. I decided Friday 17 August would be our last day at Hissarak. But we would make one last trip to the fort, despite the seeming dormancy of the battlefield.

On the way there, we came on a large group of people in the village we always passed through, attending the funeral of a young farmer who had been killed in the abortive attempt to take the fort three days before. The coffin had been left open so that the mourners could pay their last respects. His features looked composed and his lips had been painted red. Members of his family, who had brought us food under the shady village trees, were distributing money to the poor who had come to mourn.

The coffin, a simple thing of raw boards, was closed and carried up the sandstone ridge to the graveyard on top of the hill. We were told not to follow as it was in full view of the fort and liable to come under fire. Like all village graveyards it consisted of an odd assortment of undressed stones set perpendicularly in the hard ground. Sometimes a scrap of white or green cloth was attached to a pole stuck in the ground. It looked sad and neglected with no flowers and no inscriptions, in keeping with the harshness and simplicity of the land itself.

152

At the fort, once again, there was little activity all day until, at about half past four, a lone Mi8 appeared and everyone scrambled to action stations. Eventually, when it was directly overhead but very high, the SAM operator switched on his battery, which had a life of only sixty seconds, and the launcher came to life with a hum. In that minute, the missile's heat-seeking radar had to lock on to the target, and it could then be fired. But our operator never achieved lock-on, presumably because the Mi8 was too high, and although he pulled the trigger, nothing happened: the missile refused to launch. The Mi8 proceeded to rocket the Dashaka positions twice – once very wide – and our SAM team tried again, but with the same result. The missile was activated, as the jargon has it, but failed to get lock-on. Eventually the helicopter flew off, unscathed, still very high, and judging by the inaccuracy of the second rocket strike, Faisan said, it must have been an Afghan pilot. We also presumed that he intended to land at the fort, since gunships on a mission always travel in pairs. There was another alert at six, when two Mi24s flew far to the north of us, specks in the sky, in the direction of Jalalabad.

We tramped the now familiar path through the village and along the gully, glad to be leaving behind us the scene of so much waiting and so little action. We were given horses at one point, which made the journey easier, until the inevitable argument developed about the way across the Surkhot River, a wide, fast-flowing flood of grey water. In the course of it, my horse and another stallion decided to have a fight. Mine had no bit, merely a halter, and in the effort to control him, I tore the scabs off my barely-healed mosquito bites. At that moment, the man who had been instructed to carry the camera came and dumped it on the stones of the river bed beside Paul and strode off again, blowing us a raspberry, an insult which until then I had not seen in Afghanistan. Needless to say, neither Din Mohammed nor Faisan were anywhere to be seen, and in desperation I ordered the boy leading my fractious brute to give me the camera. Holding it on top of the beast's withers, and determined not to drop it in the Surkhot River, I gripped ferociously hard with my legs, having no saddle, and no stirrups to give me any purchase. On the far side of the river, we were faced with an almost sheer incline, but somehow boy, stallion, camera and I managed to scramble up it without parting company.

At the top of the slope, a pretty arbour greeted the eye, and there, within it, we found Din Mohammed, sitting under a trellis, awaiting the call for lunch. This turned out to be in another arbour, with a fine view over the river. Our host had been in the Ministry of Frontiers when the Communists took over in 1978 and had been jailed for a year on suspicion of being a mujahideen sympathiser. He said he had been tortured and showed me a thumb which, he said, had had an electrode attached to it. The only odd thing about it I could see was that it had a very short nail. He also indicated other places where the torturers attached their infernal devices: his cheeks and temples, but not, fortunately for him, his testicles.

After lunch we rode on to another village where a farmer proudly showed us how he had fashioned a piece of unexploded Russian bomb into a steel blade for his old-fashioned wooden plough. Over a cup of tea we were just discussing – rather bad-temperedly, everyone being tired – whether we should film this piece of Afghan ingenuity, when the sharp ears of the mujahideen picked up the sound of helicopters. We pulled on our boots and hurried outside, following one of the SAM teams. A small group of mujahideen, including the man with the SAM, made for a small conical hill a few hundred yards away, standing on its own in the middle of the plain.

We went farther, to the cover of a small clump of trees, from where in the distance we could see two helicopters, Mi24 gunships, circling over Hissarak. We had only just

154

1 The battle for the Newport Bridge, Saigon, 1975

2a Sandy Gall's last interview with President Zia of Pakistan shortly before his plane was blown up in August 1988

2b Zulfikar Ali Bhutto, former Prime Minister of Pakistan, deposed by General Zia in 1977

3 Filming in Hanoi, capital of Vietnam, 1980

4a Water buffalo pulling ox carts in Cambodia, 1980

4b Filming in the Killing Fields, Cambodia, 1980

5a Afghan mujahideen armed with a SAM 7 anti-aircraft missile, near Jalalabad, 1984

5b Three young Russian soldiers who gave themselves up voluntarily and fought with the mujahideen

6a The Kuwait Sheraton Hotel, destroyed by the Iraqis during the Gulf War, 1991

6b Saudi troops cross the border to liberate Kuwait

6c The first Iraqi prisoners to be seen by the West, filmed by ITN on the first day of the ground war

7a A Kuwaiti hardened aircraft shelter, used by the Iraqis in the Gulf War

7b Inside a hardened shelter destroyed by allied laser-guided bombs. The bombs penetrated two metres of reinforced concrete and one metre of sand

8a Sandy Gall in the studio with Carol Barnes presenting News at Ten

8b Sandy Gall receiving the Lawrence of Arabia medal
from His Royal Highness the Prince of Wales

reached the trees when I suddenly noticed a third helicopter, an Mi8, flying towards us very low, only about fifty feet
above the ground. Paul, who was standing just in front of
me beside a tree, immediately started filming as it
approached so close I thought the pilot must see us. Another
Mi8 followed a hundred yards behind. Paul panned round
with the lead helicopter and as it drew level with the little
hill I saw a belch of smoke. Too low for a SAM, I thought.
In fact, it was an RPG, and missed by a yard, the mujahid
said afterwards. Behind and above came the two Mi24s,
flying cover, and only a second or two later the SAM fired
at the first gunship. I saw something leave the missile tube
and fall only fifty yards away; it turned out to be the sender
component, not the missile.

Surprisingly, none of the helicopters reacted to the presence of the three or four mujahideen on the top of the little
hill, although an RPG and a SAM were aimed at them, and
both must have been clearly visible. When we examined the
video later, we could just see the blast made by the RPG,
which exploded harmlessly about four hundred yards away.
When I asked the mujahid who fired it what range he had
selected, he said 'Three hundred metres'. This probably
explains why he missed: to me, the range looked more like
one hundred metres. To have had a near-perfect target, and
to have scored one near miss and one malfunction was
immensely frustrating all round. I felt keenly disappointed
as well. Not only would a 'kill' have made superb television,
it would have done wonders for the morale of the mujahideen in their uphill struggle against the might of a
superpower.

The only people who were not sorry about our failure
were the villagers who, I discovered later, pleaded with the
mujahideen not to shoot down the helicopters, saying that
if they did, the Russians would come and bomb the village.
It was a not uncommon argument, and one the Russians
repeatedly drove home with bombing raids and the whole-

sale massacre of villagers. The views of the villagers would certainly influence local mujahideen, who might otherwise have been tempted to have a go. It turned out that the appearance of the helicopters was not unusual. Faisan told us they always flew this route on their regular supply runs to Hissarak, following the old Kabul to Jalalabad road across the plain. This was either amazingly careless or over-confident; unless, of course, the pilots knew that they would not be attacked.

We now set off along the old road ourselves, through the golden evening light, to Gandamak, where the Afghans had slaughtered the remnants of a British army in 1842. Of the three wars the British fought against the Afghans in the nineteenth and early twentieth centuries, the first was the most disastrous, and Gandamak was its painful end. We arrived very late, stumbling along dark paths into the village, which was deserted. Having tried to find some-where to sleep, and failed, we flopped down exhausted and bad-tempered in the village square. As we lay on the hard ground drinking tea before going to sleep, a young Afghan who spoke a little English approached and squatted down beside me. 'Are you British?'

'Yes, we are,' I said wondering if we would now be asked to leave.

'Welcome to Gandamak,' was the reply. 'You know, this is the place of Macnaghten.'

I must confess I was astonished. Sir William Macnaghten was Britain's political representative in Kabul during the first Anglo-Afghan War, 1839–42, and was murdered there by Akbar, the son of Dost Mohammed, the Afghan ruler whom the British had forced off the throne. Shortly after Macnaghten's death, the British withdrew from Kabul in the dead of winter, suffering terrible casualties on the way; and it was at Gandamak that the stragglers of a once proud army made their last stand. All were killed or taken prisoner, except for one man, Surgeon Brydon, who despite being

156

wounded, managed to reach Jalalabad to tell the terrible tale.

'I'm surprised you know his name,' I said.

'Oh, we all know the name of Macnaghten here,' the young man replied, bidding me good night.

Next day, just outside Gandamak, we came to a long, rectangular-shaped stone wall beside the road. We stopped. 'This where British die,' Din Mohammed said, grinning, although not unkindly. 'Long time ago.' The wall, still quite solid but not very high, and enclosing a space about one hundred yards long by fifty yards wide, was all that remained of the old British fort, but not the site of the last stand, according to Din Mohammed. We saw that later, farther east, the Afghans pointing out a small hill called *Kafir hundi*. It was here, on a bitter January day in 1842, that twenty British officers and forty-five other ranks, most of them from the 44th Regiment of Foot, formed a square and with only twenty muskets between them and two rounds apiece, hopelessly outnumbered, fought to the death. One officer killed five Afghans with his sword before himself being cut down. Of the sixty-five Britons who took part in the last stand, only four were taken prisoner: the rest were slaughtered. From where we stood, on a hot summer's afternoon, it was too far away, in time and place, to feel any real sense of drama. But you did not need much imagination to visualise what it must have been like to fight for your life, on that lonely hillside, in the freezing cold of an Afghan winter's day, the snow all trodden down and red with blood.

A little further on, the rotor blade from a Soviet helicopter, shot down they said by Engineer Mahmoud, the barbecue specialist, lay beside the road. I was never sure whether to believe these tales. Was the helicopter shot down, or did it crash? Only the rotor blade remained. All the rest, the engine and the fuselage, had been removed for sale, at good prices, in the bazaars of Peshawar and other Pakistani border towns.

157

Chapter
11

Soon after I returned to London, I received an invitation to have lunch with the head of MI6. It was very informal, the cook was off, so we had cold meat and salad, with plenty of wine. He wanted to hear what I had to say about the war in Afghanistan. I was flattered, of course, and anxious to pass on what I could in terms of first-hand knowledge. I also decided early on in the lunch that M, as Ian Fleming called him in the James Bond books, or C, as he really is, was unlikely to tell me anything. I therefore resolved to be completely frank and as informative as possible, and not try to prise any information out of him in return. This is not normally how a journalist's mind works, but I calculated that avuncularly charming as C might be – he looked rather like a high-class bank manager – he was far too experienced to let slip anything he did not wish to.

Much of the conversation concerned the morale of the mujahideen and the effect on it of Soviet air power. I described how the only SAM we fired had malfunctioned, and how easy it should have been to shoot down at least one of the Mi8s or Mi24s that flew past us that day near Hissarak. I added that, in my view, only one thing really worried the mujahideen: Soviet air power, especially the Mi24 gunships. The fact that they had no weapon which could counter them, made them all the more terrifying. I

158

ended up by saying, 'The mujahideen desperately need an effective ground to air missile. They say the SAM 7 is no good: the kill ratio is only about one to ten. They need something better. If they don't get it, their will to resist the Russians may weaken, perhaps disastrously.'

I know my friends in MI6 saw my documentary, *Allah Against The Gunships*, which was networked on ITV that November, and that they made it available to their colleagues in the CIA. I do not know, naturally, what effect either it, or my talk with C, had. Not very long afterwards, however, the Americans, who were clearly also concerned about the damaging effect of Soviet air power on Afghan morale, asked the British to supply the mujahideen with Blowpipe, our ground to air missile first used in the Falklands. The British agreed to the request and a limited number were supplied, although apparently not to Masud. At least, when I asked him much later if he had received any, he said no. This surprised me, because he was the commander the British thought most highly of – the second Tito. But then I realised the CIA would have delivered the Blowpipes to the Pakistani ISI, who would have given them to their favourite commanders, who did not include Masud. Blowpipe was not much of a success in Afghanistan, being too complicated and needing, apparently, a great deal of training before it could be used effectively. But that did not matter. The CIA wanted it supplied for one reason, and one reason only: so that they could use it as a lever to persuade Congress to give the mujahideen the Americans' own much more sophisticated ground to air missile, the Stinger. The stratagem worked, sensationally well, and by the end of 1986 it was in service with the mujahideen.

Stinger made an immediate impact, and revolutionised the war. Until they could devise counter-measures, which inevitably took time, Russian helicopter pilots took to flying either very high or very low, or not flying at all. Overnight the helicopter gunship, which had given the Russians air supremacy from the start, became almost a liability. The effect on the Afghan air force, which did not have much stomach for the fight anyway, was even more devastating. For the first time, perhaps, instead of looking like losing the war, the mujahideen and their backers began to believe they might actually win it. The advent of Stinger almost certainly forced Mikhail Gorbachev, the Soviet leader, to take the decision he had been hesitating over ever since he came to power. Eventually, he made the fateful announcement that the Soviet Union would leave Afghanistan, beginning its withdrawal on 15 May 1988 and completing it nine months later. It had been apparent for some time that although Soviet losses – more than 13,000 dead and several times as many wounded – were never as high as the Americans' in Vietnam, the war had become increasingly unpopular at home and destroyed what little credibility the Kremlin had left. News of the forthcoming withdrawal was received with equal satisfaction, ironically, by the Russian people and the mujahideen: the only people who were distinctly unhappy were the hardliners in Moscow, and Najibullah's Communist government in Kabul.

Gorbachev's announcement of withdrawal was seen in Washington, understandably, as a great victory for the United States, while in London Mrs Thatcher and her government derived a good deal of quiet satisfaction from the knowledge that their support had been low-key but decisive. The French too, who had done so much for the Afghans through their medical charities like Médicins sans Frontières, Médicins du Monde, and Aide Médicale Internationale, had a right to congratulate themselves; but above all there was cause for celebration in Zia's Pakistan. The Brezhnev Doctrine had been turned on its head and the invincible Red Army had been shown to be very vincible when its heart was not in the job. In the general euphoria generated by Gorbachev's admission of defeat, the CIA jumped to several conclusions, most of them wrong. The most serious was the belief that without the backing of Soviet bayonets, the Najibullah government would not survive very long. Some experts put it at weeks; and it was said that even the Russians themselves did not expect the Kabul regime to last more than a few months. On the other hand, they did everything they could to shore it up, handing over enormous numbers of tanks, jets, helicopters, and other equipment, and continuing to subsidise Kabul to the tune of about $300 million a month.

There were plenty of arguments in favour of the collapse theory. Ever since the start of the war in 1979, the Russians and their Afghan allies had never been able to control the country outside the towns and their own bases. Even on the main roads, as we had seen previously, they were always liable to ambush, while the mujahideen could move almost anywhere, unhindered. Then, the Communist regime had never been popular and never would be: the deep-rooted Islamic faith of the vast majority of Afghans guaranteed that. As the Americans discovered in Vietnam, bombing does not break the spirit of resistance, it hardens it, like steel in a furnace. By the time the Russians finally left Afghanistan, they had succeeded only in arousing the most violent hatred among ordinary Afghans. No, it was not the collapse theory that was wrong, it was the strategy that was so woefully inadequate.

The plan the Americans and the Pakistanis concocted to exploit the Russian withdrawal was based on a military offensive to capture the regime-held city of Jalalabad, less than 100 miles east of Kabul. A composite force of mujahideen would launch an attack on the airport and military base of Samarkhel, both on the eastern outskirts of the city, only forty miles from the Pakistan border. Once Jalalabad had been captured, the road would be open to Kabul, and final victory. If the plan had worked, it would have brought the Afghan war to a resoundingly successful close. But there were many dissentient voices among the mujahideen themselves, who had no confidence in ISI planning and resented the way they and their CIA colleagues seemed hell-bent to manoeuvre the extremist, Gulbuddin Hekmatyar, into power at all costs.

It was against this background that early in the New Year, 1989, ITN decided that the Soviet withdrawal from Afghanistan after more than nine years of brutal occupation merited blanket coverage. Paul Davies and a crew were sent to Kabul, our man in Moscow was sent to the Soviet-Afghan border, and a *News at Ten* team consisting of a producer, fixer, two crews, an editor and myself were sent to Peshawar. But we had a secret weapon as well, which we hoped would scoop the BBC and every other news rival. This was a mobile satellite ground station which we planned to take across the border and broadcast live from Afghanistan for the three days leading up to the moment when the last Russian soldier left Afghan soil. Normally, this would have been an impossible endeavour, since it needed the permission of both the Afghan and Pakistan governments, who were not on speaking terms because of the war. But, by an extraordinary combination of circumstances, we were in a unique position to exploit the situation. Several years before I had got to know Lord Cranborne MP, eldest son of the Marquis of Salisbury, who founded the Afghanistan Support Committee in the early days of the war. The Committee had a charity arm called Afghanaid, which for a time oversaw a charity I had started, called Sandy Gall's Afghanistan Appeal.

Robert Cranborne, an ardent supporter of the mujahideen, hit on a scheme to publicise the Afghan cause by beaming reports of the war, by satellite, from mujahideen-held Afghanistan to the outside world. He found a brilliant engineer who built a ground station which, they said, could be broken down and transported into the interior on the backs of two or three horses. I was sceptical for two reasons. I had travelled through the Hindu Kush, and I knew how

162

daunting the mountains were; but also, even if you got the equipment to the right place, I did not see how it would be practical, at that time, to produce live reports from inside Afghanistan which companies like ITN would be prepared to broadcast. Live television needs a big occasion, and in the mujahideen camps and villages in the depths of the Afghan countryside, the only big occasions were Russian bombing raids. The chances of being in place to capture one of those, as it happened, must have been about as likely as winning the pools.

There was another small difficulty. Any such venture would have to be launched from Pakistan, and that meant getting General Zia's approval first. Robert took a long time persuading the canny Zia, but he did in the end, shortly before the President and nearly all his generals were killed in a plane crash, in mysterious circumstances, on 17 August 1988. But, as the date of the Russian withdrawal approached, and the ISI plans for the attack on Jalalabad gathered momentum, what had originally seemed pie-in-the-sky, now began to look like a stroke of genius.

The portable satellite existed, it worked, and Robert's company had permission, thanks to the late Zia, to use it; and although we would be operating on Afghan soil, without permission, there was nothing the government, or the Russians, could do about it. The reason was simple. In the closing weeks of 1988, as the Soviet and Afghan garrisons pulled back from their outlying positions, the mujahideen had succeeded in capturing the Afghan border post at Torkham and a string of other strongpoints on the road which ran from the border to the outskirts of Jalalabad. Thus, the portable ground station could be driven in a Land Rover over the Khyber Pass and up the road to Jalalabad, without any obstacle.

I flew to Pakistan on 1 February, took a taxi to the Holiday Inn, the best hotel in Islamabad, and there met one of Robert Cranborne's aides, Richard Cleghorn-Brown.

'The ISI want to see us,' he said. 'Just to sew up a few details.'

Richard looked like a rather easy-going housemaster at a minor public school, but he had pushed through the satellite project with a good deal of persistence. He had also done his homework with the ISI. I had been in their large block of offices in the centre of Islamabad several times before, most notably when General Akhtar, who had been killed with Zia, was in command. My name must have been on their files as a friend of the ex-President. And yet, the two colonels to whom Richard now introduced me both looked at me with suspicious eyes.

After Richard had explained my role in the operation, one of the colonels demanded, 'What sort of line will you be taking in your reports, Mr Sandy Gall?'

'Why, the same as I always do,' I answered rather pompously. 'I shall be impartial.'

I realised from the way the colonel pursed his lips that this was not the answer he wanted to hear. 'We hope you will be positive, very positive, Mr Sandy Gall,' he said with what sounded like a not very veiled threat.

Richard broke in smoothly. 'Oh, yes, you don't need to worry about that, Colonel. Sandy has been reporting the war from the mujahideen side for a very long time now . . . since when exactly, Sandy?'

'Since 1982, as a matter of fact.'

'Since 1982. Longer than any other Western journalist. Sandy was also a personal friend, as you know, of the late President Zia. So you see, gentlemen, we are very lucky that he's coming with us.'

The colonels muttered to one another in Urdu, but Richard's little speech had carried the day.

'You will contact our colleague in Peshawar, Major Ali, on this number, please. If you have any problems, please let him know.'

They saw us out, but they did not smile. Perhaps they

had a foreboding of the disaster that was about to engulf the Jalalabad adventure. We drove to Peshawar that afternoon, to find, ensconced in a large villa which Richard had rented, the rest of the ITN team: Nick Pollard, the senior producer of *News at Ten*, Mike Nolan, from the foreign desk; two cameramen, Phil Bye and Bernie Glancy; an editor, Fred Hickey; and several engineers. Richard and his technician who operated the satellite were just round the corner, and there was also a Pakistani driver who doubled as major-domo, and a cook who, we discovered, liked the bottle. My eldest daughter, Fiona, who had worked at ITN and was now running our charity in Peshawar, lived quite close and often came round to the house. So we were quite a jolly party.

Nick Pollard and Mike Nolan had not been idle in the preceding days, digging up a lot of excellent war footage shot by Afghan cameramen working for the Afghan Media Resource Center, a media company run by Afghans and funded by an American university. The cameramen went out regularly on operations with mujahideen groups and brought back reports which were then edited and sent to various foreign television companies, including ITN. Nick and Mike found that the centre was not very good at keeping track of its material, and that some of the best footage had not been distributed. Between them they dug out several good action reports, Nick edited them, and I wrote the commentary and voiced them. One of the most exciting showed a mujahid using a British-made Milan anti-tank missile to knock out a Russian tank. But there were others which demonstrated the often low level of training: for example, when one mujahid's mortar failed to work, he kicked it in frustration. In the next few days, we ran a number of these special reports on *News at Ten*. News programmes often carry footage shot by freelance camera-men or agencies, and the standard rule is to flash a 'super' on the screen saying 'amateur video', 'official film', or whatever it might be, so that the audience is made aware that it comes from an outside source. Normally, ITN is punctilious about following this practice, but for some reason, probably pressure of events, the relevant super, either 'Afghan Media Resource Center', which was a bit of a mouthful, or 'mujahideen video', was left off on a couple of occasions.

It was a fairly trifling oversight, but the reaction was extraordinary. Channel 4 broadcast a programme by Tariq Ali, the well-known Marxist, in which he accused me of 'spicing up' my reports by pretending that the Afghan footage had in fact been shot by ITN. Not content with that, the programme makers leaked the story to Rupert Murdoch's *Today* newspaper which came out with banner headlines saying ITN and I were 'faking' our reports from Afghanistan. I was furious and wanted to sue both Tariq Ali and *Today*, but ITN's lawyers, like most lawyers, advised caution, on the grounds that to sue and lose, always a possibility with anything as unpredictable as libel proceedings, would be worse than not suing at all. Since there was no truth in the allegations, I concluded that Tariq Ali, given his left-wing views, was motivated by feelings of solidarity for the poor misunderstood Russians, to whom everybody was being so beastly. But *Today* had quite different motives. They were not hard to find: Sky TV, also owned by Mr Murdoch, was losing a great deal of money, so *Today* and other Murdoch tabloids hoped to launch a counter-offensive against ITN, one of Sky's main competitors.

Luckily, all this transpired several weeks later, too late to interfere with the immediate task of reporting the Jalalabad offensive. Having harvested the fruitful field of the Afghan Media Resource Center, I set off on Monday 6 February for Afghanistan. I took with me one of the more colourful and westernised of mujahideen commanders, Brigadier-General Safi, formerly of the Afghan army, and then a senior officer

166

in Pir Gailani's National Islamic Front of Afghanistan [NIFA]. Gailani was a friend of mine, pro-Western and a moderate.

It was a cold, sparkling day, the mountains standing out sharply against the pale blue sky as we climbed up the Khyber Pass. This is one of the oldest, and most spectacular roads in the world. Alexander the Great's troops came through the Khyber on their way from Afghanistan to India, and over 2000 years later, the British fought their way up and down it countless times. At nearly every bend in the rocks, we passed a plaque to regiments which had sweated and shed blood. As we negotiated the hairpin bends, I tried to read the roll call of illustrious names: Khyber Rifles, North-West Frontier Force, Royal Engineers, the Gurkhas, and many more.

Almost every mountain overlooking the road had an old stone-built British post or picquet on top of it, with the great fort at Shagai commanding the head of the pass. Home of the Khyber Rifles, Shagai was built in 1927, when I first saw the light of day in far-off Penang, and I was not sure which of us had worn better. We swooped down the other side to the border at Torkham where General Safi, who told me he had been trained by the SAS at Hereford, talked us through the checkpoints. With his jaunty beret, and neat white moustache, he looked as if he had just stepped out of the In and Out. On the Afghan side, we filmed the first signs of the recent fighting; several knocked-out tanks and APCs and a large self-propelled gun abandoned by the gate. As we bowled along the tarmac road, liberally pitted with potholes, General Safi began his conducted tour. First stop on the right was the old Russian brigade headquarters. When they withdrew, they handed it over to the Afghan army, from whom the mujahideen had captured it. It certainly looked as if it had taken a pasting, with gaping shell holes in the walls and rubble choking the courtyard. The green flag of Islam flew from the highest point. A few

167

kilometres further on we came to a Russian T-55 tank slewed across the road; another lay in the field below.

'This was the Milan,' the general said. 'Jolly good missile. Easy to use, you can't miss it.' He meant, miss *with* it. We walked round the tank on the road; there was a gaping hole through the thick steel of the hull. The one in the field had had its gun turret blown off. 'They used three missiles, actually. One for each tank. The third one missed, and the tank got away.'

On both sides of the road, the fields were littered with the debris of the Russian and Afghan retreat. At the end of a long straight stretch of road, shaded by magnificent trees, we came to a vast state farm, built by the Russians in the reign of King Zaher Shah. It had produced millions of oranges and lemons for the Soviet market, but now the acres and acres of citrus trees were either dead, or dying of neglect. General Safi said the farm had been used as a rest centre for Russian officers and their families during the war. When the Russians left, the mujahideen overran it, destroying most of the buildings and equipment; broken machinery lay everywhere, including dozens of Soviet tractors; and the workshop was a graveyard of smashed lathes. The damage, which at a rough guess would have cost more than a million pounds to repair, seemed to have been completely wanton, and was the sort of mindless destruction which sensible commanders like Masud were so opposed to.

Over lunch, General Safi told us more about himself. He had originally trained in the Soviet Union, with the Spetsnaz, the Russian Special Forces; then at Hereford with the SAS, in 1972–73; and later in America, with the Green Berets at Fort Bragg. On his return to Afghanistan, King Zaher Shah asked him to raise and command a special forces unit in the Afghan army. In 1973, Zaher Shah was overthrown by his former Prime Minister and cousin, Daoud Khan. Not long afterwards, Daoud had the general arrested, perhaps because he was a staunch royalist, but he escaped to Iran

168

and made his way to Britain, where he settled, buying a flat in Shepherd's Bush. Daoud was himself overthrown, and killed in the Communist coup of 1978. Shortly afterwards, when most of the country's Islamic leaders declared a *jehad* (holy war) against the Marxists, Safi returned to Pakistan, joining the Gailani party as military commander.

I said we needed some pictures of Jalalabad, so after lunch Safi sent us off in a lorry with a few mujahideen, including the local commander, Syed Mohammed Pahlawan, while he sensibly returned to Peshawar. The driver, who had just defected to the mujahideen with his lorry, drove us a few miles and then told us we would have to get out and walk. It was a pleasant stroll in the afternoon sunshine until we came to a wide river, the Kunar, which was too deep to ford. Our mujahideen soon found a local boatman who was prepared to ferry us across on a raft made of inflated oxskins, lashed together with rope, very like the rafts Alexander the Great's army used to cross the Oxus in 329 BC. One of the skins was slightly under-inflated, and our boatman got down and blew it up with mighty breaths. Then, climbing aboard gingerly, we sat with the water lapping our feet as the grinning boatman paddled us out to where the current caught the raft and swept it across to the far bank. He had to make two or three trips to get us all across, for which we paid him the equivalent of a few pence, and then waving the friendly fellow farewell, we walked westwards into the sun, towards Jalalabad.

But there were more, smaller arms of the river to be forded, an experience so painful with bare feet that at the last crossing I kept my boots on, squelching along until they dried out. Nearer Jalalabad, we passed several groups of refugees, travelling on foot with very small children. One man with a child in his arms stopped to talk to our mujahideen, saying they had left Jalalabad because of fighting between government forces and the mujahideen. The women veiled themselves and sat silent on the ground behind. We were supposed to stop for the night at the local headquarters but missed the turn-off, and after another hour of walking in the dark, stopped at a farmhouse, occupied by a few mujahideen. Like ourselves they were birds of passage, and seemed to have no food or cooking facilities; so there was nothing for it but to munch the bar of chocolate given to me by Fred Hickey, our editor, and bed down on his inflatable mattress, which Wilfred Thesiger, the great explorer, would have considered 'pansy'. But I still slept badly, being on a slope, and my new sleeping bag proved unsatisfactory.

Next morning, still without food, we climbed to the top of a steep rock behind the farm from where we hoped to get a good view of Jalalabad. It was a beautiful day, the air clear and the sky blue, but Jalalabad remained obstinately hidden among trees, in its saucer-shaped depression. Phil Bye took some long-lens shots of Samarkhel, the former Russian base on the eastern outskirts of the city, and of the airport; in the distance, to the south, the high mountains shone white, covered in snow. To my surprise, Pahlawan, the commander, said there was no plan to attack Jalalabad, as this would lead to heavy civilian casualties. Messages had been sent to the garrison asking them to surrender and join the mujahideen, and he expected an answer in about a week's time. I asked what would happen if the garrison refused to surrender. Then, said the commander, they would have to fight. But he seemed reluctant about it and obviously hoped jaw-jaw would prevail over war-war.

On our way back, we managed to find the post we had missed the day before, and stopped for tea and a typical mujahideen lunch of rice and *nan*, which hunger made delicious. By following a different route, we managed to ford the river higher up and after walking most of the way back to the state farm, found an ambulance to take us on to Peshawar. Over the next few days, I made another couple of trips to the battlefront, once with a local Jamiat com-

170

mander who was extremely energetic and enthusiastic. He took us to another vantage point, on the top of a stony ridge, from where we could look towards Jalalabad, although again it was impossible to have a clear view. This time, most of the Peshawar team came along, including both cameramen, Phil and Bernie. We walked for miles, through villages and across the flat, bare hills which flank Jalalabad to the south-east, but saw little sign of the build-up of men and equipment needed for a major attack. Even at the state farm, which was supposed to be the joint mujahideen headquarters, there was no sense of an offensive in the making.

Instead, all the mujahideen leaders were summoned by the Pakistani authorities to Islamabad where, after much argument and arm-twisting, an Afghan Interim Government was formed and presented to the world. Most Afghan leaders were appalled by the way the conference was manipulated by General Hamid Gul, General Akhtar's successor as head of ISI. One of them, Pir Gailani, told me in disgust, 'The whole thing's a farce, orchestrated by the Pakistanis.' Nick Pollard and I drove down to cover the event and while there, we went to see my travelling companion of five years before, Din Mohammed. Since his party was the strongest in the Jalalabad area, I presumed it would have the prime role in the coming offensive. Would they, I asked, take us with them when they attacked Jalalabad? And was my old friend, Engineer Mahmoud, the barbecue specialist, going to lead the troops into battle?

Din Mohammed could not resist making a joke at my expense. Giving his high-pitched giggle, he said, 'Sandy Gall, I think you are too old to want to go to Jalalabad.'

'Nonsense, Din Mohammed,' I said crossly. 'I'm just as fit as you are.'

He play-acted disbelief but then became serious. 'We are not taking part in the Jalalabad plan,' he said.

171

'Why not? You are the biggest party in the region, are you not?'

'Yes, we are. But they do not want us to lead the operation.'

'Who? The Pakistanis?'

Din Mohammed shrugged and gave a little smile.

'Why?' Then I understood. 'Ah, I see. They have put someone else in command of the offensive? Gulbuddin. Is that right?'

Din Mohammed merely smiled, turning the palms of his hands eloquently upwards.

It came as no surprise. From the start of the war, the Pakistanis – with the Americans following suit – had always preferred Gulbuddin Hekmatyar to any other mujahideen commander, despite the fact that most Afghans detested him for his ruthlessness and extremism. One reason the Americans always gave for supporting him, as their Consul in Peshawar once remarked to me, was that 'he kills more Russians than anyone else.' This would have been a telling argument if true, but it was just as bogus as the body-count fallacy which obscured reality for so long in Vietnam: everyone knew that Gulbuddin's men spent more time fighting, and killing, other mujahideen than they did the Russians. The real reason for the unwavering Pakistani, and hence American, support was very simple. Since the days of Bhutto, Gulbuddin Hekmatyar had been 'Pakistan's man', prepared to further Pakistan's interests provided they also furthered his own: to be the ruler of Afghanistan. In fact, Gulbuddin is on the record as saying that he wanted to incorporate Afghanistan in a Greater Pakistan.

Gulbuddin's appointment coincided with a period of bloody unrest. The long list of victims included people as disparate as Andy Skrzypkowiak, a British freelance cameraman and a personal friend, and Professor Majrouh, a Kabul intellectual who edited an exile monthly, the *Afghan Information Centre Bulletin*, in Peshawar. Majrouh infuriated a

172

well-known mujahideen leader by conducting an opinion poll in the refugee camps which showed the vast majority of Afghan refugees were in favour of the return of the king. One day, there was a knock on his front door and when Majrouh answered it, he was shot dead on the doorstep. The gunman was never found, but the Majrouh family had no doubt as to who was behind the killing.

In another incident, the Farkhar massacre, one of the bloodiest of the war, Hisb-i-Islami's complicity was never in doubt. Despite a letter of safe conduct, more than twenty of Masud's commanders were seized, tortured and killed in an ambush in Tangi Farkhar (Farkhar Gorge), in Takhar Province, northern Afghanistan, in 1988. The perpetrators, led by Gulbuddin's local commander, were tracked down, arrested, tried by an Islamic court, found guilty and the main accused executed.

But the murder of Andy Skrzypkowiak, whose only crime was his friendship with Masud, was in another category of political gangsterism. Andy, whose father was a Polish army officer who was murdered by the KGB, grew up in Britain and joined the Parachute Regiment. Exceptionally fit and tough, he was recruited into the SAS, in which he served for seven years. After leaving the SAS, he became a freelance cameraman and, inevitably, was drawn to the Afghan war, which he started covering in 1981. I met him first in 1982 and over the years he supplied ITN and the BBC with first-class combat footage, including the famous sequence of a Russian convoy being ambushed by mujahideen near the Salang Tunnel. In 1986, Andy, Noel Smart, a documentary cameraman, and I spent nearly three months in Afghanistan making a documentary on Masud's guerrilla operations in the north.

In 1987, Andy went back to Afghanistan on special assignment for the BBC, and it was while he was travelling through Nuristan on his way to meet Masud that he was kidnapped and murdered. The culprits, led by a man called

173

Luqa, a Hisb-i-Islami party member from the Panjsher, Masud's home valley, were arrested by the Pakistani police in the northern hill town of Chitral a few months later trying to sell Andy's expensive, French-made Aaton camera. They were also carrying a large amount of money belonging, the police established, to a team of French doctors they had robbed in the same area in which Andy was killed.

It was early in 1987 that Luqa and his group of about a dozen men established themselves in Kantiwar, the capital of Nuristan, on the main route from the Pakistan border to the Panjsher Valley, and the north. Their mission was to stop any aid reaching Masud, which included foreign aid workers, doctors and journalists. Apart from waylaying and robbing the French doctors, they targeted AfghanAid, which was known to support Masud, its monitors often carrying in large sums of money. One of them, Julian Gearing, was stopped on his way out and had to stand by while his Afghan escorts – Masud supporters from the Panjsher – were beaten up by the Luqa gang. Overhearing that the gang intended to come back, possibly to finish them off, Julian Gearing decided to make a run for it. Another monitor, Rory Peck, who was on his way in at about the same time as the French doctors, told me he managed to avoid the gang by making a considerable detour. (Sadly, Rory Peck was killed filming the siege of the White House in Moscow in October, 1993.)

Andy reached Kantiwar in September, which was late in the season, and he was in a hurry. Travelling alone, apart from a Panjsheri horseman, he was stopped by Luqa and his men and ordered to turn back: he was forbidden to go to the Panjsher, they told him. Andy gave them the slip, leaving the village early in the morning with his horseman and heading for Kantiwar Pass, about twenty miles to the north, at the head of the valley. It was a route he had travelled many times before and he and his horseman would have made good time; Andy always prided himself on being able to outwalk any Afghan. But they were overtaken, it

174

seems, at the foot of the pass, by Luqa and three of his men on horseback. There was a struggle, and when they tried to seize Andy's camera, he hit one of them. Unarmed and outnumbered, the fight was soon over. The horseman was told to go on, alone, and Andy was forced to walk back to Kantiwar, a prisoner.

According to a member of Luqa's gang, a boy who later made a confession in the form of a sworn affidavit to a diplomat from the British Embassy in Islamabad, Andy and his captors got as far as the village of Chaman, just north of Kantiwar, where they stopped for the night. At this point, the road into Chaman runs across green meadows, close to a beautiful, limpid river, ideal as a camping spot. The drystone walls which surround the fields of maize are high and solid, and it was apparently at the foot of one of these that Andy, exhausted by what must have been a forced march of forty miles, spread out his sleeping bag. The boy says that he heard Luqa and his henchmen discussing what they should do with Andy.

He recalls phrases such as 'He is not like the French doctors. They were frightened. This one is not frightened. He is different.' It was as a result of this discussion, the boy says, that they decided to kill Andy, but not to shoot him, since the noise of the shot would have been heard by the villagers. Instead, while he slept, they lifted a boulder from the great drystone wall and dropped it on his head, crushing his skull and killing him outright. Then, the boy says, the three or four involved in the killing carried the body, still in its blue sleeping bag, across the river and buried it among some trees on the far bank.

Despite the incriminating evidence of Andy's camera which they were trying to sell in Chitral, Luqa and the others were eventually cleared of the murder and released. A year or so later, Zia sent me to meet General Hamid Gul, General Akhtar's successor as head of the ISI, and I asked him why they had not been put on trial. The general denied

175

categorically that they, or the Hisb-i-Islami, had in any way
been responsible.

'But,' I protested, 'the British have a sworn affidavit from
an eyewitness saying exactly what happened. The people
who killed him were a Hisb-i-Islami group led by a man
called Luqa.'

'I can assure you, Mr Sandy Gall,' the general said, 'that I
have personally investigated the matter and there is no truth
in that story whatsoever.'

'Then how do you account for it?' I asked, flabbergasted.

'Your friend was killed by agents of the Kabul Government, the Khad,' the general said, looking me straight in
the eye.

I knew he was lying, but I also knew that the ISI would
never allow Gulbuddin to be implicated. He was, after
all, 'Pakistan's man', and had paid, it was alleged, a huge
bribe of several million rupees to get his men out of jail.
Needless to say, he has always denied any responsibility.
For a long time, the British Ambassador, later High Com-
missioner, Sir Nicholas Barrington, raised the matter repeatedly with the Pakistani authorities, but never obtained any
satisfaction. He also raised it with Gulbuddin, but to no
avail. I sincerely hope that one of these days, when some
stability has returned to Afghanistan, Andy's murderers will
be brought to justice before an Afghan court and suitably
punished. It is ironic that it was his pictures, as much as
anyone else's, which ensured that the world did not forget
the Afghan war, and which helped to bring about the
common policy of Lord Carrington, General Zia, and Mrs
Thatcher.

The favouritism shown to certain mujahideen commanders had serious military implications. By insisting on giving
Gulbuddin such huge quantities of arms and money, the ISI
and the CIA starved other equally or more deserving parties
of support, delayed victory and increased the number of
Afghan casualties, not least because the Hisb-i-Islami used

176

its greater firepower to attack rival mujahideen rather than government forces. The row caused by British opposition to the ISI–CIA policy became so bitter at one stage that the CIA demanded the recall of a senior MI6 representative in Islamabad. Naturally, it was refused, but the row reverberated to the very top and rumbled on for a long time. It was only very late in the war – about 1990 – that the CIA, astonishingly, admitted to the British that they had made 'a mistake' about Gulbuddin and asked the British for their advice as to what they should do now. The temptation to say 'We told you so' must have been overwhelming, but it was then too late, and the damage had been done. Even six years later, in mid-1993, as I write, Pakistan is still trying to push Gulbuddin Hekmatyar into power, despite it being abundantly clear that he is totally unacceptable to the majority of Afghans.

But at the time of the Jalalabad offensive, the Americans had still not seen the light as far as Gulbuddin was concerned, and they wanted quick results. Ideally, they hoped the mujahideen would capture Jalalabad as the last Soviet soldiers crossed the Oxus on their way home, and march on Kabul immediately afterwards. They refused to listen to commanders like Masud who said it would take three years for the mujahideen to make the leap from guerrilla to conventional warfare: from ambushing convoys to capturing cities. And when Masud refused to cut the Salang Highway as his contribution to the Jalalabad plan, with which he disagreed, the Americans and Pakistanis retaliated by cutting off his arms supply for the rest of the year. I know this is true, because I travelled north to see Masud at the end of 1989 and he confirmed it to me personally. The Foreign Office knew about the cut-off, but my report on *News at Ten* gave them the opportunity to send a telegram to Washington asking pointedly if it was true, and if so, why? Deliveries resumed the following year, but the cut-off slowed down Masud's offensive in the north.

My immediate concern, however, was to report the Soviet withdrawal from inside Afghanistan, and on Tuesday 14 February, St Valentine's Day, our improbable convoy of one Land Rover full of satellite gear, and one Landcruiser full of people and camera equipment, drove out of Peshawar, through the Wild West territory of the Tribal Area, over the Khyber Pass, and into Afghanistan. Thanks to the clearance organised by Major Ali, we were whisked through the border to pick up our mujahideen escort, armed with Russian Kalashnikov automatic rifles, on the Afghan side. Their leader, Mustafa, the local Jamiat commander, had the bushy black beard and flashing black eyes of the archetypal Pashtun warrior. A three-jeep convoy now, we sped out of Torkham and up the road towards Jalalabad, past the sights made familiar by General Safi's conducted tour. To those who had missed the original, I did my best to provide an admittedly less colourful substitute. We drove as far as the state farm, where there seemed to be more mujahideen than on our previous visit. As we passed one group, Mustafa warned, 'Please do not take pictures of Hisb Gulbuddin people, they do not like it. Nobody else mind.' We were originally going to set up our satellite equipment at the state farm, but Mustafa decided it was too insecure: the Russians, or the Afghan Air Force, had already dropped a few bombs in the area, killing and wounding several mujahideen.

'I take you now to my village,' he announced. 'There much better for you. No one see what we do.' Looking round conspiratorially, he lowered his voice. 'Here, too much spy. Too much. My village much better.'

We followed him back along the road we had come, the afternoon sunlight filtering serenely through the long avenue of casuarinas. We passed whole families returning to their homes, driving flocks of goats and sheep; camels loaded with household goods paced regally in front, small children rode donkeys, and the men and women walked behind. About five or six miles from the state farm, we

178

turned right up a dusty track and a few minutes later came to the village, a collection of mudbrick houses each surrounded by a high wall.

Mustafa led the way to the edge of the village, and after some shouting to the inhabitants within, the gates swung open and we drove inside a compound surrounded by a fifteen-foot wall and guarded by a machine-gun post reached by a ladder. If not an impregnable fortress, at least Mustafa's house would give us protection from the prying eyes of government agents. When the satellite project was first discussed, I had raised the question of how easy it would be for the Russians to intercept our transmissions and pinpoint our position.

'Quite impossible,' I was told by the engineer who designed the dish. 'The beam is so narrow that it is virtually impossible for anyone to intercept it and be able to get a fix on it.'

Although ignorant of satellite technology, it seemed to me that any beam as powerful as the one we were sending 120 miles into the sky must be detectable.

'No, no,' the expert said, 'I can assure you, nobody can pick up our transmissions. You're quite safe.'

I remembered this conversation as we started to unload and set up the satellite dish and all its component parts, taking over Mustafa's *q'ala* as television crews do, running cables across his courtyard and into the house, and filling the air with the fearsome racket of our portable generator. The trickiest part was positioning the beam to coincide exactly with the orbiting satellite, invisible above us in the immaculate pale blue of the Afghan sky. We never met the women of the house, although we knew they were there when a generous dinner of mutton, rice, *nan* and tea was served soon after nightfall. But I did meet one of Mustafa's uncles, who to our surprise accosted us in English, speaking with a strong Yorkshire accent. I asked him how he had acquired it.

'I once lived in Bradford,' he confided. 'When I used to do spare parts. You know. Second-'and. For motor vehicles.'

'Motor vehicles?'

'Aye. Bedford lorries mainly, but some cars and buses as well.'

I knew that most of the lorries in Pakistan and Afghanistan were Bedfords, their high wooden sides, decorated with garish paintings of animals, flowers and sometimes war scenes, perambulating exhibitions of pop art. I asked him how long he had lived in England.

'I lived ten years in Bradford, off and on. I'd spend a few months there in the winter, buying spare parts, then I'd come home in the summer. But that was before the bloody Communists took over. Here, have some grub.'

That night, we broadcast live for the first time from inside Afghanistan, with Alastair Burnet at the other end of the satellite link-up. The *News at Ten* audience saw me sitting on the carpet in Mustafa's living-room, dressed in Afghan clothes, and surrounded by a lot of armed, wild-looking mujahideen. We probably all looked sleepy, too; it was three in the morning, our time. Next day, Mustafa came to us and said he thought we ought to move to another, less populated village. 'You know, there some people here who are government people. Maybe they spy for Kabul.'

I thought he was being over-protective, but he seemed so sensible in other ways that we did not argue. The engineers took little more than an hour to dismantle the satellite and load the cases back on the Land Rover. An hour later we were in our new village, a few miles away in a dry, dusty valley, well off the road. The place looked as if it had been bombed, and many of the houses were empty, which pleased Mustafa. No doubt he had been told by the ISI that if anything happened to us or the satellite equipment, he need not bother coming back to Pakistan. I had to do a live interview for ABC's breakfast show – it was already late afternoon with us – which consisted of one question and a

180

time limit of one minute for my answer. Eventually, over my earpiece, I could hear the introduction from the studio in New York. After saying that the last Russian troops would complete their withdrawal that day, the presenter went on, 'With us this morning we have ITN's correspondent in Jalalabad, and she [*sic*] joins us now from Afghanistan, live. Good morning, Sandy, what is the situation like out there?'

I was tempted to say 'I'm a he, not a she,' but let it go, knowing that in America Sandy is a girl's name. Instead, I said, 'The mujahideen have Jalalabad surrounded. There's some fighting on the outskirts but no signs yet of a major offensive. Generally, as seen from here, the Russians seem to be completing their withdrawal without much opposition . . .' and so on for the requested sixty seconds. When I felt my sixty seconds were up, I stopped and the presenter in New York said, 'Thank you, Sandy Gall, for that . . .' and went on to something else, leaving me wondering if he was asking himself, 'Was that really a dame? She sure has a deep voice.'

Once again, the satellite communications worked perfectly and we fed the report we had made earlier in the day of a mujahideen patrol, led by Mustafa, probing the outer defences of Jalalabad. That night, *News at Ten* ran 'back-to-back' reports about the Soviet withdrawal from Kabul, Moscow, Friendship Bridge at Termesz on the Soviet border, and Jalalabad. Then Alastair Burnet came live to me – it was again three in the morning with us – and we tried to sum up what the Russians had achieved: the answer, apart from the deaths of thousands of Afghans and the destruction of their country, was nothing.

It was only after we had been back in Peshawar for a couple of days, packing up to go home, that Mustafa and some of his mujahideen arrived at the villa. Apart from wanting to bid us farewell, Mustafa said they had something to tell us.

'You remember when I say we must move to other village.'

'Yes, I remember. Why do you ask?'

'That night, after we leave my village, the *Shuravi* [Russians] come and bomb. One plane drop one, two bomb on my house.'

'On your house, Mustafa!'

'Yes, where you stay. They kill one old womans and wound another one.'

'Good Lord. Do you think they knew we had been there?'

'Yes. I tell you, Sandy Goll. There plenty spy in that village.'

I recalled the confident assurances of the engineer who had told me that it was 'quite impossible' for the Russians to intercept our transmissions and work out where we were. Had he been shooting me a line? Or were the agents of Kabul really everywhere, even in Mustafa's own village?

Chapter
12

When Saddam Hussein invaded Kuwait on 2 August 1990, ITN, like everyone else, was caught on the hop. No one had expected the Iraqi dictator, despite all his bombast, to do something so patently idiotic. Only the day before, high-level Kuwaiti and Iraqi delegates had been meeting in Saudi Arabia to argue about outstanding Kuwaiti loans to the Baghdad regime; Kuwait, like many other Gulf states had pumped millions of dollars into the war against Iran. At the end of the meeting, the delegates broke up saying they would meet again the following week. Nor did the big powers of the region, the Saudis and the Egyptians, believe Saddam would invade. Indeed, the Iraqi President had gone out of his way to assure both King Fahd of Saudi Arabia and President Mubarak of Egypt only a day or two before that he had no aggressive intentions vis-à-vis the Kuwaitis. King Fahd, the richest and most powerful ruler of them all, was particularly upset about the invasion.

But in Jordan, to which I flew a couple of weeks later, there was a very different feeling: far from being an aggressor, Saddam was the darling of what Arabs call 'the street', and demonstrations were being staged every day to glorify his stand. These were Palestinian-inspired, not officially organised, and the reason was not hard to find. The vast majority of Jordanians are Palestinian refugees and they looked up to Saddam as the only Arab leader who was openly committed to destroying Israel, whatever the West might do or say. Western condemnation of his aggression in Kuwait was rejected out of hand as anti-Arab. Even King Hussein, the great survivor, was not immune to the general hysteria, although there may have been method in his madness.

Rumour had it that Saddam's real objective, once he had digested little Kuwait, was to get his hands on the vast oil fields of Saudi Arabia, the world's richest, which lie mainly along the Gulf just south of Kuwait, in the Kingdom's Eastern Province. Saddam was said to have offered King Hussein and the Yemenis a share of the spoils, in Hussein's case possession (or perhaps one should say re-possession) of Mecca, the holiest city in Islam and the capital of the Hejaz. Significantly, it was the Saudis who had driven Hussein's family, the Hashemites, Sherifs of Mecca for centuries, from the Hejaz. The Hashemites, the argument ran, as former guardians of the Holy Cities of Mecca and Medina, were the most distinguished family in Islam, compared to whom the Saudis were mere upstarts. Not only was the king descended from the Prophet but, as one of Hussein's former private secretaries, Moraiwid Tel, explained to me, the Prophet was a member of the king's own tribe, which went much further back.

The story of the planned carve-up may have been apocryphal, but many Gulf Arabs, including the Saudis, undoubtedly believed it. One thing was incontrovertible. Relations between the Gulf rulers and Jordan, one of the poorest countries in the Middle East, had been bad for some time; the once liberal handouts of cash had all but dried up and on at least one occasion Hussein had been humiliated by having to kick his heels waiting to see the Emir of Kuwait. He had become fed up with having to kowtow to the ruling families of the Gulf, whose arrogance was matched only by their wealth, itself an accident of geog-

184

raphy. It was rather like an impoverished but grand English duke having to go cap in hand to some uncouth, self-made Texan oil millionaire for a loan. Whereas Western leaders like President Bush and Mrs Thatcher, it was explained to me, saw Saddam as a Hitler figure, whose aggression must be halted at any price, King Hussein saw him much more as an Arab Robin Hood, robbing the filthy rich Kuwaitis to give to the poor, whether Palestinians, Jordanians, Yemenis or Iraqis. The fact that Iraq was almost as rich in oil as Saudi Arabia was beside the point.

The rift between the Gulf rulers and King Hussein made Saddam's blandishments all the more difficult to resist, despite recent history. It was, after all, Saddam's predecessor Colonel Kassim who in 1958 overthrew the Iraqi monarchy, murdering King Feisal, Hussein's cousin, and most of his family in a coup that was exceptionally brutal even by Middle East standards. Relations did not really improve until the early 1970s, when Hussein went to Baghdad on an official visit and came back, according to a Saudi diplomat I met in Jordan, with a large chunk of money, partly for the Jordanian exchequer, and partly for his own private purse. Saddam continued to cultivate Hussein assiduously, and cleverly. Although it was the revolutionary Baathists who had assassinated Hussein's relations, this did not deter Saddam, now head of the party, from erecting a lavish memorial to the Hashemites in a belated attempt, it would seem, to make amends for his predecessors' bloodthirstiness.

Thus an unlikely personal relationship blossomed between these two: the brave little king (Harrow and Sandhurst) whose very Englishness almost conferred honorary membership of the British royal family; and the ruthless, mafioso-style dictator who had started his career as a party hit man and gone on to execute hundreds, possibly thousands of political opponents, including his own brother-in-law.

When Saddam invaded Iran in 1980, the alliance with Hussein became vital; it was only through Jordan's southern port of Aqaba that Iraq was able to import the massive shipments of arms and other supplies it needed for its war effort. Aqaba was to become Saddam's lifeline, with fleets of huge lorries ferrying tons of equipment north up the Desert Highway, day and night. Over eight years, the Aqaba traffic earned Jordan a lot of money; $650 million by the end of the war, which Iraq was still repaying in instalments of $12 million a month and shipments of cheap oil.

After the Security Council in New York gave Saddam the first ultimatum, withdraw from Kuwait or else face the consequences, one of my Jordanian friends, who had also worked for Hussein as his private secretary, told me he was convinced the king would gradually distance himself from Saddam.

'The word has already gone out from the Palace,' he said.

I was puzzled. 'What does that mean exactly?'

'The Palace passes the word as to what it wants done, and the message gets handed down, so everyone knows the score. For example, the papers are already playing down support for Saddam – you won't see any more demonstrations on television. Finally it gets to the street and then everyone's wise.'

'What happens if the street does not like what it's being told?'

He smiled. 'It doesn't work like that.'

But for some reason, the system did not work this time, or else Hussein changed his mind. Far from distancing himself from Saddam, His Majesty seemed deliberately to dig himself deeper and deeper into the Iraqi foxhole. He got a flea in the ear from both President Bush and Mrs Thatcher; and British diplomats began to make irritatedly disparaging remarks about 'the brave little king' who kept coming to Downing Street to preach the same unacceptable message. But he refused to be deterred. Perhaps the almost blanket

186

consensus at home, and his own apparently genuine admiration for Saddam as 'a true patriot and worthy representative of the Arab nation', blinded his usually astute political vision. Not that this was not the first time Hussein had let his feelings get the better of his judgement. In the Six-Day war in 1967, he had allowed himself to be talked into a disastrous alliance with President Nasser, committing his army and air force to 'the Arab cause' on the very eve of the battle. Nasser had telephoned the king in Amman to ask: are you with us, yes or no? Explaining the reason he had made the disastrous decision which led to the virtual destruction of his armed forces, Hussein said later he had asked Nasser, 'Can you guarantee air cover?'

'Yes,' said Nasser over the line from Cairo. 'You will have all the air cover you need.'

'I am with you and my Arab brothers, then,' Hussein replied. Next day, in a devastating pre-emptive strike, Israel bombed the Arab air forces, including Jordan's, into virtual oblivion, thus paving the way for the annihilation of the Arab armies, including the flower of Hussein's army, the Arab Legion. I saw Hussein a day or two later and although he insisted the redness of his eyes was due not to weeping but to lack of sleep, he was clearly deeply shocked, like a man who has just seen his family killed in a car crash. And yet here he was, twenty-three years later, ready it seemed to make the same mistake again. Almost, but not quite. He did not commit his army and air force this time, as he had in 1967, and when Saddam finally plunged to the defeat long seen as inevitable in the West, Hussein managed to avoid being dragged down in the maelstrom.

One of my last jobs in Jordan was to drive to the Iraqi border to intercept and interview the first convoy of British refugees from Kuwait. I got a tip-off fom the British Embassy in Amman that a busload of Britons were due some time in the next twelve hours and so with Bernie Glancy, an old friend from Afghanistan and one of ITN's most experienced cameramen, we hired a taxi and set off on the four-hour journey across the desert. It was a long hot drive, the road at one point traversing a stony plain which T. E. Lawrence describes crossing with the Arab army in 1917 on the way to Damscus. He says it was one of the most gruelling journeys he had ever had to make and one could see why. The desert was so completely covered with millions of closely-packed rounded stones that to walk over them must have been sheer agony to man and camel alike; we imagined, from the comfort of our taxi, the purgatory Lawrence and his Beduin comrades-in-arms must have endured as they stumbled over miles and miles of what looked like giant marbles.

The border itself runs through featureless desert, but the last Jordanian checkpoint lies some distance back from the actual demarcation line. Normally, there would have been nothing there except a few concrete outposts in the waste of sand; but the invasion of Kuwait had produced an avalanche of humanity, thousands of Palestinian, Egyptian and Indian refugees who had managed to escape the approaching Armageddon and were camped here in primitive conditions, wondering rather desperately how to reach safety. They came walking over the desert, sweating in the heat of high summer under bulging suitcases, and having at last arrived on Jordanian soil they found themselves paying over the odds for a bottle of water almost too hot to drink.

Bernie, who had already been to the border several times, spotted some of the American Embassy people and went to talk to them: the British did not bother to monitor the border on a daily basis. With the Americans were one or two Red Cross officials, who had apparently only just arrived; arrangements to cope with the flood of refugees seemed to be minimal. With luck, they might be able to get on a bus to Amman, but equally they could wait in the queue for twenty-four hours. The Americans told Bernie they had heard the British convoy would arrive at around midnight, so we drove back to a small supermarket a few kilometres

188

down the road where, at exorbitant prices by local standards, we purchased bully beef, cheese and biscuits plus a bottle of Soave, and made ourselves as comfortable as we could. For a brief moment of magic, dusk stole across the desert, turning the sky from pale orange to lemon, until the arc lights came on, dissipating it abruptly.

I was asleep in the front seat when Bernie materialised at the window and said, 'I think the convoy has just arrived. They're parked round the back, in the lorry section. They didn't come through the main checkpoint.'

We walked silently through the dark to an outside slip road where a long line of lorries was parked; right in the middle, lights doused and showing little sign of life, was a large, travel-stained coach. We approached cautiously, just as one or two people got off to stretch their legs. Delicately, we inquired: were they British, from Kuwait? Surprised, and possibly annoyed at having their anonymity blown so soon, they veered away like frightened fawns. Then someone said, 'Yes, we are British, or British dependents, and we've just had a bloody awful journey. Twelve hours from Kuwait!'

There was nothing for it. We climbed up into the bus, Bernie switched his camera light on and to gasps of surprise and irritation we filmed the huddled passengers, mainly the wives and children of the few British still remaining in Kuwait. Then some Embassy type came up and said we could not film on the bus. Would we mind getting off?

Playing for time, I said, 'There's great interest at home in the refugees, as you know, and these people are the first group to leave, aren't they?'

'Yes, but for all sorts of security reasons, we would rather you didn't film them.'

'Got it all, anyway,' said Bernie out of the corner of his mouth.

We left the bus as requested, but found that most of the passengers, their secret out, were happy to follow and one

189

or two even to talk. They included the attractive wife of a British businessman who had stayed behind – from her accent she might have been Lebanese, or possibly French – and a friend of hers, an older woman, a Yugoslav who had spent years in Kuwait and knew all the gossip. She had been an active member, or possibly employee of the Equestrian Club, frequented, she said, by many rich and powerful Kuwaitis. Her stories were unusable on ITN, but made fascinating listening.

'You have no idea of what goes on,' she said. 'I could tell you lots of things.'

'What sort of things?'

'They are mad about Western women, you know. They bring them in secretly, lots of them. There was this friend of mine, a very beautiful Scandinavian girl, blonde, very good figure, you know . . .'

We stood in the dark, beside the bus, the arc lights making a white patch in the sky a few hundred yards away. All round us there was a low murmur, like the sea lapping on a sandy beach; it was the nighttime sound of thousands of refugees, eating, talking, even sleeping. I could hardly see the face of our Yugoslav informant, but I guessed her shortish hair was blonde and that she been good-looking when younger; and I could picture her in well-cut jodphurs.

'Well, my friend was working in Geneva and she met this minister from Kuwait. He was very important. He liked her very much and invited her to Kuwait. She wasn't too sure at first, she has a boyfriend, you see, but the minister was very persistent. He gave her a first-class ticket and made all the arrangements. So she caught the plane and flew down and was met at the airport by a Filipino, a sort of secretary . . .'

'A minder, you mean.'

'Yes. Sorry, my English is not so good. [It was in fact extremely good.] This man took her to a house where there were already a number of other girls, all young, foreign and

190

good-looking. There were very strict rules. They were not allowed to go out on their own, nor to use the telephone without permission. They would have parties, in the evenings, when the Kuwaiti men would come, and sometimes they would stay all night . . .

'During the day, she went shopping, with the Filipino. They would go to jewellery shops and she was told to choose whatever she liked. Then they would go back to the house. One night, my friend rang me up. She told me she was bored and she would like to see me. We arranged to meet. Well, they found out about it. They asked her lots of questions. Who had she telephoned, why, and so on. They were very angry that she taken a taxi to come to my flat. They were so angry that next day they put her on the plane back to Geneva.'

'Why were they so angry?'

'Because they didn't want anyone to know that she was in Kuwait, that any of these girls were in Kuwait. Normally, the girls would come for a week, see only the Kuwaiti men who brought them over, go shopping with the Filipinos, and then go back on the plane. Nobody was supposed to know they were here. When they discovered my friend knew someone in Kuwait, and might have told her – me, in other words – who had brought her over, they got in a panic. They're very secretive, you see. They don't want anyone to know what they're doing. But it goes on all the time. Quite frankly, I don't have much sympathy for what's happened to them.'

We watched them drive away, Bernie getting a last shot of the bus going through the checkpoint. Then we walked back to our taxi and set off on the return journey. It was nearly three in the morning.

I returned from Jordan and took up my post again at *News at Ten*. I was approaching the end of twenty-one years' newscasting for ITN. I found it hard to believe that it had been such a long run, that it seemed to have passed so

191

quickly – every old man's complaint – and that now, almost unthinkably, it was practically over. The withdrawal symptoms would come later, but fortunately, I was born an optimist and they were never very serious. As a career in television journalism, it had been at its best enormously exciting – sometimes almost too exciting – and worthwhile; at its worst pedestrian but nearly always interesting. The news is one of the few live programmes on television, and that gives it bite, even on a quiet night. What I enjoyed most were the occasions when I was freed from the desk and the restrictions of the studio and allowed to roam abroad. There had been a few times on air in the early days when the nerve almost failed, but I used to tell myself that if I had not been frightened when the Vietnamese Communists rocketed the American fire base at Rockpile, there was no need to panic when I made a cock-up in the studio in London.

'Know thyself,' is the great Buddhist injunction, and one which, although not a Buddhist, I find admirable if difficult to attain. But is not every counsel of perfection equally unattainable? Being a presenter of a news programme on national television gives one a certain, if ephemeral fame, although in my case I think my work as a foreign correspondent has opened more doors; lunch at Chequers, dinner at Downing Street, the award of the CBE, the Star of Pakistan, the Lawrence of Arabia Medal: the first from the Queen, the second from President Zia, the third from the hands of Prince Charles, patron of the Royal Society for Asian Affairs. Life as a foreign correspondent has also brought, in my case at least, friendships in every part of the world, with diplomats and businessmen, journalists and writers and foreign leaders. Being a 'face' on TV certainly does open most restaurant doors, but it can also be embarrassing; prices tend to go up when you heave into sight and you are always recognised when you wish to be incognito.

I made my last newscast with my old and good friend, Sir Alastair Burnet, on 4 January 1990. Alastair is the most able yet modest of men, extremely good company, convivial in the extreme and generous to a fault. He is also witty. When he had the misfortune to collide with a lamppost in a badly-lit street and gave himself a black eye, his response to an over-intrusive journalist who asked him if it was true that he drank a bottle of whisky a day, was typical. Where a lesser man might have blustered and bullied, he smiled disarmingly and urbanely replied, 'That, I'm afraid, is altogether too flattering.'

On our last night together on *News at Ten* Alastair, predictably, paid me an extremely generous tribute. It was brief, but beautifully turned, every word in place: as other men always have every hair in place, Alastair always has every word in place. We had a couple of Scotches afterwards, as we often did, and I went home as I had done for years in a car with a driver – it took an hour – where dinner was waiting and a bottle of claret. I read for a bit, unwound, went to bed about one, listened to the world service for five or ten minutes and slept like a baby. Five days later, on Wednesday 9 January I caught a plane for Saudi Arabia to start, or rather renew, my career as a reporter, covering the Gulf War.

A few months before, when I had been in Jordan, I had applied for a Saudi visa, without success, although I had spent an interesting hour with the diplomat who was so knowledgeable about King Hussein's friendship with Saddam Hussein. One reason I failed to get the visa, I discovered on return to London, was that the Saudis do not in general like giving them to people outside their own countries. Since I was no longer tied down by my newscasting commitments, and since it looked pretty likely that there was going to be war in the Gulf, I decided to try again. Luckily, I had a friend, high up in the Foreign Office, willing and able to work the oracle. No sooner requested than arranged. 'Go and pick it up whenever you want,' I was told. This was extremely important because the Saudis, who are paranoiac about the media and hardly ever give visas to journalists, were being very cagey about changing their policy, despite pressure from Washington and London. Like every one else, ITN was finding them deaf to all requests.

Now it happened that about this time, *News at Ten* held its annual party in a small trattoria near Wells Street, where ITN then had its studios. We foregathered a little after ten thirty for a drink, sitting down at about eleven for a late dinner of pasta and wine. About midnight, Nigel Hancock, then News Editor, came in with a couple of cronies and installed himself near me. Somehow the conversation turned to Saudi Arabia and the problem of visas.

'It's bloody difficult,' Nigel declared, 'No one can get visas.'

'I can,' I said. 'I can get one tomorrow.'

'Forgive me for saying so, Sandy, but I'm bloody sure you can't!'

'I'm bloody sure, I can, Nigel,' I replied. 'I have a firm promise that I can go in and pick it up any time I want.'

Nigel laughed knowingly. 'I'm sorry to have to repeat myself, Sandy, but I bet you can't.'

By this time we had all had a few, and I must confess that, irritated at being contradicted, I snapped. 'I bet you I can.'

'How much?'

'A hundred pounds.'

'Right, done,' Nigel said. There was a brief pause; it was a rather larger figure, perhaps, than I would normally wager, and no doubt Nigel, too. Then the conversation switched to other things.

A week or so later, I got a message from the Saudi Ambassador's secretary to say that if I wanted my visa I should come straightaway, as only the Ambassador could sign it and he was leaving for Saudi Arabia in a couple of days' time. I went round next morning, had the priceless document stamped in my passport and took a taxi back to the office, where I happened to meet Nigel Hancock.

'Got something to show you, Nigel,' I said finding it hard to keep the triumph out of my voice. I opened my passport to show him the full-page red and green open-sesame with the big green 50 riyal stamp at the bottom, bearing the insignia of a palm tree and crossed scimitars and the magic words: Entry Visa, Kingdom of Saudi Arabia.

A few days later, I flew to Riyadh, the Saudi capital. A small ITN team of Peter Allen, a political correspondent, Mike Jermey, a *News at Ten* producer, an editor and a film crew were already installed in the Hyatt Regency. Also, and most importantly, we had a share of a satellite dish on the hotel roof which meant we could go to London live at virtually any time.

Mike Jermey was waiting to meet me, which I thought exceptionally courteous, and we were soon in the back of a large American taxi, on our way into Riyadh. First, if very superficial impressions suggest that Saudi Arabia is really a piece of America in the Middle East. Riyadh reminded me of both Phoenix, Arizona, which is also built in the desert, and of Los Angeles with its vast sprawl, although the Saudi capital's wide, superbly engineered freeways are almost certainly in better shape. As you near town you could be forgiven for thinking you were watching a Hollywood film; the road is lined on both sides with second-hand car showrooms. One sign read 'Joe's Used Cars – As Good As New.' There was almost no traffic, which was refreshing after the overcrowding of southern England, and the temperature was pleasant. The Hyatt Regency, predictably, was wholly American, and completely peaceful. The only hint of crisis was the presence on the door of armed American military police, who checked our credentials as we went in. A few yards down the street, lights blazed late in the Saudi Defence Ministry, where General Schwarzkopf, I was to discover, had his headquarters. Apart from the MPs, there was no sign of war nerves, no blackout, no panic.

Inside, the Hyatt was brilliantly lit and boasted all the usual amenities: an American-style coffee shop, with a self-service buffet, an Italian restaurant, a Japanese restaurant, a French restaurant (closed) and an outdoor swimming pool. The ITN office was on the fifth floor, the VIP floor, and you needed a special key to stop the lift there. Up on the ninth were the American and British forces' information desks, and most of the ground floor, where the Saudis had their desk, was given over to a press centre where the daily briefings were held. Apart from large numbers of American officers and a smaller number of British, the hotel was packed with journalists, photographers, television crews and producers from all over the world, the majority, of course, American, but a lot of British as well. There were also a considerable number of Kuwaiti refugee families in residence, the children amusing themselves by riding up and down in the lifts non-stop. Being Kuwaitis, the parents were rich enough to stay in the Hyatt, which charged New York prices. In one respect only did the hotel fall woefully short of the American norm: in conformity with Saudi law, it was completely dry and few journalists, if any, risked instant expulsion for being caught smuggling in a drop of the hard stuff.

Next day, I went to call on the British Ambassador, Sir Alan Munro, a friendly, knowledgeable Middle East hand who was clearly on good terms with the Saudi Establishment and was said to be one of the architects of the £20 billion Yamanah agreement, under which we undertook to sell ships and a large number of aircraft, including our hottest property, the Tornado fighter-bomber, to the Saudis in the largest defence contract ever won by Britain. It was one of the great commercial successes of the Thatcher Government, achieved in a notoriously fickle and competitive market and I presumed that the Saudi ambassadorship was part of Alan Munro's reward.

He received me affably, in red sweater and slacks, and

196

over coffee and shortbread in his office spoke of King Fahd's great contribution in 'stabilising' Saudi Arabia and the Middle East generally by his moderate, sensible policies. He found King Hussein's support for Saddam Hussein 'inexplicable', and in the same vein said that Yasser Arafat, by committing himself and the PLO so unreservedly to Saddam, had thrown away all the support he and it had gained in Saudi Arabia and the rest of the Gulf from their recent more moderate line. He also talked of the shape of things to come, which was really a forecast of growing Saudi influence and a new Riyadh–Cairo axis, with the Saudis' vast wealth and growing political clout being married to Egypt's traditional role as the leading Arab country, with the biggest population and the biggest army after Iraq's.

That evening, after eating an Arab chef's not altogether brilliant rendering of *tortellini alla Romana* in the Giuliana restaurant in the hotel, a group of about twenty of us boarded a bus for the Conference Palace where James Baker, the American Secretary of State, on one of his frequent, hectic shuttles to Middle East capitals, was meeting King Fahd. Like many Saudis, and indeed many Arabs, the Saudi monarch likes to do business at night, the later the better, a habit many Westerners initially find baffling. They soon learn, however, that hard though it may be to reach an important Saudi in his office in the morning, the closer the sun sinks to the horizon, the more accessible he becomes, until by ten o'clock at night he is positively holding open house. Perhaps because of ancestral hot weather habits, and despite the ubiquity of air conditioning today, the Arabian day often seems to be for sleeping and the night for working and playing.

So it was not until about 11 p.m. that we reached our destination, one of the many palaces in Riyadh built in the grandiose Arab manner by famous architects, with no expense spared. Such is the Conference Palace, with its acres of priceless carpet and what must be the biggest chandelier in the world, a huge, glittering inverted cone of cut crystal floating high above the vast, circular entrance hall.

After waiting patiently for some time, we were told by an American diplomat travelling with Baker, whom I had known slightly when he was an Afghan watcher in the Consulate in Peshawar in Pakistan, that unfortunately the Secretary of State would not be able to talk to us. After our small display of disappointment, another, plump diplomat appeared and told us that doubly unfortunately, the State Department spokeswoman, none other than the redoubtable Margaret Tutweiler, had decreed there would indeed be a briefing, but only for the correspondents travelling with Mr Baker. Howls of indignation and protest followed, mainly from the British journalists, who of course had no representative on the Baker plane, and several of whom had come up specially from Dhahran, 250 miles away to the north-east.

The situation showed every sign of turning nasty, but the plump diplomat, quiet-spoken and polite, managed, with admirable aplomb, to defuse the situation. Finally, more out of exhaustion than anything else, there was nothing left for it but to go home. Cursing American arrogance and incompetence, and with the nasty feeling that the Special Relationship did not count half as much as we liked to think, we climbed wearily back on the bus and left the Conference Palace behind us, chandeliers blazing with a prodigality that made one realise just how far the Saudis had come, from the poverty and hardship of the desert to wealth of Croesus-like proportions, all in the space of a few short years.

Chapter
13

I had only one high-level Saudi contact, Prince Abdullah bin Feisal bin Turki, a charming man known to his friends as AFT. His father sent him to Nottingham University where he took an engineering degree, and then did a year's practical, working on the shop floor of a local factory. This must have been a fairly harsh experience but he makes light of it, merely saying he always felt exhausted and that he used to to lock himself in the lavatory and fall asleep on the loo. One piece of advice his father gave him was that on arrival in London he must pay a visit to Soho, which in his father's day was still the most cosmopolitan place in Britain, full of foreign restaurants where you could eat cheaply and well. His father did not say anything else about Soho, so the young Abdullah, only eighteen at the time, made his way there on the tube with high hopes and expectations, very much, as he admits, the innocent abroad.

Arriving in Soho, he stopped at a street corner to get his bearings, and was pleasantly surprised when a good-looking young woman, dressed in a very short and tight miniskirt, approached him with a smile. After a word or two of badinage, in which she called him 'love,' she asked, as he understood it, 'And, how's your father?'

Although slightly baffled that she should know his father, he replied that his father was very well and politely returned the compliment. At that point, he says with a chuckle, a man who clearly had some connection with the young lady, approached him and started to address him in an over-familiar manner. When it began to dawn on Abdullah that the young lady was in fact not the slightest bit interested in the health of his father, but had other designs on him, he began to retreat, whereupon the man switched to abuse, pursuing him down the street with language which the young Saudi had never heard before, but which he guessed to be extremely rude. AFT puts it all down to experience and remains very fond of the British, perhaps because he shares our sense of humour.

On his return home as a qualified engineer, Prince Abdul-lah soon rose to prominence in his profession and by the time I met him was in charge of Saudi Arabia's two largest industrial complexes, the port cities of Jubail and Yanbu, one on the Gulf, the other on the Red Sea, known as the Royal Commission for Jubail and Yanbu. When I rang him at his office in Riyadh, he invited me to lunch in the desert the next day. 'There are quite a few friends coming,' he said, 'diplomats and so on.' He then added with true Arab hospitality, 'Bring your crew, as well.'

We all assembled for coffee at the house of Brigadier Nick Cocking, a British officer who was head of the advisory mission to the National Guard, a paramilitary force often seen as a counterbalance to the army. There, I met an old friend from the British Embassy who offered me a lift in his Range Rover. It was an enjoyable drive, bowling along the wide, empty desert highway for fifteen or twenty miles before turning off into the desert and following a sandy track to the prince's camp: despite the dramatic change in their way of life, most Saudis still consider their roots are in the desert and feel the urge to go there periodically to commune with nature. We passed a small herd of camels and sheep and a handful of Arab horses before stopping beside a big tent where we would have lunch, and an open reception area with carpets spread on the sand. The prince, dressed in flowing white robes, came forward in smiling welcome, hand outstretched. I had last seen him in Western clothes at a Foreign Office lunch at the Savoy. We were offered small cups of the bitter desert coffee poured from a long-necked pot wielded by a retainer in a blue robe. The sun was warm, the sky blue, the desert dunes rolled away empty into the distance. Only the sound of a generator which supplied the camp with power broke the silence.

I was standing with Hugh Thomson, an ITN cameraman with whom I had last worked eleven years before in Vietnam and Cambodia, and a young sound recordist, when a small, hawk-faced Arab came up to us and asked, 'Do you know why we serve our guests coffee in such small cups?'

'No,' I said. 'Why?'

'Because, in the days when Saudi Arabia was a very poor country, we could not afford to drink coffee very often. So we made it rather weak, as we still do, and offered guests only one small cup. Although Saudi Arabia is now a rich country,' he grinned like a schoolboy, 'we still stick to the old habits.' I discovered later he was a prominent government minister.

Just before lunch, the prince summoned half a dozen of us to his trailer, parked a hundred yards or so from the tents. Mounting the steps to the trailer we found ourselves in a small group which included the British brigadier, one or two foreign diplomats and two or three Saudis, including a wealthy and well-connected businessman called Teimour Alireza, whom I had met in St Moritz: as far as I know he is the only Saudi who is a member of the St Moritz Tobogganing Club, better known as the Cresta. One of the other Saudis now took charge. 'Gentlemen, there is a very important question I would like to ask you all, in turn. It is very simple. Is there going to be a war in the Gulf, or not?'

'Let me start with you, sir.' He turned to Brigadier Cocking. 'Do you think there is going to be a war?'

201

The Brigadier paused for a moment. 'Yes, I do, if Saddam doesn't withdraw.'

The Saudi turned to my embassy friend. 'What do you think?'

He did not pause very long. 'Yes, I agree, I think there will be a war.'

Then it was my turn, but I backed away. 'Pass, if you don't mind. I plead journalistic impartiality.'

The questioner went through the rest of the guests, and not one disagreed. They all thought that if Saddam did not withdraw from Kuwait, there would be a war. Then something interesting happened. One of the Saudis whose name I did not know, burst out, 'It's not just a question of whether there *will* be a war. There *has* to be a war. We *have* to get rid of this bloody man or there will *never* be peace in the Gulf.' There was a chorus of agreement from the other Saudis and I suddenly understood just how frightened all the Gulf states, including the Saudis, were of Saddam. The invasion of Kuwait had opened their eyes, it would seem, for the first time. The prince cut short further discussion by announcing it was time for lunch. On the way back to the tents we passed the 'kitchen', a shallow depression in the desert containing the red-hot embers of a wood fire over which several Beduin had just finished roasting a whole baby camel. As we passed by, clouds of steam and loud hissing noises rose in the air.

The prince himself carved the camel, which turned out to be delicious, very like veal but a little stringier. I interviewed him afterwards, and he was much more cautious than his friends in the trailer had been, saying he thought there was still a chance that Saddam would see reason and withdraw from Kuwait. But I knew he was being diplomatic, and that he really did not believe what he was saying. He was too intelligent a man not to realise that only a miracle would prevent war now.

A day or two later I flew down to Dhahran, on the Gulf,

202

to attend a reception for the press given by General Sir Peter de la Billière, the British Commander. A hero of the SAS, the most decorated man in the British army, he was especially famous for master-minding the storming of the Iranian Embassy in London in 1980. It was said Mrs Thatcher was so impressed by his handling of a tricky political as well as military operation that she pushed for him to be given command in the Gulf, despite his imminent retirement. General Peter, as his staff called him, had the reputation of being shy to the point of near-invisibility, but perhaps this was only to be expected in a soldier who had spent most of his life in a cloak-and-dagger organisation. It was also said that he did not get on well with the press, and this seemed to be borne out at the beginning of the evening when he gave the assembled hundred or so British media representatives a ten-minute pep talk.

My heart sank as I thought for a moment I was back in the headmaster's study, being told I would have to pull my socks up, put my back into it and really try and do better next time. To use army parlance, I thought it was long on bullshit and short on humour. But I blamed the general less than his advisers, which was disappointing in itself because, although the British army, traditionally, had always been bad at press relations, Northern Ireland seemed to have changed all that. There, for the first time, young officers were allowed to speak to the media directly, without refer-ring first to higher command. The result, seen most dra-matically on our television screens, had been straight talking by the men on the spot, telling the British public what it was like to fight a guerrilla war in the back garden. And now, here we were, apparently back at square one.

Afterwards we trooped into a marquee filled with round tables each seating about ten people, queuing up to be served army style as we filed in. A PR officer whispered in my ear, 'Would you like to go to the table right at the end? General Peter will come and join you in a minute.' Kate

Adie, Martin Bell, myself and half a dozen others dutifully took our places as instructed and in a minute or two the general arrived and joined us. To my surprise, he showed an entirely different side of his character. Where he had been rather pompous and school-masterly before, he was now delightfully natural. In fact, he could not have been nicer, and it was now some of my colleagues who proved to be bores. One radio correspondent did his best to monopolise the general and then Kate Adie, for whom I have the highest regard as a trouble shooter, for some strange reason took it upon herself to answer questions put to him. Someone, for example, wanted to know what, in his opinion, the Arabs would think of this or that move by the West?

Without giving the poor general a chance to open his mouth, and in magisterial tones which would have done credit to Mrs Thatcher, Kate Adie held forth not only at inordinate length but with a conviction that brooked absolutely no gainsaying. Sitting only two seats away from her, the general was the model of tact, showing not the slightest sign of impatience, never for a moment daring to interrupt the lady, and giving his opinion – when he could – with admirable modesty. Then, perhaps feeling his time would be better employed elsewhere, he got up and departed for another table. I was left wondering if Miss Adie, having been isolated for some time in one of the desert media pools, had contracted a nasty case of verbal diarrhoea.

Inexorably, the UN deadline for Iraq's withdrawal from Kuwait came closer, without any sign that Saddam would climb down. We debated it endlessly, will he or won't he, along with the other chestnut: would the allies be able to crush the Iraqis by bombing alone? As my colleague Mike Jermey pointed out, bombing (excepting the atom bomb) had never done the trick before; witness Vietnam. Further, if the allies were then forced to go in on the ground to finish off the Iraqi army, the fourth biggest in the world as we were always being told, would they suffer unacceptably heavy casualties? I thought the answer to the first question was, yes, not because modernisation had advanced so far – no one, apart from the experts, knew just how devastating the new technology would prove to be – but because, even to a layman like myself, the sheer power of the allied air forces, easily the greatest ever assembled, must inevitably crush an army operating in a country as bare of cover as Iraq.

The Security Council ultimatum expired at midnight on Tuesday 15 January New York time, which was 8 a.m. the following morning in Riyadh. I and most of my colleagues spent the rest of the day wondering when the first blow would be struck. Would Saddam make a pre-emptive attack? Would the allies, having already waited so long, decide to delay another day or two to keep the Iraqis guessing in a war of nerves? Or would they decide to launch the air war at the earliest possible moment, namely early the next day? I went to bed at about one o'clock in the morning, these questions still chasing one another in my brain, and all unanswered. Just as I was falling asleep, I was jerked awake by the roar of an aircraft's jet engines passing directly overhead. As I lay there wondering what was happening, another plane followed the first, as if taking its bearings from the hotel, so low that the roar of the engines was deafening. As soon as that faded away, another aircraft followed, and another, six or seven in all. By the sheer volume of noise you could tell they were heavily loaded, but with what; bombs?

As the din of the last one died away, I switched on the bedside light and looked at my watch. It had just gone 1.20 a.m. local time, 10.20 p.m. in London, almost the end of *News at Ten*. I rang the American and British information desks upstairs but got no reply: everyone had gone to bed. It was only later that I discovered the planes I had heard were KC-135 tankers, whose job was to refuel the fighter-bombers before they crossed the Iraqi border. The only

205

surprise was that they were airborne so early, because the first air strikes – again, as we discovered later – were not due to start until one minute past three local time, 0001 GMT, Thursday 17 January. Not being able to raise anybody, and by this time finding it impossible to stay awake, I rolled over and went back to sleep. An hour and a half later the first RAF Tornados, each loaded up with the ultra high-tech JP233 runway-cratering bombs, were streaking low over the desert at 500 miles per hour towards their Iraqi targets. In their survival kits each crewman carried £800 in gold and a chit promising that the British Government would pay a reward of £5000 to anyone who returned a downed airman safely. At the same time, jets and Tomahawk cruise missiles were being launched from American carriers in the Gulf in the first strikes against Baghdad. To anyone there, it must have seemed like the end of the world.

By breakfast time, as General Sir Peter de la Billiere states in his account of the war, *Storm Command*, the allied air forces had flown 352 sorties against 158 targets and only one aircraft was missing. Such was the sense of occasion at the morning briefing in the British headquarters that the Chief of Staff, Air Commodore Ian Macfadyen, quoted to the assembled company the words Shakespeare has Henry V say before Agincourt.

> *We few, we happy few, we band of brothers;*
> *For he today that sheds his blood with me*
> *Shall be my brother; be he ne'er so vile*
> *This day shall gentle his condition;*
> *And gentlemen in England now a-bed*
> *Shall think themselves accurs'd they were not here,*
> *And hold their manhoods cheap whiles any speaks*
> *That fought with us upon St Crispin's day.*

By ten o'clock, according to my notes of the first wartime press briefing, the United States air forces alone had flown 750 sorties; other sorties had been flown by the RAF, the

206

French, the Saudis and the Kuwaitis. The first assessment was 'very encouraging', with 'minimal resistance' reported although, unfortunately for the British, the only serious casualty was the loss of a Tornado over Iraq. The crew, Flight Lieutenants John Peters and Adrian Nichol, ejected safely, but both were captured, beaten and paraded on television. In the days of intense bombardment that followed, Britain lost five more Tornados, making six in all. These were the heaviest losses of any of the Coalition air forces, partly because the Tornados had to fly very low, in pitch darkness, through heavy anti-aircraft fire.

Saddam Hussein's response to the first air strikes was swift, launching his first Scud missile attack against Riyadh on Thursday night. I had just gone to bed when I heard the siren go off; it brought back faint memories of a German air raid on Aberdeen which I witnessed as a small boy in, I think, 1940. Scrambling out of bed, I struggled into my chemical warfare suit and climbed up the stairs – the lifts were out of action – to the roof, where in a blaze of lights, television crews were milling about frantically, trying to get into position to film the incoming Scuds. Some people had donned their gas masks, moving about like zombies and occasionally mumbling incomprehensibly. I wondered if I should put on my mask, but seeing a number of other people had not bothered to do so, decided against it: no Scuds had arrived, as far as we knew, so there could be no gas about. The logic seemed irrefutable and yet, I had to admit to a slight feeling of unease.

A few minutes later, as the first Scuds did begin to arrive like gigantic fireworks, the decision was made for me. I tugged on my mask, holding one hand over the air intake at the bottom and sucking in my breath, as instructed, so that the rubber clung to the contours of my face, at the same time peering through the Perspex visor to see what was going on. Suddenly there was a distant roar, like an express train approaching, and a bright orange light appeared,

207

descending lazily from a great height: everyone was pointing excitedly. So this was what a Scud looked like. I wondered rather nervously what the best thing to do would be if it came straight for the hotel. But as we watched, eyes riveted on the incoming missile, we saw, far below it, first one and then a second shooting star rise from the ground to meet the invader. As they climbed above the desert to the north of Riyadh, there were several distant but still loud bangs: the Patriot anti-missile missiles going up against the Scud. It was almost like a video game, far away in the night sky and unreal enough to make it all seem harmless.

The Patriots were still climbing but the Scud had disappeared behind a bank of cloud. As I peered to locate it, there was another express train roar and another bright star appeared high up. This must be a second missile. Shortly afterwards, the first Scud reappeared and there was a bright flash; then darkness and, eventually, a dull report. The Patriots, locked like bull terriers to the space invader – the roar, of course, was the noise of the Scud's re-entry from space – had taken out the first one. Seconds later there was a loud bang, which I presumed was the missile, or what was left of it, hitting the ground. Now the focus shifted to the second incoming Scud and possibly a third as well: it was hard to tell precisely how many were in the sky at one time. The Patriots were still rising and, again, with a flash and a bang, the interception was made and, for the first time for what seemed half an hour, but could have been only five minutes, the sky was empty.

One of the ITN team came running up to me excitedly. 'A Scud has landed in the middle of town. Could you go and see what's happening?' I had my mask off by this time and there remained only the question of a crew. Hugh Thomson was busy on the roof, so I took a freelance who was helping us out and our Filipino driver and set off. The city was innocent of traffic, except for the odd police car with siren wailing, going in the same direction as ourselves. The

208

Filipino driver, a resourceful fellow, knew roughly where the Scud had fallen.

'Near Sheraton,' he said. 'Other driver tell me.'

We came to an intersection and could see a considerable commotion on our left. 'That's it,' I shouted from the back, but the driver had also seen it and swerved into the side. We ran back to where a knot of Saudi police and troops were making a half-hearted effort to cordon off the street; but the combination of camouflage chemical suit, press pass and journalistic assertiveness got us through.

About a hundred yards down the street, in the dim light of dawn, a great, long tarnished silver tube lay in the middle of the road, smoke and fumes still rising from its corpse, the first Scud to fall on Riyadh. We approached it gingerly, just as a figure in full NBC (nuclear, biological, and chemical) gear with a Geiger counter was completing his checks. I nodded to the cameraman to switch on and went up to him. 'You getting any reading?' I asked. He shook his head and replied tersely in an unmistakably English voice. 'No, it was a conventional warhead, no biological or chemical component.'

'What is it?' I asked, feeling rather foolish but wanting to be sure.

'Scud,' he said shortly. 'Possibly the Hussein. There are two versions with an extended range, the Hussein and the Akhtar. I think this is the longer one.'

We filmed the smoking monster for five minutes, I did my obligatory piece to camera, and then sped back to the hotel. By now it was after six and the city was coming awake. It was still the middle of the night in London but by editing the package right away, we would have it in ITN in good time for our first news broadcast of the day, which went out shortly before TV-am went on the air. We then came back on the air after TV-am signed off at nine o'clock. As soon as we were able to talk to London over the satellite

209

they said they would like to do a live two-way interview with me on the subject of the Scud attack.

There was plenty of time, so I went down to our office on the fifth floor and had a cup of tea and a sandwich. When it was time for the livespot, I went up to the roof again; it was a beautiful day, sunny and clear, but the wind off the desert was cold, so I kept my camouflage NBC top on. Technically, the two-way went perfectly, the interviewer wanting to know how much terror the first Scud attack on Riyadh would cause. My reaction was to play this down, not for any reason of mock heroics but because I genuinely thought, admittedly on the evidence of one night, that the Scud was an overrated weapon. It was extremely inaccurate in the sense that you might be able to hit a city but not any specific target in that city; and there had been no casualties. General Schwarzkopf, whom I interviewed a few days later, was of the same opinion. He said he thought 'an electrical storm in Alabama' posed more risk to life and limb than one of Saddam Hussein's Scud attacks. This was fine until, near the end of the air war, a lucky, or unlucky, hit on an American barracks in Dhahran killed twenty-nine Marines.

Next day, ITN's Editor, Stewart Purvis, a colleague for many years, sent a message via Mike Jermey, our producer, saying, 'Tell Sandy not to wear his camouflage chemical suit on camera in future.'

'Why not?' I asked, riled. 'We don't know if there are chemical weapons in these bloody Scuds, so it's silly not to wear the NBC suit. Also, it's damned cold up on the roof and the suit's very warm.'

Mike shrugged. 'Stewart didn't give a reason, just told me to tell you not to wear it in future.' Placatingly, he added, 'He may think you looked a bit over the top, dressing up for the part.'

I went off fuming that 'those bloody people in London' never understood the problems of the correspondent in the field, and did not wear the offending outfit for a day or so,

210

being interviewed live by the husband and wife team who presented Granada's *This Morning* show in an open-necked shirt. But as soon as the Scuds started coming over again, I donned the forbidden suit. I was damned if I was going to risk being gassed or biologically contaminated just because someone in London, even if it was the Editor, thought I was being too gung-ho.

In this first, hectic 'Scud season', hardly a day went past without the wail of the siren disrupting our lives; in fact, it became so frequent that we began to think of it as more of a nuisance than anything else. On one occasion, I had just sat down to coffee and shortbread with Sir Alan Munro when the alarm went off. Getting up briskly, Sir Alan said, 'Come with me. We have to go to the secure room.'

Before I could follow, one of his security men rushed in and snapped, 'Where's your gas mask?'

'Oh dear,' I said helplessly. 'I'm afraid I forgot to bring it.'

'You must carry your gas mask with you at all times,' the security man said severely, sounding as if he would have liked to have had me confined to barracks for the weekend, and disppointed he could not do so.

'Come along,' the Ambassador said kindly, and feeling like a naughty boy, I followed him and his secretary through the steel door into the chancery. As we stepped into the holy of holies, Sir Alan turned and said, 'You're not supposed to be in here, so avert your gaze and pretend you haven't seen anything.'

I tried as best I could, although not being a communications expert, none of the large machines which filled the room meant very much to me. Secrecy was saved, however, by the almost immediate sounding of the all-clear and we trooped back to Sir Alan's office where the coffee was still hot in its silver pot.

Usually, however, Saddam Hussein timed his Scud attacks for the hours of darkness, preferably when everyone had gone to bed. Invariably, it seemed, you were just dropping off into that first, delicious sleep when the howl of the siren jerked you awake. Cursing the Iraqis in general and Saddam in particular, I would get up, close the window in case of a gas attack, and struggle into my NBC suit; the trousers were especially difficult to get on and the boots almost impossible. Then, clutching my gas mask, I would walk up the stairs to the roof. As often as not the all-clear would sound ten minutes later and, grumbling at another broken night, we would all go back to bed. The cause of the false alarm lay not in whether there really had been a Scud launch – there invariably had – but in the tracking. The sirens went off in Riyadh even if the eventual destination turned out to be Dhahran, or an empty bit of desert. Because the radar trackers could not pinpoint the real target quickly enough, and since a Scud took only a few minutes to complete its 600-kilometre flight, they clearly thought it was better to be safe than sorry.

Irritated by these false alarms, especially at night, I developed a new drill, refusing to get out of bed until I heard the first real bang, whether it was the launch of a Patriot, an interception, or a Scud landing. As often as not, the all-clear would be sounded first, in which case I would turn over smugly and go back to sleep. If it was the real thing, I could still get to the roof in time for the action. Shortly after the start of the air war, one of the rare Scuds that did penetrate the Patriot shield hit a block of offices in the middle of Riyadh. Luckily, being the middle of the night, there was no one there except the caretaker who, poor man, was buried under tons of debris. Although the Patriots had something like a ninety per cent success rate, their relatively few failures seemed to involve the precise point of contact; they would sucessfully intercept the body of the missile but fail to knock out the warhead, which could still do a lot of damage when it hit the ground.

Very often the Scuds, being intercepted some way from the target, would fall harmlessly in the desert outside the

212

capital. One night we scoured the outskirts for an hour or more before finally finding the stricken monster lying virtually intact on the edge of the desert a few hundred yards from one of the main freeways. This time, the Saudi army was there well ahead of us and, rather over-excitedly, had cordoned off the entire area. But when the American Geiger counter team reported another conventionally-armed Scud, the initial panic subsided and we were able to get close enough to film the smoking hulk.

One night, tired of the hotel food, we decided to try a Thai restaurant about half a mile from the Hyatt. It was a pleasant, fifteen-minute walk along one of the wide boulevards, the dry desert air crisp and cold, and we had an enjoyable if not particularly Thai dinner. The walk home turned out to be unexpectedly exciting. A few hundred yards after we had left the restaurant, the stomach-curdling howl of the air raid siren burst on the otherwise peaceful night. Almost immediately the sky beyond the airport burst into a dazzling series of bangs and flashes. Since this was happening behind us, we tried to watch the firework display while walking backwards. Two or three Patriots rose into the darkness with their usual, deceptively lazy trajectory to intersect the orangey, meteor-like parabola of the falling Scuds, their re-entry into the earth's atmosphere heralded by the now customary express train roar. We were torn between the fascination of the battle in the sky behind us, as Patriot climbed to take on Scud, and the need to reach the hotel and make contact with London. Running and walking backwards, we managed to monitor the progress of the battle and reach the hotel within a few minutes. Up on the roof, every television camera was deployed, busy recording one of the most spectacular confrontations of the war. All the Scuds were shot down without, as far as I know, any casualties.

Despite an occasional miss, so disastrous in the case of the Marine barracks in Dhahran, we all thanked God for the

213

Patriot. Originally developed as an anti-aircraft missile, it was modified only just before the Gulf War for anti-missile use. In fact, the margin was so tight that Israel did not have any Patriots at the outbreak of war and they had to be flown to Tel Aviv after the first Scud attack. Luckily, the Patriot performed so brilliantly there that its success, probably more than anything else, kept the Israelis out of the war. The possibility they might attack Iraq terrified the Coalition leaders, especially the Americans. If Israel had been dragged into the fray, as Saddam clearly hoped, the more extreme members of the Coalition, such as Syria, would have walked out; the pressure on the rest of the Arabs, including the Saudis, to follow suit would have been enormous, and the Coalition would almost certainly have collapsed. Although every Patriot launched cost about £800,000, they were worth their weight in gold. Without Patriot, it is hard to see how the Coalition could have survived and Saddam Hussein been defeated.

Chapter
14

Two or three days after arriving in Riyadh, an American colonel walked into the ITN office on the fifth floor of the Hyatt Regency and asked, 'Is Mr Sandy Gall here?'

'Yes,' I said, not expecting not very much from the enquiry.

'Mr Gall,' the colonel said, looking very serious, 'how would you like to interview General Schwarzkopf?'

Rather taken aback, I got to my feet and stammered, 'Interview General Schwarzkopf? Oh, I'd like to very much indeed!'

'It'll be in the next couple of days,' the colonel added confidentially. 'We'll let you know. Oh, and by the way, it's not a one-to-one. The BBC will be there, and three or four American newspaper and magazine people as well.'

Big deal, I thought as the affable colonel made his way out of the room. A British exclusive with 'Stormin' Norman' would have been something to get excited about. But to be one of six, who included our main rivals, the BBC, was much less exciting: still, it was better than nothing.

Two days later we were told to be ready to board the bus outside the hotel at 1.30. The lucky group included Ben Brown of the BBC and myself, plus crews, an intense-looking, bespectacled ethnic Chinese or Japanese lady from *Newsweek*, a rather dour man from the *Los Angeles Times*,

215

representatives from a couple of other big American provincial papers and a local reporter from the English-language *Saudi Times* of Riyadh. General Schwarzkopf had his headquarters in the Saudi Defence Ministry only two hundred yards from the hotel, but the bus had to make a detour because of the dual carriageway system and it took us all of five minutes to drive there. We took another five minutes to negotiate security on the gate, having to get out of the bus and pass through the checks individually. We then drove across the courtyard to a side entrance. Like all Saudi public buildings, the Defence Ministry was ultra-modern and palatial. We took the lift to the second floor and were ushered into what I imagine was the briefing room.

As we waited, perhaps ten minutes, for our interviewee to arrive, I read the sheet of paper we had all been handed with details of the Coalition Commander-in-Chief's career. Born in 1935, Norman Schwarzkopf came from a typical middle American family of, as his name implied, German stock. But despite a conventional small town background, the young Schwarzkopf enjoyed a much more cosmopolitan upbringing than might have been expected. During school holidays, he and his two elder sisters would fly out to join their father, a dashing figure who spent most of his Second World War service as a military attaché in the Middle East. These trips gave the teenage Norman his first taste of the Arab world, which was to stand him in such good stead later.

With his physique and energy, he was bound to do well at West Point, graduating in the top echelon; from there he joined the Airborne, serving two tours in Vietnam, where he was awarded two Silver Stars, three Bronze Stars, and the Purple Heart. Back in Washington, he worked his way through a series of staff jobs, and although at one point his career seemed to be stalled, in 1988 came the most fateful step of his career. He was promoted to four star general and appointed to Central Command, which took in a vast area

216

stretching from the Afghan border in the north-east to the shores of the Mediterranean; the heart of the command, of course, was the Gulf. No one could have foreseen just how fortunate it was that a man of Schwarzkopf's calibre and background would find himself in charge when the Kuwait crisis eventually erupted.

He was clearly a soldier's general, someone who led from the front, a big man in every sense, built like a football quarter-back. But, man of action as he undoubtedly was, and given when provoked to 'bawling out' his subordinates, he could also display unexpected political sensitivity; he seemed to get on well with the Arabs in general and the Saudis in particular, something he had no doubt learned during those distant school holidays with his father in the Lebanon. I was prepared, then, for a large physical presence, but the man who strode into the room with a broad smile on his face was little short of a giant, six foot four and fifteen stone, with a personality to match. Not for nothing was he called Stormin' Norman. During the interview, which of course ranged over many more serious matters, I asked General Schwarzkopf what his favourite nickname was: Stormin' Norman . . .? 'Bear,' he said without hesitation. 'That's what my men always called me.'

He gave the six of us nearly two hours, a considerable amount of time for such a busy man, and impressed all of us by his articulacy and his manifest desire to try and answer the questions as fully and honestly as possible. He made one proviso: 'I'm not going to get into anything that's of potential help to the enemy. You wouldn't expect me to, anyway. But anything else, I will try and tell you exactly what I think about it, and why.' Two things emerged most clearly. First, he did not make the mistake of underestimating the enemy. On the other hand, when someone asked him about Saddam's 'elite Republican Guard', he snorted, 'Elite? They may be the best he's got but I wouldn't call them elite by our standards. But, sure, he's got a helluva big army, over a million men, that's big by any standards. And he's got a helluva lotta hardware.' Secondly, what came through even more strongly than his determination to see off Saddam Hussein, one way or the other, was his concern about the welfare of the men under his command. Several times he said, 'I want to keep casualties to the absolute minimum, that's not just American casualties, but the whole Coalition. Whatever decisions I have to make, that is always in the forefront of my mind. I don't want a single soldier to lose his life, on either side. But if we do get into a shooting war, then it's my duty to make sure our casualties are as low as humanly possible.'

Two or three days later General Schwarzkopf gave the evening briefing at the Hyatt, his first since the start of the air war. The scene was worthy of Hollywood. He drove at jogging pace the two or three hundred yards from his headquarters to the hotel in a bullet-proof limousine, several Rambo-style bodyguards in jeans and trainers running beside him, their long hair tied back with bandanas, M-16s at the ready. Springing out of the car, the General marched into the hotel, surrounded by his bodyguards, and along the lobby to the briefing room, where he took up his stance behind the podium, an impressive figure in desert camouflage with four stars on his collar. He had brought a video with him and after a positive but by no means over-confident analysis of the success of the aerial bombardment so far, demonstrated with the video just how devastatingly accurate American laser-guided bombing was. To anyone who had seen the effects of conventional bombing in Vietnam and Afghanistan, where both the United States and the Soviet Union had used their most up-to-date aircraft, it was simply unbelievable. As the general pointed out, you did not simply hit a designated building, you chose a specific window or door and put the bomb through that one. Fittingly, it was known as a 'smart' bomb. The British did not have this capability at first, since our role was to provide

218

low-flying Tornados with their runway-busting JP233s, but later, when Tornado losses started to rise disproportionately, and the Americans were unable to honour their promises to provide us with laser-designating aircraft, we had to fly out some of our ageing but still extremely effective Buccaneers.

Schwarzkopf got his biggest laugh when he ran a section of the video showing a laser-guided attack on a bridge somewhere in Iraq. As the video started, a civilian car appeared on the bridge and started to cross it at speed. At the same time the jet was diving on the bridge at 600 m.p.h. and it became a race between pilot and driver. We saw the bomb hurtling towards the bridge, hitting it right in the middle; as the smoke and dust cleared, the car came into sight, shot like a rabbit over the last span and disappeared from view. 'That,' said General Schwarzkopf to laughter, 'must be the luckiest man in the whole of Iraq today!'

After a few weeks in Riyadh, with the Scud story subsiding and the daily briefings on the air war inevitably beginning to become repetitive, I began to get itchy feet. Peter Allen, the other ITN reporter in Riyadh, was more than able to cover the briefings and anything else that might come up, so there was really not enough for the two of us to do. Prince Abdullah had several times invited me to visit the great industrial complex at Jubail, which he ran, so I decided a change of scene would be good for everybody. Mike Jermey agreed and, accompanied by Steve Harrow, with whom I was going to work for the rest of the war, I set off across the desert to Dhahran, another sprawling city on the American pattern, lying between the desert and the sea. The capital of Saudi Arabia's oil industry, equipped with an international airport and a port in the satellite town of Dammam, Dhahran was one of the Coalition's two great staging areas through which men and *matériel* flowed; the other was Jubail. It also boasted the International Hotel, the main media centre for the war where nearly a thousand

219

broadcasters, television crews, journalists and photographers worked and ate day after day for weeks on end, some of them hardly ever leaving the building. Nearly broke when the crisis started, the International was booming and must have ended the war with enormous profits. It was virtually impossible to stay there: most of the rooms had been converted into offices and all the main television companies had suites according to their pretentions, negotiating skills and budgets. The Americans, of course, had the biggest. ITN's was rather cramped.

Like every hotel in Saudi Arabia, the International was completely Americanised, with the overworked coffee shop on the ground floor providing American-style food cooked by chefs of varying nationalities – but not American nor Saudi – at all times of the day and night. Nearly the whole of the first floor was taken up by the main press centres, the Saudis' being the biggest, closely followed by the Americans, with the Kuwaitis and the British relegated to the fringes. The ITN office was next to the British press centre, which displayed a sign forbidding entrance and instructing the caller to ring the bell. Only if they knew you and approved of you, would they let you in. The BBC satellite ground station, which the other British television companies – ITN, Sky and TV-am – used on a pool basis, was sited in the garden just outside the BBC office on the ground floor and our video editors had to run down the stairs and along the corridor to 'feed' when the deadline for transmission to London was close.

Fredo Guedes, an enterprising Portuguese editor whom I had met for the first time in Mozambique in the 1970s, and who was acting as a kind of office manager, booked me in to his hotel in Dammam, twenty minutes in a taxi from the International. It was part of an Indian-owned chain, with a fountain in the vast lobby, gloomy rooms decorated in fusty colours, and to my annoyance, hermetically sealed bedroom windows. The grill room, which opened off the lobby, was pretentious, expensive and bad, and the inevitable coffee shop was downstairs, out of sight. But with hardly a room to be had in the whole place, I was grateful. Steve Harrow preferred to stay at the Palm, which was far less agreeable than it sounds; but at least it was relatively central and most of the ITN editors and crews stayed there.

Next day, we left for Jubail, driving north up the Gulf, through perhaps the richest oil-producing area in the world. The only visible sign that the sands over which we were travelling concealed huge reservoirs of crude oil was a long, low parapet of fire, like a flaming pillar laid on its side, which was the gas flame-off from one of the oil fields. It burned night and day all the time I was in the Gulf; I must have driven past it thirty or forty times in the next month or so. Further north we passed another landmark, the great cooling towers of the desalination plant at Ras Tanura, with its aircaft warning beacons flashing on and off with the mesmeric rhythm of the lights in some monstrous disco. Otherwise, the desert stretched away featurelessly to the north and west, empty apart from the occasional herd of grazing camels.

Jubail itself is a model industrial complex, comprising eight or nine major enterprises, including a petro-chemical plant and a steel mill cooled by sea water brought in by canal; turbines at the entrance provide Jubail's own power needs, which are equivalent to those of a large Western town. Add to that a handsome headquarters and first-class housing and amenities and I could see why the Saudis, including King Fahd who was then the chairman (succeeded shortly afterwards by Prince Abdullah), were justifiably proud of it. We booked in at the Holiday Inn near the beach, and rang the prince's office. 'Come and have breakfast with the prince tomorrow morning,' I was told, 'he is very concerned about the oil spill.' A few days before, on 23 January, the Iraqis had deliberately pumped a huge quantity of crude oil into the sea at Al Ahmadi, in Kuwait. Helped by wind and current, the spill, believed to be the biggest ever known, was now floating south threatening the entire ecosystem of the Gulf. This is fragile at the best of times, since the area is virtually an inland sea, and scientists were alarmed at the effect the oil would have on the wildlife: the rare Hawksbill Turtle; the even rarer dugong, or sea-cow; the huge flocks of cormorants, including the Socotran Cormorant which is indigenous to the Gulf and the Red Sea; and the thousands of other seabirds which either breed in the Gulf or migrate through it.

Peter Sharp and Chris Squires of ITN were the first to record the terrible impact of the spill and to broadcast the first, heartbreaking pictures of cormorants drenched in oil on the beach at Khafji, on the border between Kuwait and Saudi Arabia. The pictures went round the world, prompting an immediate outcry, but because Sharp and Squires were in the border zone without permission, the Saudi military authorities arrested them and took away their passes, effectively restricting them to Dhahran. Yet, the oil was advancing daily down the coast, ruining the local fishing industry – the Gulf is famous for its shrimps and prawns – and threatening to shut down the huge desalination plants farther south which provide, for example, all Riyadh's drinking water.

I immediately got the prince to make out a *laissez-passer* for Steve and myself and we set off next day to search the coast north of Jubail and film the worsening plight of the seabirds. By a stroke of luck, we met a husky young English marine biologist, working for the Saudi Government, who looked rather like Ian Botham. He was an expert on the Hawksbill Turtle and we scoured the beaches together, picking up dozens of birds, mainly Black-necked Grebes and Socotran Cormorants, but on that first day there was no sign of any turtles. Because of the huge number of birds affected, Prince Abdullah had started a wildlife rescue centre in Jubail and birds and volunteers started to pour in. There were some infinitely pathetic sights: we came across one Black-necked Grebe close inshore which was so smothered in oil that it was barely visible. We managed to scoop it out with a long pole, but it fell off the pole back into the thick oil and although we eventually succeeded in getting it out, it died soon afterwards. Only its bright red eye still blazed defiantly, as it fought desperately for its life. Many birds were already dead, trapped in the oil, as thick as treacle, which lapped the coast or washed up on the beaches. Others, still alive although badly oiled, had to be chased down among the dunes and captured. This was not as easy as it sounds, as cormorants have vicious beaks.

On one or two occasions, Steve and I fell foul of Saudi checkpoints, usually manned by ordinary soldiers or police who either could not read the prince's elegantly penned *laissez-passer*, or were simply falling back on their natural inclination of, when in doubt, saying no. Fired by the conviction that Saddam Hussein's barbarism in deliberately destroying the environment must be exposed to the gaze of an outraged world, Steve and I drove ourselves hard, travelling up and down the coast day after day, arguing and pleading at the checkpoints, mostly Saudi, but some American, to get through to the beaches. One day, hunting for a lagoon which a British employee of Aramco had told me was choked with dead birds, we were spotted and intercepted by an American unit. They came racing after us over the dunes, but when the officer in charge, a reservist, had satisfied himself we were not Iraqi invaders, he became extremely affable; unfortunately, it was the wrong lagoon.

The rescue centre was now handling hundreds of birds, and dozens of volunteers including off-duty British soldiers spent hours cleaning the victims. It was a slow, painstaking business, sometimes painful if a cormorant wriggled its head free and pecked the unfortunate hand that was trying to clean it. When the birds arrived, many with only hours to live, they were placed in a sink and the worst of the oil washed off with detergent; this could take one or two hours, depending on how badly oiled the bird was, the victim being repeatedly soaped and hosed down. When clean, they were transferred to darkened pens to rest and be fed. After a few days, if they made good progress, they were moved outside to the swimming pool, covered with a camouflage net so that they could not escape, but where they could dive and swim while awaiting release. Right at the beginning we had brought in a very badly oiled Black-necked Grebe and a week later, when Steve and I were paying another of our frequent visits, the attractive French lady in charge smiled sweetly and asked, 'Do you want to see Sandy Goll?'

'I'm sorry, what did you say?' I stammered in surprise.

'The bird,' she said. 'You remember, the grebe you brought in on the very first day? We called it Sandy Goll, after you. Look, he's getting on very nicely.'

She drew back a curtain and there he was, almost as good as new, the black fathers sleek and the bright red eye clear and unwinking. 'We'll be releasing him in a few days' time,' she said. We all smiled. It was, at least, one happy ending. Another offered itself almost immediately. Our friend, the marine biologist, said he would be releasing a turtle farther up the coast, and we could go with him. Excited, we met at a pre-arranged rendezvous the next day and followed him north, driving fast up the Gulf road for twenty miles before turning off down a track that led to a secluded beach. The sea was pale blue under the slight haze, and clean; the oil spill had not yet reached the area. He and an assistant lifted the turtle, a large male with a handsome greenish shell, out of his box and carried him down to the water's edge. Steve ran backwards and forwards getting every possible shot and then held up his hand imperiously.

'Hold on. Before you release it, I want to get into the water so that I can get a shot as it swims towards me.' Steve took off his shoes and socks, hitched up his trousers and waded into the chilly water. The turtle was carried down to

224

the sea and placed gently in the shallows. He lay there for a moment, as if savouring his natural habitat and then, with a tentative stroke of his flippers, glided forward, gathering speed and submerging as he passed Steve, who turned and followed him with the camera out to sea, until the green shell was only a faint bubble of light, gradually disappearing in the milky waters of the Gulf. We all gave a little cheer as Steve turned and waded back towards the shore. It was another small victory, of hope over despair, life over death. We left with our film for Dhahran that afternoon and sent the story to London that evening: the final shot was the Hawksbill Turtle swimming bravely out into the Gulf. It made a fitting ending, and I was pleased to have struck a blow, however small, against the nihilism of the Iraqi regime.

When we had arrived at the ITN office in the International, I found the senior producer, Sue Tinson, in a considerable state.

'I need your help,' she said. 'Peter and Chris have had their passes confiscated, and so have the other crew. Without them, they can't go anywhere. They're virtually stuck in the hotel. It means we're down to one crew, and if anything happens, we'll be up the creek . . . I'd be very grateful if you could do something, Sandy.'

'What about the Embassy, in Riyadh?'

'We're trying that, but it's here we need to be putting the pressure on. I'm just too busy to run around talking to Saudi officials, and frankly, I don't know who to talk to. I haven't been able to get out and make contacts, I've been stuck in the office all day, every day.'

I saw the problem, but did not have the answer, any more than Sue did. The Saudis were being extremely strict, and we thought unfair. CNN, Ted Turner's 24-hour-a-day news channel, was watched by every senior offical in Saudi Arabia from the king downwards, and apparently could get away with murder: no matter that most of their best reports were taken, by mutual agreement, from ITN. If, on the other hand, ITN or the BBC overstepped the mark, we were immediately reprimanded and had our passes removed. The system seemed so iniquitously unfair that the thought did cross my mind that perhaps money was changing hands. Luckily, that night, arriving late at my hotel I ran into an old friend and Arabist extraordinaire, St John Armitage. Lean and bespectacled, still with a military meticulousness about him, St John told me he had been trying to find me and had left messages in various places. He was full of what he had just been doing. The Saudi Commander-in-Chief, Prince Khalid, had invited him to his war room at headquarters at the very moment when, by chance, the Iraqis crossed the border and occupied the deserted Saudi border town of Khafji. St John, the old soldier, had revelled in the grand-stand view he had of the unfolding battle. Later, he had gone to the ITN ofice in the International to try to find me and had been able to brief ITN which had just heard about the attack.

'They were under the impression that a bloody great battle was taking place and I was able, luckily, to put them straight on that,' St John said with some satisfaction. Neither of us had eaten so we moved to the coffee shop where, St John having ordered soup and I spaghetti, I was able to explain the difficulties we were having with the Saudis over passes.

'Are you free tomorrow morning?' he asked.

'Yes, of course.'

'Do you happen to know Prince Fahd bin Salman?'

'No.'

'Well, he's Vice-Governor of the Eastern Province, a very charming man and very helpful. Unfortunately I have to go back to London tomorrow afternoon – my wife doesn't know I'm here, incidentally, so I have to get back – but I'll take you there tomorrow morning, introduce you to his press man, who's also charming, the son of a general by the

226

way, and if we haven't seen the prince by the time I have to leave for the airport, he'll look after you. I'll ring him now.'

Although it was after eleven, St John got up and went to find a telephone. He was back in five minutes, rubbing his hands gleefully. 'Good news. The prince is here and we can see him tomorrow. His secretary suggests we come about ten, although we'll probably have to wait an hour or so.' St John now gave me a little lecture on Saudi customs.

'When you first meet a Saudi he will probably ignore you altogether. The second time you meet him, he may nod at you, but won't necessarily say anything. The third time, he may shake your hand. The fourth time he may do both and the fifth time he will throw his arms round you and treat you like a long-lost friend. What people from the West don't realise is that they are not being discourteous, it's just the way their system works.

'Some people are offended if they go to a Saudi's office and have to wait half an hour, or even an hour and a half to see whoever it is. They think they're being deliberately snubbed. It's got nothing to do with that. People often don't realise that that's the way the Arab system works. They do it themselves. They will go to another man's office, or house, and wait quite happily. The great thing about their system is that even the humblest person can see the highest, such as the prince or even the king. If you go to the prince's *majlis* [audience] you'll see him receiving a whole line of petitioners, rather like an MP's surgery at home. They bring requests, ask him to intercede on this or that, it is in fact their form of government. And it works very well.'

Next morning, the prince's secretary sent a car for St John and we drove in style to the Governate. The building, an imposing mansion with a flight of marble steps leading up to the entrance, was set in extensive gardens and heavily guarded: jeeps with machine-guns mounted in the back were positioned at each corner. The secretary was waiting for us, a polite man of about forty with excellent English, which he had learned at a British university. He and St John were old friends and immediately launched into a long, animated talk. At one point, a man came in and sat in one of the semi-circle of chairs in front of the secretary's desk. After they had shaken hands, St John asked the newcomer, 'Was, by any chance, your father in the army just after the war, in 1946, or 1947?'

The man confirmed he had been.

'I thought he was. I remember him very well. You look just like him.' Astonished, the man looked from St John to the secretary and back again. Then all three burst out laughing. After an hour or so, St John said it was time he was thinking of leaving for the airport, asked the secretary to make his apologies to the prince, and wished me luck. After he had gone, and in an effort to be polite, I remarked to the secretary how amazed I was that St John had recognised his recent visitor through having known the father.

'Oh, yes, St John knows more people in Saudi Arabia than most Saudis. He remembers not only their faces, but their names and family connections. He has been coming here for a very long time and everyone respects him. You see, we consider him as a friend, as one of the family, really.'

At the end of another hour or so, the phone rang and the secretary said, 'His Highness is ready to receive you.' He got up and led me down the stairs and along the corridor to a big waiting room where perhaps twenty people were sitting. We marched through, the secretary opened the double doors at the far side and beckoned me in. It was a huge office, with vast picture windows overlooking the garden. On the far side of the room, about twenty paces away, a man in white robes and black headdress with a golden *aghal* (headcord) was sitting at an enormous desk. As I entered the room he sprang up, made his way round it and advanced towards me, hand outstretched and smiling

228

broadly. He was in his early forties, tall and good-looking, and his first words came as a pleasant surprise.

'Mr Sandy Gall, welcome to Saudi Arabia. It gives me great pleasure to see you in my office. I have often seen you on television in England.'

He indicated a seat and sat down opposite me, ten feet away across the vast desk. 'You know, I feel I already know you well. That's what comes of having seen you so often on television. In fact not so long ago, I saw you in a restaurant in London.'

'Really, which restaurant was that?'

'I can't remember. In fact, I nearly came over to speak to you.'

'Oh, what a pity, why didn't you?'

The prince laughed. 'You were with a lot of other people. I didn't like to interrupt.' His English was perfect, like his manners. 'What can I do for you, Mr Gall? I understand you have some problems.'

'Well, Your Highness,' I began, mentally taking a deep breath, 'some of my ITN colleagues are in the embarrassing position of having lost their Saudi press passes. As you know, without a pass you cannot operate as a journalist and it is seriously affecting our coverage of the war. We feel it is all an unfortunate misunderstanding and my friend, Mr St John Armitage, who has had to catch a plane back to London . . .'

The prince waved a hand. 'Mr Gall, any friend of Mr Armitage's is a friend of ours.'

'That's very kind, Your Highness. Well, Mr Armitage suggested I come and see you.'

'I'm sure we can arrange this without too much difficulty,' the prince said. 'Please give me the names.'

Having written them down, he picked up the telephone and asked his secretary to get him the Ministers of the Interior and Information in Riyadh. In a matter of seconds he had the Minister of the Interior on the line and after a brief conversation in Arabic, he put down the phone and smiled across the desk at me. 'The Minister says the matter will be resolved very quickly.' The Minister of Information, whom I knew to be a retired general, proved to be more elusive. 'Unfortunately he's out of his office, but I have asked my secretary to send him a fax which he will get as soon as he returns. In any case, you can assure your colleagues, Mr Gall, that all should now be in order. If you have any more difficulties, please do not hesitate to get in touch with me.'

I thanked him effusively and left feeling elated. It had been a good morning's work, and the Vice-Governor was undoubtedly as influential as he was charming. The passes were returned that evening, and ITN was back in business again. I saw the prince several times in the next week or so, and one night he showed me round his official residence, a handsome mansion with black leather armchairs, a swimming pool, a gym and some good English nineteenth-century watercolours of Arabian scenes on the walls. He seemed to be alone in the house, apart from servants, having evacuated his wife and children to Jeddah on the Red Sea coast, out of range of the Scuds. Over a glass of something soft, he told me a little about himself. His brother was a popular hero, a fighter pilot in the air force and Saudi Arabia's first man in space as part of the crew on an American Space Shuttle mission. The prince himself, an Anglophile with a house in London, was more interested in racing, and had forty horses in training in Wiltshire.

'Do you know Paul Cole?' he asked. Not being a racing man I didn't. 'Well, he trains for me. We are in partnership together. I helped him to set up his stables at Manton.'

I asked the prince if he rode himself. 'Yes, I love to ride, although riding race horses is a bit different. One time, at Manton, I had just arrived from Saudi Arabia, or America. Paul asked me if I wanted to ride out on a morning gallop and I said yes, on the spur of the moment. I didn't have any

230

proper clothes, just a pair of ordinary slacks and a jacket and it started to rain and I got soaked to the skin. It was so cold, I thought I was going to die.' He gave a very British laugh. 'I nearly pulled up, it was so miserable, and then I thought, damn it, I'm not going to give up, whatever happens. I thought I would fall off but somehow I didn't. When we had finished, I was so cold and my legs were so sore, you know, because I didn't have proper breeches on, I couldn't get down off the horse. They had to lift me down, I was so stiff!'

I soon realised the prince's family connections placed him very close to the centre of power in Saudi Arabia. His father, Prince Salman, was the powerful Governor of Riyadh and a full brother of King Fahd, one of the Sudairi Seven, so-called because they are all sons of King Saud's favourite wife, a member of the Sudairi clan. The seven brothers virtually rule the kingdom between them, and apart from the king and Prince Salman included Prince Sultan, the Minister of Defence, whose son, Prince Khalid, was the Saudi Commander-in-Chief. The Saudi Royal Family is huge, consisting of at least 4000 princes of the royal blood, but the Sudairi Seven are the inner core, hugely wealthy and enormously privileged. Even before the upheaval caused by the Gulf crisis, King Fahd took the view that privilege carries its responsibilities and had become increasingly sensitive to minor princelings flaunting their wealth abroad, especially in the West where their antics would be fully reported in the tabloids. The war had undoubtedly intensified this sensitivity and it was quite clear that even as privileged a figure as Prince Fahd was anxious not be seen, in any sense, as a playboy.

One day, returning to the hotel fairly late, I bought all the British papers I could find in the book shop, one being the *Daily Mail*. Out of habit, I skimmed through it page by page, including the sports section. On the inside back page my eye was caught by a headline which said, 'Generous for the

231

Derby? Saudi prince says he may enter Irish Derby winner for Epsom'. I read on, and in the body of the story it said that the well-known owner, Prince Fahd bin Salman, whose excellent colt had recently triumphed in the Irish Derby, was planning to enter him for the Derby at Epsom where he would almost certainly be favourite. The prince was quoted as saying he and the trainer were very pleased with him. I picked up the phone and rang the prince's secretary. Although it was about ten o'clock in the evening, he answered immediately. I told him about the story in the *Mail*, adding that I thought the prince might be interested. The alacrity with which the secretary responded seemed to confirm this. He would talk to His Highness and call me back.

He did so, almost instantly. Yes, His Highness was extremely interested and wondered if he might borrow the paper? I said he could have it, with my compliments. 'I'll send a driver immediately,' the secretary said. The next time I saw the prince, I realised just how careful he felt he had to be. 'If you do anything about me on *News at Ten*,' he said, 'please don't say anything about my racing interests. Normally, it would not matter. But now, with the war, it could give people the wrong impression.' He was also at pains to play down his wealth. When I remarked quite innocently that racing was, of course, an extremely expensive sport, he said, 'Yes, but you know I am not particularly rich by Saudi standards. There are many people in Saudi Arabia who are much richer than me.'

But even the authority of someone as influential as Prince Fahd appeared to have clearly-defined limits. Having admired the ease with which he handled the matter of the passes, I appealed to him for help in getting accreditation to the Saudi Army, which I was confident would be in the forefront of the battle once the ground war started. To my surprise and disappointment, he turned me down. 'I'm very sorry, Mr Gall, I cannot help you in that direction. You must

232

apply through the usual channels.' I asked him again a few days later, when the start of the ground war was imminent, this time trying to wangle an introduction to Prince Khalid, the Saudi Commander-in-Chief, his first cousin. The prince was polite but equally unhelpful, referring me to the Saudi colonel who was in charge of the army information office in the International. I was tempted to tell him that the said colonel had proved extremely unhelpful to us in the past and had been directly responsible for confiscating ITN's press passes after the Khafji incident, but I restrained myself. Perhaps he did not get on well with his cousin.

I do not know whether he regretted being unable to help me, but when I went to say goodbye and tell him I was heading north, towards Kuwait, he gave me a present: a pair of gold and ruby cufflinks from Asprey's in London. The prince did not hand them over himself. His secretary pushed the little box into my hands as he showed me out, murmuring, 'A small gift from His Highness to show his appreciation.' I protested that it was unnecessary, but saw no way of refusing – I did not know what it was at that juncture – without giving offence. I hardly ever wear them but they are very beautiful.

Chapter
15

ITN's television teams with the British army had been in the desert for so long that they almost qualified for the long service medal. We had one reporter and cameraman with the Fourth Armoured Division – they lost the coveted accreditation to the Seventh Armoured, the Desert Rats, to the BBC on a toss of a coin – and another with the FTU, the Forward Transmission Unit, so-called because of its satellite ground station which would, in theory, transmit all pool television material back to London when the shooting started. Like most things in war, the FTU did not work quite as well as had been predicted. Instead of the ITN and BBC crews being able to send back running reports as the land battle developed, the system proved virtually useless.

These pool crews and correspondents shared the troops' hardships and frustrations during the long build-up which began in the late summer of 1990 and was not translated into action until the start of the ground war at the end of February 1991. During all this time they, like the troops, slept in tents in the bitter cold of the desert winter, had cold showers and used open latrines. Even Kate Adie, one of the few women correspondents in a pool, had to rough it with the men. She drew the line, I was told, only when she heard that a man from the *Sun* was to take the place of the *Financial Times* correspondent, who was being recalled to London.

234

Apprehensive lest her most intimate personal details, down to the colour of her underwear, would be splashed all over page one, if not page three, she protested to the army and they bent the rules to keep the BBC prima donna happy. But the hardships of life in the desert were real. One of our cameramen, Paul Carleton, with whom I had travelled in the Hindu Kush in Afghanistan for a month in 1984, told me that despite going to bed in his sleeping bag fully clothed he was still so cold he could not sleep.

The rest of us who were not in one of the pools had it much easier, living in comfort in a hotel and trying to cover the news in the normal way. Not that this was always easy in Saudi Arabia where you are not allowed to film even what are known in the trade as 'street scenes' without first obtaining permission from the Ministry of Information and being accompanied by one of its minions. So ingrained was Saudi distrust of cameras and journalists, born of long years of isolation during which virtually no journalists were allowed into the country, that it was impossible to dispel it overnight. But since they were effectively forced by the Americans and the British to allow in several hundred western journalists, something that had never happened before, the Saudis were obliged to watch their system being overwhelmed. Whether they liked it or not, western journalists were going to break the rules. The only question was: would the Saudis turn a blind eye or would they try and enforce the old, outdated restrictive practices? The answer, unfortunately, and certainly in the case of the army press office, was the latter. But first they had to catch the culprits; and many of them were far too crafty to let that happen.

Among those skilled and experienced enough to outflank the censors and make their way on their own virtually all over the desert, something that was strictly against the rules, were journalists like Robert Fisk of the *Independent* and the remarkable Colonel David H. Hackworth, Defence Correspondent of *Newsweek*, who distinguished himself as a young battalion commander in Korea and ended up as the most decorated man in the American army. I could understand how Robert Fisk, thanks to his knowledge of Arabic, was able to talk himself through the various checkpoints, but I was intrigued to discover how the Colonel was able to wander apparently at will all over the country, obtaining a remarkably accurate picture of events quite independently of the official information services.

'Why, it's dead easy,' he assured me. 'I wear my army uniform and my jeep has all the correct Coalition markings, you know.' By that he meant that like all Coalition vehicles it had five inverted black Vs painted on the bonnet, back and sides. 'And here's my little secret that nobody knows about – I still have my old army ID card. So I simply drive up to an American base in the desert and show them my ID card. They usually salute and wave me through and I just drive in and go around talking to people. That way I learn a helluva lot of what's going on. Sometimes an officer will come up and say "Colonel, you shouldn't be here, I have to ask you to leave, Sir." So I leave. But you'd be surprised how often I get away with it.

'After a few days driving around talking to people, I come back to Riyadh at the weekend and file my piece to *Newsweek*. Then the following Monday, or Tuesday, I leave town again and go visit someplace else. You know, we have so many troops here in the desert right now, I can keep on doing this sort of thing for a long time.'

By dint of visiting so many different units and talking to so many servicemen, officers and ordinary soldiers, David Hackworth probably had a better understanding of the progress of the war and the likely outcome than almost anyone else in the Gulf, with the obvious exception of Generals Schwarzkopf and de la Billière and a handful of their most senior staff. Having met him by chance and shared a taxi with him, I was extremely interested to hear his assessment of the situation at a time when we were

236

clearly nearing the end of the air war and the start of the ground war.

'There's no question but that the Iraqis are taking a helluva beating,' he said. 'The destruction from the air is something else. You only have to talk to the pilots to know that. The number of sorties flown and the accuracy of the technology is frightening. The army doesn't exist that can withstand this kind of punishment for this length of time. I just don't believe that the Iraqi army – any army – will be in a fit state to fight when the air force finally tells Schwarzkopf the job is done. So, when he launches the ground war – and, in my view, it can't be far away now – I don't see it lasting very long. You know, in Korea we would rocket or bomb a target, but even if you were pretty accurate, a lot of the missiles, or bombs, would fall wide. That doesn't happen now. Every bomb or missile hits the target, not just the target but the precise part of the target that's been specifically designated.' He was right, both in his analysis of the awesome accuracy and destructive power of the laser-guided technology and in his estimate of the havoc that was being wreaked on the Iraqi war machine.

Hackworth's success in circumventing the censorship of the pool system deserves a medal, and the system itself deserves a vituperative word or two. Historically, and certainly for most of the twentieth century, the British army always distrusted what was then the press, and is now the media. The Americans, on the other hand, have always been much more open, partly because the freedom of the press is enshrined in the American Constitution and, therefore, incontestable. But in the search for a scapegoat after the Vietnam débâcle, the American establishment, especially the top brass in the army, convinced itself that the only military defeat in United States' history was the fault of the media. Was it not true, the argument ran, that in Vietnam, the first television war, the media were given almost unlimited access?

237

As they cast around for ways to deny the media such freedom ever again, the Pentagon was delighted to discover that the British had already found an answer: the pool system. Under it, the only media representatives to have access to the battlefield – accredited war correspondents – would be few in number, strictly regimented and herded together in 'pools'. They would be subject to military discipline, and needless to say, military incompetence.

It was significant that, during the Falklands War, the Royal Navy tried to prevent an ITN team being allowed on board the flagship *Ark Royal*, on the grounds that there was 'no room', and it was only the intervention of Downing Street which persuaded them to change their minds. Don McCullin never did succeed in reaching the Falklands, convinced that he was deliberately excluded because of his reputation for always being in the thick of the action; his skill as a war photographer might have proved too embarrassing when the casualties started to mount.

The Americans embraced the pool system enthusiastically, found it kept the media under firm control in Grenada and Panama and, naturally, when the Gulf crisis came along, put it to work again in conjunction with its inventors, the British. I made only two direct requests of the British army in the Gulf; one produced a perfect example of the deeply-ingrained British establishment belief that no news is good news; the other fell foul of the pool system. In the first, I asked for an interview with General Sir Peter de la Billière, mentioning the fact that I had already been invited to interview General Schwarzkopf. I was told by a toffee-nosed colonel that 'there is a long waiting list of people in front of you.'

'Yes,' I said, 'but I am asking on behalf of ITN, not just any tinpot little outfit.'

Nothing happened. Later, I asked the same colonel, who seemed to consider his role as one of preventing rather than encouraging the free flow of news, if he could arrange for

238

me to visit the RAF Tornado pilots at Tabuk air base, in the north-west corner of Saudi Arabia. This was right at the start of the air war when we sustained a whole string of Tornado losses, much higher proportionately than those of any other Coalition partner, and the cause of considerable concern at home.

'I'm afraid I can't do that,' the colonel said. 'Under the pool system, TV-am is the pool crew at Tabuk.'

'So?'

'So that precludes an ITN team going there as well.' I do not know if TV-am ever did a story with the Tornado pilots, but whether they did or not, ITN were effectively blocked from reporting one of the most important episodes of the war. I gave up asking after that. Although, individually, most of the British press officers were extremely helpful and friendly, I soon realised that the pool system, certainly as it was being operated in the Gulf, was the negation of good journalism.

The restrictions imposed by the system, and the example of David Hackworth and Robert Fisk set me thinking how ITN, and particularly myself, could best plan our coverage of the ground war. Although it was clearly much more difficult for a television team to talk its way across the desert, it should not be impossible. I started planning several lines of attack. First I tried the Kuwaiti option, reasoning that for compelling political reasons – it was the invasion of Kuwait, after all, which had ignited the whole crisis – the Kuwaitis would have to be among the first to liberate their own capital. Steve Harrow and I made the rounds of the Kuwaiti army, where we were met with courtesy, some bafflement and little success; the officers did not seem to know themselves what was going to happen.

On the political side, and although advised by a high-powered American PR agency, the Kuwaitis seemed to have no real plan for press coverage of the coming liberation, apart from inviting every journalist in Saudi Arabia to put his or her name down on a list. How the four of five hundred applicants would eventually be transported to Kuwait, and under what system of priority, remained a mystery. Part of the problem lay in the remoteness of the Kuwaiti leadership, marooned in the hilltop Sheraton Hotel in Taif, a mountain resort south of Jeddah, where it remained effectively cut off from the day-to-day running of the war. Security outside the hotel was so intense that it was extremely difficult to get inside, and once inside to find anyone in authority.

Reluctantly, I abandoned the Kuwaitis, despite the friendliness and eagerness to help of their head man in the International, a large, heavily moustached, and charming gentleman, and switched my attention to the Saudis. Despite having no success in arranging either an introduction to Prince Khalid, the Saudi Commander or, at a lower level, accreditation to the Saudi forces, I remained convinced that the Saudis, as the principal Arab partner in the Coalition and the host country for the whole allied force, must be the favourites, ahead even of the Americans, to enter Kuwait first. My hunch was reinforced by a historical parallel I found irresistible. Just as in 1944, towards the climax of the Second World War, the Allies made sure that the first troops seen to liberate Paris were the Free French led by General de Gaulle, so, I reasoned, the same Allies would see to it that Arab troops were the first into Kuwait.

By a process of elimination, I decided that the best solution might be the simplest. The shortest and most direct route from Saudi Arabia to Kuwait City lay up the main Gulf coast road to Khafji and then across the border and along what had been a dual carriageway to Kuwait. The only other obvious approach was from the main forward logistics base at Hafar al Batin, fifty miles to the west and roughly speaking in the centre of the front; but we already had another team trying to go from there with an American Special Forces unit. Having talked my plan through with

240

anyone who cared to listen, Steve Harrow and I drove our four-wheel drive Toyota Landcruiser emblazoned with the obligatory five black inverted Vs to a supermarket in Al Khobar, Dhahran's main shopping area, and bought enough tinned food and water for a fortnight in the desert. This amounted to a considerable quantity, since the team had now expanded to four: apart from Steve and myself, we had acquired a sound-recordist-cum-editor, Duncan Jones, and a young producer, Mike Gillings.

The Security Council's final ultimatum to Saddam Hussein was due to run out at 8 a.m. local time on Sunday 24 February and by the Saturday the Iraqi dictator had given absolutely no sign of any last minute change of heart. On the contrary, practically everyone I spoke to thought that, in his pig-headed arrogance, Saddam would refuse to budge, daring the Coalition to come and get him. Even if he no longer thought that he could win the war – and it is hard to believe, after the terrific pounding of the air offensive, that he still clung to his delusions – to back down at this stage would have meant a disastrous loss of face. Convinced that Saddam would ignore the deadline and that General Schwarzkopf would launch his offensive immediately, I was busy making final preparations when the office in Riyadh told me London was extremely agitated about my trip.

Nigel Hancock, the Chief News Editor, wanted me to ring him immediately to discuss my plans, which he had just heard about. Like every other television executive, he was very conscious that much earlier in the war a CBS reporter and crew had been arrested on the border by Iraqi troops and taken to Baghdad, where they had spent most of the war. Nigel was all the more concerned because the Editor, Stewart Purvis, was out of the country at the time, and he was in charge.

'I'm very concerned about your plans, Sandy,' he began. 'In fact, I am against you going. It sounds to me as if you're

241

taking a very considerable risk and we're all very conscious here of what happened to the CBS crew.'

'Honestly, Nigel,' I heard myself shouting down the line, 'it's really not at all like the CBS business. I'm convinced the Saudis will be among the first troops to reach Kuwait and we're going to try and go with them. But if things get too hairy, you have my guarantee that we'll pull back. Don't worry, I'm the biggest coward around. I've no intention of getting shot up at my time of life!' Then in an attempt to clinch the argument, I added, 'You have my absolute assurance that I won't let anybody take unnecessary risks.'

There was a moment's pause, then a somewhat mollified Nigel Hancock said, 'All right, Sandy, in the light of your assurances, and now that I understand what you're planning to do, you have my permission to go ahead. But take bloody good care, won't you?'

'Of course, Nigel, please don't worry.'

The main problem we faced in getting to Khafji lay in the series of Saudi checkpoints dotted along the main Gulf road north. At the start of the air war they had been comparatively casual, but in the past two or three weeks they had become progressively stricter and, on the eve of almost certain war, I expected them to be a serious obstacle. To increase our chances, I suggested that everyone should wear his camouflage NBC suit and steel helmet, although this was strictly contrary to the Saudi guidelines for 'freelance' journalists. Steve, who was going to drive, was convinced that the only way we would get through without having to show passes, which would immediately have given the game away, was by pretending to be Americans. So, just as it was getting dark, we slipped out of the hotel car park in our travel-stained Toyota, minus the identifying orange cloth on the roof, and headed north towards Jubail and the border.

Steve tackled the first roadblock, not far outside Dhahran, in a very good imitation of a gung-ho GI, slowing down

242

only long enough for the rather bewildered Saudi MP to take in the fact that we were all in uniform and to be treated to a raucous, pseudo-American greeting. 'Hi, guys,' Steve boomed, showing all his teeth in a huge smile, 'you okay?' and without waiting for the answer gunned the engine and roared off up the road. Slightly intoxicated by Steve's high-handedness, I grinned and hugged myself. It was almost too good to be true. The next roadblock was a long way ahead, so I settled down if not to enjoy the drive at least to register the by now familiar sights of the Gulf coast: the monster disco flash of the warning lights on the huge desalination plant at Ras Tanura and the long bank of orange fire which flared off the oil field gases in the desert on our right. There was little traffic on the road and no moon, the headlights revealing only the black tarmac and the fringe of the desert as we sped north through the darkness. As the next checkpoint approached, my sense of apprehension rose; it would be disappointing in the extreme to be turned back now.

Steve seemed oblivious of the risk of failure. He slowed down reluctantly, like a man to whom roadblocks did not apply. As soon as the vehicle in front was waved on, Steve followed, all smiles and self-confidence. The MP took a step forward, hand half raised to stop us, but we were already past him, picking up speed. It was brilliantly done, without the slightest hesitation, but I noticed as we shot forward that the MP gave us a dirty look. I wondered if he would be efficient enough to radio ahead to have us stopped; but I doubted it. The third and fourth roadblocks fell to the same tactics, and we were left, we suddenly realised, with poss-ibly only one more to go, the checkpoint at Mishab, only a few miles south of Khafji. We had had problems at Mishab before, being sent on a wild goose chase across the desert to find an American headquarters and ending up by having to explain ourselves to a Saudi base commander. I prayed the Americans would not be too vigilant tonight. It was one

243

thing to bluff a Saudi; quite another to take in an American Gunny sergeant.

As we approached the last hurdle, I advised the others to put their helmets on, hoping it would made us look as if we meant business. I need not have worried. Steve rose to the occasion magnificently. Like a great comedian he had perfected his act to such a degree that it had taken on a kind of inevitability. There was no sign of any Americans – perhaps they had moved out already in preparation for the coming offensive – and the Saudis quickly capitulated. We were through the last checkpoint and rolling up the almost empty road towards Khafji. I could hardly believe our bluff had been so successful, and that we had surmounted four or five major obstacles without once being stopped, on this of all nights, the eve of the start of the ground war. But I don't think any of us felt smug. There might, after all, be more checkpoints we did not know about. So we drove on in sober mood, into territory that was new to all of us, passing a deserted oil installation on our right, and then a mile or so farther on, an equally abandoned petrol station. There were no lights and no sign of life anywhere. To our right lay the sea and to our left the desert, both silent and both apparently peaceful, although we knew the desert contained half a million men and more of the Coalition forces, ready for the battle.

We rounded another bend and there ahead of us, standing out clearly in the Toyota's headlights, was what looked like a triumphal arch. I wondered if it had been put up by the Iraqis to celebrate their short-lived and ill-fated intrusion; beyond lay the darkened and deserted city of Khafji. We drove slowly up the main street, noticing the bullet holes in the walls and then, on the left-hand side of the road, a dark shape, spreadeagled: a camel, its stomach hugely swollen. The road bent to the right and then to the left, giving a glimpse of the battered Khafji Beach Hotel. Another hundred yards and we suddenly found ourselves

244

leaving the town behind, with open space on either side of us.

'Hold on,' I said. 'We seem to have run out of town and we don't know how far the border is.'

'Or if there are any Iraqis this side of it,' someone added.

We turned and drove slowly back the way we had come, slightly unnerved by the emptiness of the town and the possibility that Iraqi troops might suddenly materialise out of a dark side street. I was almost glad to see the poor camel again, because it meant we were almost out of the town, in open country. We drove slowly back down the main road until we reached the petrol station.

'Let's pull over and spend the night here,' I suggested to Steve. He swung the wheel and drove fifty yards beyond the pumps, so that the petrol station was between us and the border. As we turned to face the road, our headlights lit up a long line of American cars, many of them new, parked between the petrol station and the sea. All of them bore Kuwaiti number plates and I suddenly realised they had been dumped by their fleeing owners in the mass exodus that followed the arrival of the Iraqi army in Kuwait the previous August. As I walked along the line of cars a dog, abandoned by its owners no doubt, began to bark nervously from somewhere near the petrol station. It was now after eleven and we settled down to get some rest, Steve and I in the front and Mike and Duncan in the back. I longed for a cup of tea, for lack of anything stronger, but neither Steve nor I had been efficient enough to bring the necessary apparatus.

As our senses became accustomed to the dark and the silence, we realised there was a checkpoint of some kind about one hundred yards away on the far side of the road, and occasionally a snatch of music floated towards us. The lights of a lorry appeared from the direction of Mishab and after a brief stop at the checkpoint turned off into the desert. We deduced there must be a military camp there, either

245

Saudi or American, but they were certainly paying no attention to us. I dozed off, and slept fitfully, getting up to answer a call of nature in the early hours. As I sniffed the night air, I became aware of what I at first thought was a thunderstorm further up the coast. Great flashes of light lit up the night sky and what sounded like thunder growled in the distance. The night being fine, I realised this was no thunderstorm but an extremely heavy artillery barrage, perhaps fifteen or twenty miles to the north.

The distant thunder of multiple rocket launchers, a giant version of the Second World War Stalin Organ, accompanied me back to the vehicle as I reflected that I was listening to the start of the great offensive. Saddam had refused to withdraw and Armageddon was now upon him. A couple of hours later, we were all awake as a raw, grey dawn broke over the desert, and glad of our charcoal-lined NBC suits, which made you grubby but kept you warm. We were munching chocolate and biscuits – I silently cursed Steve, and myself, for not having bought a primus in Al Khobar to brew tea – when we became aware of a high-pitched hum approaching from the south, the sound of a vehicle driving fast. It was another Toyota Landcruiser, but maroon-coloured and, unlike ours, carried none of the Operation Desert Storm markings.

'Who the hell are they?' Steve demanded. 'They seem to know what they're doing, though.' There was a pause as we all watched the Toyota go careering past in front of us. Then he added excitedly, switching on the engine. 'They must be journalists. Let's follow them.' With that he let in the clutch and we shot out onto the road in hot pursuit. The maroon Toyota was already round the next bend and Steve had difficulty catching up until it slowed slightly at the entrance to Khafji. Whoever was driving certainly knew his way, taking the two right-angle turns in the middle of the town so fast we barely had time to notice that the plate glass front of the Khafji Beach Hotel had been completely shat-

246

tered. As we emerged on the north side of the town, the maroon Toyota was accelerating up the dual carriageway which led to the border.

'They know exactly where they're going, they *must* be journalists,' Steve shouted excitedly. I was not so sure. 'Don't get too close,' was all I could think of saying, 'just in case.' The maroon Toyota was doing about eighty up the empty dual carriageway when a large rectangular gateway came into view: the border. For a moment it looked as if our guides were going to stop in front of the deserted border post, but instead they swung left and left again and started back down the dual carriageway. If they had not seen us already, they must have noticed us now as we executed the same manoeuvre and sped after them, towards Khafji. The chase was becoming almost too exciting and I held on tightly as the Landcruiser rocked wildly.

Suddenly the vehicle in front swerved right-handed down a rough track into the desert, where, to our surprise we found ourselves on a well-made road bulldozed across the sand. The Toyota was almost out of sight as we passed several armoured personnel carriers and lorries, and not wanting to lose it now Steve put his foot hard down. We swooped into a dip still accelerating, and came up over a ridge just in time to see the Toyota swerve off the road and stop. 'Slow down,' I shouted unnecessarily, my nerves getting the better of me. Steve was already braking hard, and we came to a halt with a jolt.

Out of the maroon Toyota now stepped, not the journalists Steve had so confidently predicted, but four senior Saudi officers. Sheepishly, I got out and sauntered towards them. One, a tall, thin colonel, turned and asked frostily, 'Who are you?'

'We're British.'

'British what?'

'British television, actually,'

'British television?' He looked as if a bad smell had passed under his nose. 'You shouldn't be here, in fact.' He turned and spoke to his colleagues in Arabic.

'Oh, really? We'd better be leaving, then.' I turned and whispered urgently to Steve. 'Come on, let's get out of here before they bloody well arrest us.'

The Saudis were still deep in discussion as we got into the Landcruiser, turned and drove off. The colonel, frowning, looked up as if trying to decide what to do; but he had missed the moment, and in any case probably had more important things on his mind. As we drove back over the ridge and down into the dip on the other side, I realised we had gotten lucky, as the Americans say. Very lucky. Stopping at the bottom of the dip we looked back; we were completely hidden from the Saudi colonel and his friends, and thanks to their involuntary assistance, we had stumbled right into the middle of the Saudi build-up. As Steve pulled the camera out of the car and set up the tripod by the side of the road, an armoured personnel carrier loomed out of the early morning mist above us and went trundling away across the desert. More APCs followed and after ten minutes it became clear that the main action was behind us, on the other side of the ridge. We looked at one another. We decided to go and have a look.

We drove cautiously back over the ridge peering apprehensively ahead in case the colonel was still about. But there was no sign of the maroon Toyota, and much more interestingly the whole desert was filling up with tanks, APCs and lorry loads of Saudi infantry. We stopped and got out, and as soon as Steve put the camera on his shoulder, Saudi soldiers started to crowd round. One bearded character, who had obviously learned his English in the cinema, stood in front of me waving his fist. 'This bloody Saddam, we gonna kill the bastard. We gonna kill him for what he's done to Kuwait. Yes, sir.' His mates chorused their approval. In the distance, a battery of multiple rocket launchers suddenly opened up, the rockets howling over

248

our heads in the direction of occupied Kuwait, salvo following salvo with a roar like an express train. It was a fearsome sight and I pitied whoever was on the receiving end.

As the sun came up and the desert turned a pale, shimmering gold, the great cavalcade of tanks started to move ponderously towards the north. I glanced at my watch. It was almost eight. We climbed into the Landcruiser and followed the lead tanks, weaving our way through the mass of armour and infantry. Jubilant Saudi soldiers waved and shouted at us in excitement, as if the battle was already won. We waved back, equally excited and then, peering ahead, I shouted, 'Look there's the bloody berm!' This was Saddam's vaunted defensive system, two great walls of sand with between them a ditch which he had threatened to fill with blazing oil to repel the allies. Now, as we approached, caught up in a great mass of tanks, I saw that the berm had been bulldozed flat the width of a dual carriageway, and that on either side, the ditch was dry: no oil, no flaming inferno. Here, at least, Saddam's threats had turned out to be empty bluster; a pipeline had been partly laid but never connected up. As the lead tanks crossed the berm with almost insolent ease, meeting no opposition – indeed there was no sign of any Iraqi presence at all – I knew that no one was going to stop us filming the allied invasion of Kuwait now.

Chapter
16

As the Saudi tanks fanned out across the level desert, dotted with small green bushes of camel thorn but otherwise bare, I urged Steve, who was driving, 'Keep in the tank tracks. You never know, there could be mines.' But surprisingly, in this strategic stretch of desert, only a few miles west of the main coast road and eighty miles south of Kuwait City, the Iraqis did not seem to have laid any mines at all. A few miles north of the border, we climbed a sand slope and, looking back, saw a long column of armour and soft-skinned vehicles snaking across the desert behind us. After another mile or two, we crossed the main road and came on some empty foxholes and abandoned tank emplacements. But it was only when we had gone about twelve or fifteen miles into the Kuwaiti desert that we saw the first real sign of Saddam Hussein's army. A burst of small arms fire sent us racing forward to where a group of Saudi tanks and APCs, drawn up in a rough semi-circle, had just captured an Iraqi outpost. A makeshift white flag flew from a stick, suggesting that the Iraqis had decided to surrender without a fight.

Running forward from the Landcruiser, Steve filming as he advanced, we saw a small group of prisoners being marched across the sand at gunpoint, hands tied behind their backs, to join a group already squatting on the ground.

Most of them were in their thirties or forties, and all of them looked dirty and demoralised. I had heard that Saddam's policy was to deploy his worst troops on the borders, cannon fodder for the initial attack, and keep his best troops, the Republican Guard, back in reserve. I could well believe it; these troops looked very second-rate. One man had been shot in the stomach and seemed badly hurt; several others were less seriously wounded. The Saudis looked panicky. One man was shooting up an apparently empty under-ground bunker with automatic fire so ineptly – as he fired, the muzzle of the carbine lifted dangerously, the bullets thudding into the sand at the top of the bunker – that I stepped back nervously. 'Watch out,' I told Steve, who was busy filming beside me. 'I don't trust this cowboy.'

I suspected that the Iraqis had not offered any real resistance, but that the Saudis, being basically untried troops, had shot them out of sheer nerves and incompe-tence; perhaps the Iraqis had been slow about surrendering. We must have arrived within five or ten minutes of the capture and the hunt for prisoners was still in progress. A few yards away, another wounded man crawled out of his bunker clutching a leaflet dropped from the air which called in Arabic on all Iraqi soldiers to surrender. He too looked extremely scared, no doubt fearful that he might be killed rather than taken prisoner. There was one touching moment when a wounded Iraqi, his arm round the shoulders of two Saudis who were helping him to an ambulance, turned and kissed one of his captors on the cheek, rather as a dog licks its master after being scolded.

I was anxious to begin the long journey to Dhahran. We undoubtedly had a first-class report on the start of the allied invasion of Kuwait, but as every journalist knows, it is not enough merely to get the story, you have to get it back. I had been busy consulting my watch and doing sums, urging that it was time to turn round and head for home, but Steve, to his credit, had insisted on keeping on until we had the

251

climax to the story: the capture of the first Iraqi prisoners. Now, however, was the time to break off; it was eleven o'clock and we were four and a half or five hours' drive from the International Hotel. We climbed into the Landcruiser and started off in the direction from which we had come. This proved to be quite difficult. So much traffic was now pushing north, as the invasion gained momentum, that we were like a swimmer breasting the tide. Hundreds of vehicles were pouring across the desert: tanks, APCs, and lorries full of Saudi and Kuwaiti troops, flying their respective flags. We had been battling through the press for half an hour when suddenly, we heard a loud shout.

'Hey, you guys, where the hell's your goddam orange cloth?'

It took me a moment to locate the source of the unmistakably American voice. It came from a Special Forces officer in camouflage uniform, hair tied back with a bandana, driving a jeep flying a Kuwaiti flag and crammed with Kuwaiti soldiers.

'What orange cloth?' I countered.

'On the goddam roof' – he pronounced it ruf – 'for Chrissake! You're supposed to have an orange cloth on the roof. You nearly got blown away!'

As he spoke, I glanced behind him and saw a young American soldier standing in the back of a pickup with a heavy machine-gun pointing straight at us. I felt a moment of chill, and anger. I clearly remembered asking someone if we needed an orange marker on the top of the vehicle and being told no.

'We don't have any orange cloth,' I shouted, rather obviously.

'Here, for Chrissake.' The Special Forces man with the bandana jumped out of his jeep and started tearing his own sheet of thin orange plastic in half. He handed me one of the pieces. 'Tie that on the roof! You sure as hell nearly got blown away that time!' I thanked him profusely and

252

watched them depart while Steve tied on the strip of plastic. We were the only vehicle going against the stream of traffic and in the general confusion and excitement it was only to be expected that some trigger-happy young American should think we were Iraqis. We completed the rest of the journey to the border without further difficulty, except for the traffic jams caused by the flow of petrol tankers, ammunition trucks and more lorries full of troops. By the time we were on the tarmac heading south, it was nearly midday and we had a long drive ahead of us.

Steve drove fast, the roadblocks hardly holding us up at all, and we were outside the International in Dhahran by three. We had no idea how exclusive our material was, and I tried to banish the thought that we might just be the first with the story. We ran up the stairs and hurried into the office where we were met by Sue Tinson, the senior producer. 'Hello love, what have you got?' she asked, realising we were extremely excited about something.

'We've got the Saudis invading Kuwait,' I gasped.

'Great. You're the first with the story. And what's more, Schwarzkopf has imposed a 24-hour news blackout, so none of the pools will have anything.'

Peter Read, the senior editor, was already working on another item with Jeremy Thompson, so we moved to another editing table, at the end of the room, and Duncan, who had trained as an editor, sat down at the video machine while I started to write the story.

Sue poked her head round the corner of the cubicle. 'Just before you start, and I won't interrupt you any more, you have just over half an hour to feedtime for the lunchtime news and they're holding the lead open for you.' Half an hour is not very much time to edit a package, but just enough, if you know your business. We took it chronologically; the Saudi tanks rolling across the bulldozed berm; the multiple rocket launchers hurling their salvoes into Kuwait; the interview with the Saudi soldier describing what they

253

were going to do to Saddam; myself on camera in the rain talking about the ease with which the invading force had crossed the undefended border and looking, as a friend said later, rather like a drowned rat; the armour fanning out across the desert; the capture of the Iraqi outpost; and the taking of the first prisoners. We completed the edit and the commentary with only minutes to spare and Duncan had to race down the corridors to the BBC office to feed. We watched anxiously as the package was beamed up to the satellite by the mobile dish just outside the window, the first television pictures of the liberation of Kuwait.

Within minutes it was going out from the ITN studios in London to an audience of a couple of million tuned to the lunchtime news on the ITV network. Only two or three minutes after that, the time it took CNN in London to record the ITN report and satellite it to America, where it was re-broadcast from CNN's headquarters in Atlanta, it was being seen by many millions in countries all over the world, including of course Saudi Arabia.

We swiftly became aware of that when an agitated Saudi official, the very same colonel we had had rows with before, came storming into our office demanding to see the report. He was torn between official anger and private delight; outraged that we should have circumvented the system and evaded army censorship; and yet secretly elated that the first pictures of the ground war should show the Saudi army in so flattering a light. We ran the package for him again and when we came to my 'into camera', in which I said that Saudi tanks having crossed the border were now heading for Kuwait, he gave an agitated cry. 'No, no, no, you can't say that. You must cut out the reference to Kuwait! Immediately!'

'Where else would they be going?' I said.

There was a brief argument, but he was so wrought-up that we conceded the point, rather than risk a total ban, and he departed, still torn between anger and pleasure. ITN

254

made the most of our exclusive, running the story on all bulletins, including the main evening news which at that time had an audience of around twelve million, usually the highest of the week.

By the time it was all over, I felt completely exhausted and wanted nothing more than a large Scotch, a bath and bed. The first was unobtainable, but the latter two were easy. As I was about to leave the office to get some sleep, the ITN press office came on the phone and said *The Times* wanted me to write a one-thousand-word article about the invasion. I said, 'No, I simply can't. It would take me two hours and I must get some sleep before going back up there tomorrow.' I felt my first duty was to the story, and to ITN, however gratifying it would be to see myself in print in *The Times*. Unknown to me, however, someone at ITN in London wrote it instead, under my name, which I thought was a questionable practice, although perhaps understandable in the circumstances. But his version was completely inaccurate on one point. My ghost writer had me saying it was the most nerve-racking experience of my life. On the contrary, it was a piece of cake.

Having settled, as I thought, the matter of *The Times*, I found myself embroiled in a brief argument about who should go back into Kuwait the next day. Sue wanted to send someone else but I said, 'No, this is my story and, having done all the donkey work, I'm damned if I'm going to hand it over on a plate to someone else.' I was determined that, having engineered the scoop, I should be allowed to follow it through. It also made sense. Steve and I were a team: he was the roadblock expert, I knew this particular story better than anyone else.

Since we were in different hotels, Steve and Duncan dropped me off first and arranged to pick me up at eight the next morning. On the TV in my room, CNN was still running our package, so nothing fresh had materialised to overtake it.

Next morning, having decided, because of the distance to the front, to operate a shuttle service, we set off in two vehicles. Steve negotiated the roadblocks with his customary dash and we reached the shattered Khafji Beach Hotel, where we parked the spare Toyota, shortly after midday. From there it was only a few minutes' drive to the border, where we found the traffic using the old gateway, and threaded our way through the remains of the Iraqi fortifications on to the dual carriageway. Only one side was in operation, the other lane having been been dug up at intervals by the Iraqis to make tank emplacements, now empty. After twenty minutes we passed the place where the invading column had crossed the road the day before and after about another thirty minutes caught up with a small detachment of Saudi tanks; they were parked on the right of the road looking across a shallow depression to the outskirts of a small town on the coast. In front of the tanks, an American Special Forces team was studying the area with a sight which gave them the exact range of whatever they were looking at. As we were filming, a small group of journalists, mainly French, came up and introduced themselves; I presumed they had been alerted by our report on CNN. But there was so little activity, either hostile or friendly, that we left them to it and drove on up the road, passing one rusty, burnt-out tank, probably Kuwaiti.

Not long afterwards, we caught up with the Saudi spearhead, twenty or thirty tanks and APCs drawn up in loose formation across the desert; they had not covered many miles since we had left them the day before. As we drove slowly between them over the firm sand, wondering why they had stopped, a shell exploded about two hundred yards away, on our left. We stopped and examined the situation with renewed interest. Another shell landed, slightly closer this time.

'Bracketing,' I said, pretending it was all fairly routine. Steve had the camera out and was trying to work out where

256

the next shell was going to drop. The answer was, still closer, about one hundred and fifty yards away. A couple of the APCs nearest the point of impact started to reverse. 'What's known as a tactical withdrawal,' I joked. No one seemed to think it was very funny. 'Come on,' I said to Steve. 'Let's do a camera piece right here.' An APC was conveniently parked only ten yards away. The next shell took us by surprise. It flew over our heads with a menacing, high-pitched scream and landed with an angry *crump* a hundred and fifty yards behind us. The one after that landed a bit shorter. We could not see who was shelling, but about a mile in front the road disappeared over a low ridge and the Iraqis must have been dug in behind it. Sitting in the front seat of the Toyota, I unzipped my laptop and started typing a script. As I worked, shells kept landing behind us, but luckily did not come any closer. Ten mintues later, with the Saudis showing no signs of dislodging the Iraqi gunners and time beginning to run short, we set off for Khafji to record the commentary and despatch Mike Gillings, the young producer, to Dhahran. He would have to drive flat-out to make the early evening feed. On our way back to the border, we passed a big mobile rocket launcher, a cluster of barrels occupying the back of a lorry, labouring across the desert on its way, I presumed, to silence the Iraqi gun. I wondered why they did not assault the ridge with their tanks; it would have been much quicker and cleaner; this was like taking a sledgehammer to crack a very small nut.

We recorded the commentary right beside the once limpid, blue waters of the Gulf, at the back of the Khafji Beach Hotel, which must have been a pleasant enough place before the Iraqis smashed it up and flooded the beach with oil. Then, after eating a quick snack we separated, Mike to drive to Dhahran and Steve, Duncan and I to head back to the front. We wished him luck. I was worried that he would be stopped at one of the roadblocks and our report delayed; I realised, of course, that every time we made the run to

Dhahran, the shorter the odds against us would be. I did not, however, expect them to have shortened quite so dramatically in another direction. As we headed north along the now familiar dual carriageway, only about forty miles from Kuwait City, our luck ran out. Passing a number of vehicles parked at the side of the road, I noticed one of them was a press bus and simultaneously, my glance fell on the Saudi colonel who had censored our report the day before. Even as I sighted him, he turned and spotted us, and as we drove by, still within earshot, I heard him shout. 'Stop, stop that car. You have no right . . .'

Steve's reaction was to put his foot down. As we gathered speed along the road, a siren started to howl behind us. Steve pressed harder on the acccelerator. The howl of the siren rose to a crescendo and a Saudi military police jeep shot past and then cut in sharply in front of us. The driver, an MP wearing a red beret and clutching an automatic weapon leaped out of the jeep, gun pointed.

'Stop,' I shouted. For a panicky moment I thought that Steve was going to try to drive through him, or over him.

We skidded to a stop and the MP poked his gun angrily through the open window. 'Stop!' The gun gestured peremptorily to us to get out. 'Passport!'

'Give him the lot,' I said, thrusting my Saudi press pass and nice blue British passport at him. For a moment I thought the MP's fury might get the better of him and that he would shoot us on the spot. Instead, there was the thud of running feet and a very irate colonel appeared, almost incoherent with rage.

'Stop! You are all under arrest. Mister Gall,' he rhymed it with Val, 'I warn you yesterday. I am confiscating your press passes. Please!' He held out his hand.

'Why, what have we done?' I asked, all innocence.

He rounded on me, almost apoplectic. 'You ask stoopid question. You break all rules. You wear uniform. You know that not allowed. You drive through roadblocks without stopping. Oh, yes, Mister Gall, we know all about you. You lucky you not get shot!' He snatched the passes, pausing only for one parting comment. 'You wait here! You under arrest!' he snapped and stormed off, his back expressing a mountain of insult and rage. It did seem that our luck had run out rather spectacularly.

We waited beside our Toyota while the colonel and his minions tried to establish how much further it would be safe to take the press bus. One or two journalists came and spoke to us, but for the most part we were ignored, although not sufficiently to make a run for it. Eventually, after an hour or so, orders were given for the press bus to proceed – in fact, they eventually got about as far as we had earlier in the day. Rather than wait for the press party to return, which might take hours, we managed to persuade one of the officials to let us drive back towards Dhahran, although the colonel refused to return our passes.

It was at the second or third roadblock, not entirely unexpectedly, that we came to grief. An MP in a red beret demanded to see our press passes and when we were unable to produce them, refused to let us proceed. In desperation, we tried to argue, explain, plead and cajole, to no avail, and finally Steve's patience snapped and he employed a four-letter word. Despite the MP's almost total lack of English, this was one word he did recognise and he immediately became extremely angry, launching into an indignant flow of Arabic, in which the four-letter word featured repeatedly. Then, holding his automatic in one hand and crooking the forefinger of the other at Steve, he marched him to a sentry box and motioned to him to go inside. Steve was now apologising abjectly, but the MP, his manhood impugned, was adamant. Sensing further prevarication might only make things worse, I urged Steve to yield. 'I'm afraid, old boy, you'll have to sit in the bloody thing for a bit, until he cools down.'

Reluctantly, and no doubt feeling extremely foolish, Steve

stepped inside and sat down – luckily there was a chair – while the MP ceremoniously fastened the chain across the doorway. Symbolically, at least, he was a prisoner. The MP then motioned to us that we should move away, as if to emphasise the incarceration of this passless infidel who had insulted the manhood of a proud Saudi soldier. Slowly, and with rather forced smiles, Duncan and I sauntered slowly back to our vehicle. There was nothing to be done but wait, and hope that that other proud Saudi, the colonel, would soon return to release us. It was a forlorn hope and we whiled the time away as best we could, making periodic visits to cheer up Steve and trying to think of ways of escape. Security in the roadblocks was undoubtedly much stricter, no doubt as a result of our escapades, and a French journalist was also stopped for a time, although he still had his pass. He seemed to know the area well, and I talked to him at some length about possible routes across the desert to the border, avoiding the main road. A plan was already forming in my mind as to how we could get to Kuwait despite the loss of our passes, which I now took to be permanent. One thing was clear. If what we had seen on the coast road was typical of the speed of the Coalition's advance, it would not be long before Kuwait was liberated, and I wanted to be there.

We had been waiting for about five hours when the press bus and the colonel eventually appeared, releasing poor Steve from his sentry box and permitting us to drive on to Dhahran, where we arrived after midnight, weary and still passless. The drawbacks of such a condition were immediately manifest. The American sentries on the door, who checked everyone and everything going into the hotel, made their customary request.

'ID, please sir.'

'I'm awfully sorry, Sergeant, the Saudis have taken our passes away.'

'Okay, sir, you have an office number in the hotel?'

I supplied the ITN room number and two minutes later,

Jonathan Monro, our young number two producer, appeared all smiles and escorted us through. 'You been bad boys, again?' he joked as we went up the stairs two at a time. 'You've got half an hour to revoice your earlier piece, and we've got some good, fresh material as well.' He meant for *News at Ten*. Peter Read had cut and fed the original version for 'the early', the 5.40 evening news, with plenty of time to spare, thanks to Mike Gillings who had driven flat out to reach the International in a record three hours. The *News at Ten* version was even better, improved by the addition of French Television pictures of an air strike against the Iraqi position which had been shelling the Saudi tanks. The French must have shot it shortly after we left and, because of the informal camaraderie which exists between TV companies in the field, had offered it to ITN in return for past favours or in anticipation of those to come.

It was after one in the morning by the time we had finished and I was too tired to lie awake worrying about the loss of our press passes. Just before I fell asleep I thought of appealing to Prince Fahd bin Salman again, but decided that even he might be unable to save us this time, and that in any case it would almost certainly take too long. During the night my subconscious must have continued to work for in the morning I arose with a full-fledged, if simple, plan in mind. We would fill the Toyota with petrol, stock up with provisions and set off across the desert for the Kuwaiti border, passes or no passes. By eleven, having discussed with the office what we were planning to do, I was waiting outside the hotel ready to leave when Duncan told me a problem had arisen and suggested that I go back upstairs. A little earlier, Sue had suggested to me that another, more senior producer, Bill Taylor, should go with us instead, replacing Mike Gillings. I knew Bill well and welcomed the idea, but while I was waiting outside, Steve had raised an objection.

When Duncan and I arrived, a heated argument was in progress on the dimly-lit landing outside the ITN office.

261

Steve was insisting, vehemently, that Sue should change her mind and reinstate Mike who, in Steve's view, deserved to be rewarded for his sterling efforts of the day before by remaining part of the team. Sue's point was that Bill had been stuck in the office for weeks on end, wanted a break and deserved it. I could see the strength of both arguments, but not an obvious solution. It required a Solomon-like wisdom which was not available and eventually, with time pressing Steve's emotional barrage won the day: Mike stayed and Bill walked back, looking upset, to the gloomy dungeon he inhabited with the rest of the team.

The Frenchman I had met the day before had told me that if we could reach the main east–west desert road about fifty miles north of Dhahran, head west for a few miles and then strike north on another desert road we should be able to reach the Kuwait-Saudi border without too much difficulty. Although I was doubtful that it would be that easy, I knew we had no alternative. The first problem, having no passes, was to reach the turn-off without being stopped at a road-block. In the event, our luck seemed to have recovered, and we had no trouble negotiating the only roadblock, just north of Dhahran. But half-way to the turn-off, things started to go wrong. We were speeding along the almost empty dual carriageway when a loud hissing noise caused Duncan to pull over. It sounded as if the engine was boiling over: it turned out to be air escaping with great force from a back tyre. We had a flat. Some kind Saudis stopped and helped us to change the wheel, and half an hour later we arrived at the turn-off, in the middle of a small town which we had passed through at speed on our frequent journeys to and from the border.

It was a typical Saudi desert townlet, ugly and dirty, with a few scruffy shops, a garage and a mosque. The garage sold petrol but did not repair tyres and we were directed to a workshop. Unfortunately it was now lunchtime, or prayer-time, and both are immutable in Saudi Arabia. The first workshop was about to close, and we were directed to another, which turned out to be already closed. A man standing nearby said the owner had gone off with the key – to lunch no doubt – and he did not know when or even if he was coming back. We stood for some time beside the road in this dusty, fly-blown dump, debating our next move. On the plus side, we had successfully reached the turn-off and could see the east–west road disappearing into the desert, with no roadblock in sight. On the minus side, we had one flat tyre and no means of getting it repaired. In other words, we were proposing to cross a sizeable chunk of desert with no spare, something that no person in his right mind would normally contemplate. But these were not normal times, and after railing briefly at the shortsighted-ness that had led us to set off across the desert with only one spare, we elected to go on. The alternative was an ignominious return to base.

The desert road, which I imagined was the main highway to the huge Coalition staging point of Hafar al Batin, was almost deserted and we sped along it meeting hardly any other traffic. We passed a fairly impressive road on our right and wondered if this was the route north. Our sketchy map was not much use and we decided to go on, finally stopping at a small military outpost to ask directions. Unfortunately, the Saudis who emerged were friendly but uncommunica-tive. We made one or two other abortive attempts to fix our position but finally, frightened that we might run into someone who wanted to see our passes, decided to go back to the road that had looked so promising. It started well, running due north according to Duncan's compass, but then began to veer east, towards the coast road and its road-blocks. Coming to a crossroads, we stopped to consult the map.

'I think we need to head more west again and then north,' Duncan suggested. The map was now virtually useless since these desert roads were all new, presumably bulldozed by the Saudis specifically for Desert Shield. The only reliable piece of equipment we had was Duncan's compass. I thanked God under my breath that he had had the foresight to bring it. In the disorganised scramble of our departure, there had been lamentably little of that commodity. 'Look, the road we're on is heading almost due east now.' He demonstrated with the compass. 'If we keep following it, we'll soon be back on the coast road.'

'Which we don't want,' I said firmly.

'Exactly. So we should turn left here, keep heading in a westerly direction and eventually hope to pick up the road to the north which your French chum was talking about.'

I peered at the map. 'There's a town called Wafra just over the Kuwaiti border, twenty or thirty miles from the coast. I think that's where we should be heading for.' A thin, red line ran north from roughly where I imagined we were towards Kuwait. According to the map, it bypassed Wafra and continued towards Kuwait City. 'If this road exists, it would do us very well.'

'Okay, let's turn left here and see what happens.'

Infuriatingly, after running west for a short distance, the road started bending south. We slowed down, perplexed. The largely featureless desert stretched away unhelpfully in front of us.

'We need to take a right at some point fairly soon,' Duncan said, studying his compass. Shortly afterwards, a track appeared obligingly, running north. It even bore signs of being recently used; at least one set of tracks was clearly imprinted in the sand. This was reassuring, because we were all conscious, at the back of our minds, that the Saudis might have laid mines anywhere in the area to deter an Iraqi invasion. We followed the track for several miles with growing optimism until, breasting a ridge, we saw it dipping down and disappearing into a swamp. Steve, who was driving, approached cautiously, too cautiously. Realising what was was about to happen, Duncan shouted 'Go on!

Put your foot down!' But it was too late. We barely succeeded in fording a shallow pool of water with soft mud
underneath, and stalled on the incline on the far side. By
now the sky was overcast and threatening rain; it was after
four, so we had only two hours of daylight left. The ground
squelched beneath our boots. 'Here, let me drive,' Duncan
said. 'I'm used to these kind of conditions.' He took the
wheel, slammed the gears into four-wheel drive and
shouted 'Push!' Slowly, with three of us straining every
muscle, the vehicle started to emerge from the morass, and
the wheels began to bite.

Duncan drove with considerable skill, keeping to the high
ground as much as possible and when forced to cross the
swampier patches building up enough speed to slide and
skid his way through them. Eventually, after almost an hour
of driving across country on a compass heading, we saw the
road ahead of us and gratefully rejoined it. It was now
almost dark, so we parked on the hardest patch of ground
we could find and prepared to camp for the night. We had
seen no living thing, except the odd bird, for several hours
and the landscape around us was innocent of any human
habitation. I reflected that we were living the dream of many
romantically-minded young adventurers; camping out in
the desert. In fact, it was disappointingly dull and
uncomfortable. I announced I would have a tin of baked
beans, but Steve, suddenly bossy, vetoed the idea.

'These stores may have to last a week or more,' he
lectured. 'You can only have half a tin.' I meekly accepted
the diktat and munched my cold baked beans as the damp
dusk started to close in. Steve had managed to lose my
borrowed sleeping bag in the chaos of provisions and
camera equipment that filled the back of the Landcruiser so
I was obliged to make my bed on the sand, with only my
red and white checked *keffiyeh* as a ground sheet; luckily,
the ground was soft.

A light drizzle woke me at dawn and forced me to take

refuge in the Toyota where we munched a frugal breakfast. Again, we had neglected to bring a stove to make tea, a serious shortcoming which my Afghan friends would have failed to comprehend. The Afghan war, I thought miserably, was fuelled by tea. With nothing to delay us, we were ready to depart as soon as it was light. My watch told me it was Wednesday 27 February 1991. At least it was not raining.

Chapter
17

The road ran due north, over undulating desert, and fortunately we seemed to have left the swamp behind us. I could just make out the line of the coast to our right, the Gulf a blue smudge in the far distance. After driving steadily for about an hour, we ascended a slight slope and were suddenly confronted, to our complete surprise, by a stretch of smooth, black tarmac. We bumped up to the top of the ridge and found ourselves on one side of a dual carriageway, not knowing whether to turn left or right. The road was completely empty and there were no signposts. Where were we, and in which direction was Kuwait? Duncan produced his compass and declared that the road ran roughly east and west and so, if we turned right, we should come to the sea. Rather hesitantly, not knowing what we might find next, we drove down the road, until after about half a mile, Duncan suddenly shouted, 'I know where we are, this is the road to the border.' We were in fact, about half-way between Khafji and the border. We must have emerged from the desert very near the point where, three days before, we had watched the Saudi tanks assembling for their assault on Kuwait.

Despite the setbacks of the day before, and thanks to Duncan's compass and a bit of luck, we had made it. We were now on familar ground and nothing, it seemed, stood between us and Kuwait City. As we pushed further up the road towards our objective, only eighty miles from the border, we began to overtake a lot of military traffic going north; very few vehicles were heading south, which was just as well because in many places the dual carriageway was reduced to two lanes. We must have covered half the distance to Kuwait when our guardian angel, who had watched over us so devotedly, either deserted us or nodded off. The Toyota lurched, yawed and from somewhere at the back there came a loud banging noise. 'Bugger! Puncture!' Duncan exclaimed, as we rolled to a halt at the side of the road. We now had two flat tyres and no spare.

Our only hope was that some friendly member of the Coalition would take pity on us and stop. As we stood by the side of the Toyota looking helpless, I noticed that the road was littered with empty cartridge cases and jagged bits of shrapnel, one of which had undoubtedly finished off our tyre. Quite soon, a jeepload of Saudis drew up but not being able to offer any real assistance drove on again. A lot of traffic was heading for Kuwait, but nothing else stopped and time was slipping away. The frustration of having broken down only forty miles from Kuwait, on liberation day, and to be unable to extricate ourselves became almost unbearable. As if all that was not more than enough, Nemesis, who had clearly replaced our guardian angel, hit us below the belt. Among the stream of traffic moving in front of us I noticed an army bus, but it was only after it had gone past that, in rapid succession, I realised three things; first, it was the press bus; second, the angry features glaring at us out of the window belonged to none other than the colonel; and third, and most alarming, the bus was stopping.

'Look out,' I said. 'You'll never guess who's just arrived.'

With the kind of helpless horror with which a rabbit watches a stoat, we saw the colonel and an assistant descend from the bus, climb over the barrier that divided the dual

268

carriageway and hurry towards us, their body language indicating the threat of at least a court martial if not a firing squad at dawn.

The colonel opened hostilities while a full five yards away, his voice thick with rage. 'You again, Mr Gall.' (He still rhymed it with Val.) 'You break the rules once more. I have told you three times already, you are not allowed to wear this uniform . . .'

Everyone started talking at once. 'Just a minute, Colonel . . .' 'Look here, Colonel . . .' The colonel's face became extremely red for a Saudi. He too was trying to make himself heard. When there was a lull, I seized my chance. 'Colonel, we've had two punctures and we are stuck. Can you please help us?'

'No!' the colonel said, with a certain satisfaction, I thought. 'No help. You break the rules again. You have many warnings. No help. Now it is finish.'

Steve put into words exactly what we were all thinking. 'Why don't you f— off, then?'

From being merely angry, the colonel became apoplectic. Although quite a small man, he swelled visibly with rage. 'How dare you use that language to me? I will have you arrested! You come here and break the rules of our country. And then you insult me, with this . . . feelthy language. This is too much!' With that, he turned and stormed off along the road, his dramatic exit slightly spoiled by the rush of the passing traffic. Steve and I ran after him, Steve apologising abjectly.

'Colonel, Colonel, I didn't mean that. Please accept my apologies, please!' But the colonel ignored him, leaving me to make one last attempt. Matching him stride for stride, I exerted every ounce of persuasiveness I was able to muster. 'My dear Colonel, please accept my apologies on Steve's behalf. It was said in the heat of the moment. He's said he's sorry.' The colonel strode on, apparently too angry to speak. Keeping in step beside him, as if we were on parade, I put my arm round his shoulder. 'Come on, Colonel, we are all on the same side. We're allies, after all. We're only trying to do our job and tell the world about the liberation of Kuwait!'

Shrugging off my arm, the colonel kept walking. 'No, Mr Gall. It is too late now. It is finish!' Then, with all the dignity he could muster, he threw his leg over the barrier and mounted the steps of the bus without looking back.

'What a rotten bastard,' someone said as the bus ground off up the road towards Kuwait. I watched them go with a mixture of contempt and anger; how could they be so petty? A thought struck me. 'Anyway, it's none of their business now,' I said. 'After all, this is Kuwait, not Saudi Arabia.' Luckily, some of the colonel's fellow countrymen were inclined to look more kindly on a Western ally. Not very long afterwards, another Toyota pulled up alongside and two Saudi soldiers got out. After a brief discussion, they drove off with one of the flat tyres, returning half an hour later having mended the puncture and, in a final generous gesture, proceeded to change the wheel for us.

Having lost the better part of three hours, we sped on towards Kuwait, noticing on our right, the closer we got, the smoke from the hundreds of oil fires the Iraqis had started in their final, most damaging act of revenge. That day, the wind must have been from the west, and most of the smoke was blowing out to sea, but every now and then, when it changed, we caught the acrid smell of burning oil. Eventually we reached the outskirts of Kuwait, and were forced to slow down by the crowds lining the highway, waving and shouting greetings. I turned round to see how Steve was getting on with the camera. He looked worried, snapping the on-off switch several times to no effect. Finally, he looked up. 'The bloody camera's packed up.'

'Oh, shit no!' I groaned. 'What the hell's wrong with it?' I heard the anger and frustration thickening my voice.

'Dunno,' he said. 'It's taken a hell of a pounding in the desert and there hasn't been time to have it serviced.' ITN, in fact, had a young camera technician back in Dhahran, or had until he fractured his ribs in a car crash. But it was too late now. Trying to hide my disappointment, I stretched my arm out of the window and shook hands with a score of happy Kuwaitis pressing against the vehicle, their faces full of the joy of liberation. There were a lot of women and even more children, but very few men, all of them excited, laughing, cheering and waving green, white and red-striped Kuwaiti flags. There was even an occasional Old Glory or Union Jack.

'Where are you from?' they wanted to know. 'America?'

'No, Britain.'

'Oh, Britain very good. Willcome, willcome!'

I made a conscious effort not to lose my temper over the breakdown of the camera, which would have been unfair as well as pointless. I knew the others must be feeling equally disappointed: there was nothing for it but to go on. Ahead of us, the twin water towers which are Kuwait's most obvious landmark soared into the sky, apparently undamaged, although many buildings, including two big seaside hotels on our right, showed obvious signs of destruction. But it was the sight of the Kuwaitis themselves which made the breakdown of the camera so frustrating. They were not actually dancing in the streets, but they looked as if they might at any moment, and they were certainly extremely happy. The broad boulevard which runs along the waterfront from the American Embassy towards the British Embassy was thick with people celebrating their new-found freedom. Cars packed with grinning, flag-waving citizens raced up and down, horns blaring. We did not know exactly where we were going but we were suddenly rewarded by the sight of the CBS satellite dish and white Land Rover and a number of ITN people, including Alastair Stewart and Peter Sharp, clustered round them. We had shot nothing in the desert, so our interest in the satellite dish was academic. But as we stood watching the Kuwaitis enjoying themselves,

271

I suddenly spotted three young, unmistakably British women walking past.

'Excuse me, are you British by any chance?'

'Yes, we are, all of us.'

'Well, isn't that a stroke of luck. Were you here during the occupation?'

'Yes,' said the prettiest one, Lorraine. 'We were all here the whole time.'

'We're from ITN,' I said by way of an introduction. 'I'd be very interested in doing the first interview with you.'

'Yes, why not?' Lorraine said. She asked where we were going and when I said the International, offered us a lift.

'Was it pretty grim?' I asked, as we walked down the road towards their car.

They looked at one another. 'Not really,' they giggled. 'It wasn't too bad, at all.'

'Come on,' I said. 'You must be joking.'

'No, honestly, the Iraqis didn't bother us very much. It was the men they were looking for.'

I did not believe them, putting their sang-froid down to good old British understatement: I was confident that the real story would emerge later. They dropped us off at the International Hotel, opposite the American Embassy, saying they would come back and fetch us later. The hotel, that first day, was little more than an empty shell in which nothing worked: no light, water, food and hardly any staff. But within a matter of hours, the media had taken the place over and established communications with the outside world. Like so much else in Kuwait, the Iraqis had destroyed the front entrance, so we had to walk up the back stairs from the car park, emerging into the open air to the deafening roar of portable generators. Someone shouted in our ear that ITN was 'over there', in the fitness centre, next door to the empty swimming pool, and just below a convenient flat roof on which the Sky satellite dish, shared by ITN, and our INMARSAT satellite telephone, which gave us

272

instant communication with London, were already operating. It was from this flat roof that we fed all our material; our reports of the liberation of the city; and live links and interviews.

It was only as darkness fell that I realised the full extent of the shambles in which the Iraqis had left Kuwait. There was no power in the city at all, which meant no light, no water, and no public telephones. As we drove to the block of flats in which Lorraine and one of the other girls lived, we passed the still smoking hulk of the electricity generating plant which the invaders had blown up as their parting gift; and every bridge and overpass was disfigured by an ugly rash of concrete pill boxes. From the top of some of the overpasses we saw scattered points of orangey-red in the distance, our first glimpse of the oil fires burning in the desert. Lorraine was the girlfriend of a friendly Kuwaiti Air Lines pilot called Aws, pronounced like house in cockney, who had also stayed on, and acted as a courier for the resistance. When he discovered that Steve and I had nowhere to stay, he offered us beds in the empty flat below his and said we could eat with them. He also offered us the first drink we had had in months, which was hugely appreciated. More than that, Aws and a friend volunteered to act as chauffeur-guides for ITN, driving us around the city in their own cars. When I suggested to Aws that we should pay for the service, he waved it away. 'No, we don't want any money. We're glad to see you here and we're happy to do it for the country.'

Next day, the British Ambassador, Michael Weston who, with his consul, Laurie Banks, had stayed on doggedly in the Embassy for months, despite Iraqi attempts to get rid of them by cutting off their power and water supply, arrived to see Lorraine. She had acted as the unofficial chronicler of the British who stayed behind, and had kept a detailed list of names and movements. Weston did not know that we were lying in wait for him, and got a surprise when he stepped through the door to find himself bathed in the glare of television lights, being filmed by ITN. But he recovered well and gave us a good interview, the most interesting part of which was his statement that the British Government was anxious to see a rapid move on the part of the Emir towards free elections. He told me later that, although this was absolutely true, he had his wrist slapped by the Foreign Office for saying so.

The next few days were hectic and fascinating. The hundreds of journalists who had been reporting the war from various vantage points in the Gulf poured into Kuwait like an army of ants, penetrating every corner of the city, searching for stories and devouring every blade of information they came across. But almost immediately, ITN started bombarding us with requests to go to Basra where bloody fighting was reported in the wake of a Shia rebellion against Saddam.

Sue Tinson waylaid me as I walked into the office.

'London's been on again about Basra. They're desperate to get someone up there.'

'I'm quite happy to go,' I said. 'But tomorrow. It must be planned properly. Otherwise, the whole thing will end in tears.'

I had just interviewed a young friend of Aws's, called Al Khubaisi, who said he had been arrested as a suspected member of the resistance and beaten up by the Iraqi army. On a day made as dark and cold as a January day in Britain by the pall of smoke from the oil fires hanging over the city, he led us to a sports centre where, he said, suspects had been interrogated. He himself had been held in one of the changing rooms under the squash courts.

The place was deserted, and over it hung something of the sinister silence that I remembered from Tuol Sleng, the Khmer Rouge interrogation and extermination centre in Phnom Penh. 'This was the main entrance where we were checked in,' he said pointing to an office behind a huge plate glass window. The whole window was sandbagged, from floor to ceiling, leaving only the door free. As we stood beside it, wondering how we were going to get in, we noticed a black electric wire running from under the door to the far end of the entrance hall.

'Don't touch the door,' he said. 'You never know, the bastards may have booby trapped it.' He disappeared downstairs and a few minutes later shouted up to us. 'It's okay this way, you can come down.' There were several rooms at the foot of a narrow staircase, half underground. He opened one door, carefully. 'This is the room where I was kept,' he said, looking round the bare walls. 'This is where they beat me up. They took us out to interrogate us, one at a time. If you didn't give them the answers they wanted, they hit you. With their hands, with a stick, with kicks. There were three or four of them, they took it in turns. This went on for several days, but I didn't tell them anything and then, one day, they released me. I don't know why. I think they just got bored.'

On the way back to the International in his big black Japanese four-wheel drive, I mentioned the Basra idea to him. 'Do you know anyone who could take us, who knows the area?'

'Sure,' he said. 'I'll take you.'

'That's very kind, but can we get across without being arrested?'

'Sure, we can. When you wanna go?'

'Tomorrow.'

'Fine.'

When we got back to the office, I introduced him and mentioned that he was willing to take me to the border. I was busy for the next hour, editing his story and writing the commentary. In the meantime, unknown to me, he was asked if he would go with Andrew Simmons and Mike Gillings, agreed, and they left almost immediately. When I found out what had happened, I felt quite relieved. I knew, instinctively, that it was going to be a nasty assignment. I also understood the reasoning behind the decision: they were free, I was busy, and we were under intense pressure from ITN in London to cover the Basra rebellion which, with the war now over, was the big story.

As promised, Al Khubaisi took them to the border, but in the general confusion, was unable to prevent them being arrested. After waiting at the border for some time, he drove back to Kuwait and reported what had happened. I asked him what had gone wrong. 'I told them not to go over the border,' he said. 'I saw those Iraqi army guys standing on the border and I knew they were bad news. I was in front, see, and when we reached the border post, I stopped. But your friends came up and passed me and then drove over. I tried to warn them, but either they didn't hear or didn't understand what I was saying. After they were arrested, they were driven away and I didn't see them again. I'm sorry for your friends, but there was nothing I could do.'

Simmons and Gillings were taken to Basra and held by the Iraqis for what must have been a very frightening ten days. Luckily, they emerged unscathed, losing only their jeep, which predictably the Iraqis stole.

The Basra rebellion began when the Shia resistance stormed the prison, killing the guards and the governor, and liberating hundreds of prisoners, including a splendid, retired British colonel. He was one of the many British who went underground when the Iraqis invaded Kuwait, hiding in his own house and being supplied with food and drink by Kuwaiti friends. He would almost certainly have got away with it had not a neighbour with a grudge, an Egyptian, betrayed him to the Iraqis. He was arrested and told he would be sent to Baghdad as part of Saddam's 'human shield', but for some reason got no farther than Basra where he was locked up in a hugely overcrowded cell, in filthy conditions. When the prison was seized by the rebels, the gallant colonel was freed along with hundreds of other prisoners, walking out of the jail straight into the chaotic streets of Basra.

'It was a bloodbath,' he told me, describing his escape. 'The Iraqi army were slaughtering people indiscriminately. You could get shot for nothing at all. I saw someone being killed for driving on the wrong side of the road. We managed to get out of the city, on foot and started walking in the direction of Kuwait. Luckily, after a couple of days someone came along and gave us a lift.' It had taken the colonel, who must have been closer to seventy than sixty, several days to reach Kuwait City and safety. When I saw him the day after his arrival, he looked remarkably untouched by his gruelling experience, and was impeccably turned out in immaculate riding breeches and highly-polished brown riding boots.

Having missed out on the Basra story, I devoted myself to trying to find out exactly what had gone on during the occupation. The first thing I discovered was that reports of looting, wilful destruction and sheer vindictiveness had been, if anything, underplayed. The looting and the 'trashing' that went with it were the most obvious aspects of the Iraqi invasion and, as Laurie Banks explained to me, could be divided into three distinct phases. 'First, you got what you might call the VIP looting. Saddam Hussein and his cronies earmarked certain valuable things, a big computer, racehorses, valuable *objets d'art*, whatever they wanted, and gave orders for them to be shipped out, straight to Baghdad. Then there was the army. They took the obvious things, televisions, video recorders, telephones, and cars, especially cars, thousands and thousands, a lot of them brand new, and just drove them out of the country. Thirdly, there were the organised, criminal gangs. They came down from Basra and Baghdad, in removal vans, headed straight for a warehouse and loaded up the entire contents, personal computers, fridges, you name it. The lot.'

The Iraqis were motivated by envy and hatred as well as

277

greed. Every house belonging to the Al Sabah, the ruling family, was looted and then deliberately trashed. One day, Geoff, a British expatriate who worked in Kuwait for a number of years, asked me if I would like to have a look round the city. We drove first to the centre, where the Sheraton and Meridien Hotels had been looted and then set on fire, the flames leaving great black scorch marks on the outside of the buildings. Then we drove to the Sief Palace, a pleasantly old-fashioned fortress on the sea. 'This is the oldest palace,' Geoff said. 'It's the main working palace, a bit like Buck House.' A tall clock tower rose majestically above the battlements, to the right of the entrance. The clock had stopped.

There was no guard on the gate and we simply walked in. Signs of destruction were everywhere, most of it wanton, for there had been little fighting here. We climbed the stairs, treading on broken glass and mosaics, and walked down a long, spacious corridor. 'Look at this,' Geoff said, stopping half way. I peered into a room on the left and mastered an impulse to recoil. The room was empty but carpeted, and there, in a row along one wall, were piles of human excrement. The Iraqi occupiers had used the room as a public lavatory not, I suspected, because there was no alternative, but with the express intention of degrading the palace and its owners. We walked to the end of the corridor which opened out into a large room looking out over the placid waters of the Gulf. Like the rest of the palace it had been looted but less obviously trashed, probably because it was of some practical use. 'The Iraqis used it as a look-out post,' Geoff said. 'They were pretty worried they were going to be attacked from the sea. I imagine they spent a lot of time keeping an eye on the Gulf.' He laughed.

On our way back, at the top of the stairs, we met two Kuwaitis, one of whom, as soon as he heard us speaking English, expressed his feelings forcibly. 'It is really disgusting, what the Iraqis did here. They behaved like savages. You have seen the throne room?' he asked.

'Not yet.'

'You must. It is one of the most . . .' he struggled for words . . . 'depressing sights I have ever seen. It tells you everything about these people.' We walked on a few yards, came to a large doorway and found ourselves gazing at a picture of destruction which almost beggared description: it was like a scene from the Blitz. The once handsome room had been wrecked with rare viciousness. The mosaics which had covered the walls had been ripped down and lay crushed on the carpet; a huge mirror was shattered in a thousand pieces; the furniture, including what must have been the Al Sabah's throne, was scattered and smashed as if caught in a cyclone; papers and files lay everywhere, and then in a last act of vandalism the place had been set on fire. Perhaps the Iraqis had tried to burn down the palace, but failed to do the job properly in their haste to get away.

Historically, conquerors had always razed whole cities and massacred their populations. Alexander the Great had done it when his patience snapped; Genghis Khan did it as a matter of course, believing that cities were evil, since they interfered with the grazing of his horses, on which his power was based. But Alexander lived more than two thousand years ago and Genghis Khan more than 700 years ago. Saddam had wreaked his vengeance on fellow Arabs whose only crime was to be richer and more successful than he was; and whose biggest mistake, apart from lending him money and then expecting to be repaid, was to have the temerity to exist at all. Like some Middle East Al Capone, he thought he could 'rub out' his tiny, virtually defenceless neighbour, and get away it. He was a political gangster whose only way of dealing with his opponents was to murder them.

The looting and defacing of the Sief Palace epitomised the contempt which Saddam obviously felt for the Kuwaitis, but

279

it was demonstrated in more brutal ways. In the days that followed liberation, many stories were told of how the Iraqis had tortured young Kuwaiti resistants, many of them women. In some cases, it was said, the Iraqis cut off the women's breasts and then dumped their bodies outside their own front doors, a common Iraqi tactic to cow anyone else who might be thinking of resisting.

It was Aws who had introduced me to Al Khubaisi and he now came to me with a very strange story. 'There's a girl living in this block who was a nurse in one of the hospitals. She says that she killed a number of Iraqi soldiers who were brought into the hospital for treatment.'

'Killed them? How?' I asked, disbelievingly.

'By injections. She says a lot of them were quite badly wounded. When she saw her chance, she gave them an injection. A lot of them died.'

'How many?'

'I'm not sure. Ten or twenty, something like that. You can talk to her yourself. She's an intelligent girl, from a good Kuwaiti family.'

At first sight, she looked as if she would not have the nerve to stick a pin in a pin cushion, let alone give a wounded Iraqi soldier a lethal injection. But although I talked to her and then interviewed her on camera at considerable length, I could not shake her story, although I still do not know if I believe it. She was small, demure, self-controlled, in her early twenties, dressed in drab, Arab clothes, wearing a headscarf and no make-up: not the kind of girl to make men turn their heads. She said that after the Iraqi invasion, when thousands of Palestinian and other skilled immigrant workers left Kuwait, there had been an acute shortage of nurses. Although she only had first-aid training, she answered the call for volunteers and was enrolled in one of the main hospitals where she worked under an Iraqi doctor, who had lived in Kuwait for several years.

280

'A lot of Iraqi soldiers were brought in to the hospital, some of them badly hurt. Sometimes they had been shot by the resistance, sometimes they had been in a car smash. I would wait until no one was around, then I would choose one of the soldiers and give him an injection.'

'Weren't you afraid that you would be seen by one of the other staff, and exposed?'

'We were short of staff, and very often I was alone in the ward. I would choose a soldier who was very ill, maybe unconscious. Some of them would probably have died anyway.'

'How did you know what sort of injection to give them to kill them?'

'A friend of mine, a chemist, who was in the resistance, gave me the drug and showed me exactly how much to use. You see, I had to give the patients medication anyway. Some of them received injections to make them sleep, or for some other reason, so it wasn't very difficult.'

'How many did you kill, altogether?'

She wrinkled up her brow, and without any change of tone or expression, said, 'About twenty, but I'm not sure of the exact number.'

'What about the ethics of what you were doing? As a nurse, shouldn't you have been saving lives and not killing people, even if they were Iraqis?'

She looked at me coldly. 'We were fighting a war. The Iraqis were our enemy. They tortured and killed hundreds of Kuwaitis, including many of my friends. I was fighting for my country, for the liberation of Kuwait. I did not think of myself as a nurse. I was a member of the resistance, a soldier.'

I discussed her veracity with Aws. He believed her. 'I know the family, and I know the girl. She is very independent. She has a flat of her own, she didn't want to live at home. I know she was close to the resistance, maybe the

281

Iraqis did something to her, something that affected her mind.

'You mean, you think she'd a bit mad?'

'I don't know. But I believe her. I think she's telling the truth.'

We ran it on *News at Ten*, and it caused quite a sensation. It was certainly an intriguing document.

Chapter
18

By the beginning of 1992 the Afghan war had virtually disappeared from the television screens and even from the foreign pages of serious newspapers. The much-publicised withdrawal of the Red Army in 1989 had led to a rapid decline in world interest, especially when it became apparent that there would be no quick mujahideen victory over the man the Russians left in charge, President Najibullah. Trained by the KGB and a former head of Khad, the Afghan secret police, 'The Ox', as he was nicknamed, looked increasingly secure, especially after the Jalalabad fiasco. The Russians, conscious of the knock-on effect that a collapse in Kabul would have on the rest of their empire, were generous in their support of their successor. When they withdrew across Friendship Bridge with bands playing and flags waving, they left behind hundreds of tanks, long-range guns, helicopters and even MiG fighter-bombers, with enough money to maintain them and pay the wages of the tough, tribal militias on whom Najibullah came increasingly to depend.

The Russian subsidy to the Kabul Government had been running at around £200 million a month for several years, and cannot have dropped much below that in 1990 and 1991, after the withdrawal. But then, in an agreement with the Americans for which the tortuous phrase 'negative symmetry' was coined, both sides stopped funding and supplying arms to their respective clients. The Americans made their last arms shipment to the mujahideen in October 1991; the Russians said they stopped sending arms to Kabul on 15 December, although the mujahideen disputed this and claimed there were some late deliveries. But both sides had such large stockpiles that the embargo had little immediate significance. More important was the general collapse of the Soviet empire at home and abroad, and the chilling realisation in Kabul that with the Russians unwilling and indeed unable to come to their rescue across the border, they were now very much on their own. Najibullah, who until now had played his cards with considerably more skill than the disunited and disorganised mujahideen leaders in Peshawar, suddenly started to make mistakes.

In the new climate of political uncertainty, and nervous about the reliability of his northern, non-Pashtun commanders, Najibullah decided to replace a key figure, General Momen. Momen was the commander of Hairatan, the Afghan port on the Oxus at the southern end of Friendship Bridge, opposite Termesz, the railhead in Uzbekistan. It was through the marshalling yards and harbours of Termesz–Hairatan that the bulk of the Red Army's supplies had flowed throughout the war, and the Hairatan–Kabul road was still Najibullah's lifeline. Down it came the petrol and aviation fuel which kept his army and air force in action, and when the mujahideen later cut the road, there were acute shortages in the capital and a sharp rise in the price of food and fuel. Although he had no means of knowing it, Najibullah was right in suspecting General Momen's reliability. A Tajik speaker like Masud himself, Momen had been for several years in close and secret contact with Masud, who once said to me: 'If you knew the names of all the high-ranking people who support us in Kabul, especially those in the Defence Ministry, you would be surprised.' Momen was clearly one of them.

Like most dictators who depend on their generals for their survival, Najibullah was in close personal contact with his senior commanders. He rang Momen personally to tell him he was replacing him and ordered him to hand over his command to his successor, a Pashtun. An extraordinary thing now happened. To Najibullah's surprise and fury, Momen refused to resign his command and sat tight. His fellow generals in the north supported him, including the formidable figure of General Rashid Dostam, the commander of the Uzbek militia, the most feared and most effective fighting force on the government side. Confronted with a situation that had all the makings of a mutiny, Najibullah tried desperately to reach a compromise, offering to transfer General Juma Azek, the unpopular commander of Mazar-i-Sharif, the second most important city in Afghanistan. By the end of February, negotiations were close to success when Najibullah demanded that General Dostam and other militia commanders drop their support for Momen. When they refused, the talks collapsed and Najibullah reinstated General Azek, which infuriated Dostam. Rebellion was now open, with the northern generals negotiating with Masud, who had been brought into the struggle by Momen. It was the new alliance between Masud and Dostam which was to bring about the fall of Mazar-i-Sharif, and eventually of Najibullah himself.

Dostam was an impressive figure, larger than life, who from humble beginnings had risen to be one of Najibullah's most important warlords. He was born in a small village near the town of Samangan, south-east of Mazar-i-Sharif, joined the army as a simple soldier and rose rapidly through the ranks, ending up at the head of the Uzbek militia, popularly known as the Kilim Jam. In their distinctive uniform of green and blue check turbans, long, olive-green shirts and baggy trousers, and sandals, they were the regime's shock troops, thrown in whenever the going was rough, and used to stiffen the garrisons of government-held towns like Khost, Ghazni, Jalalabad and Kandahar against mujahideen attack. Dostam boasted to me that they were never defeated. 'We drove off all the mujahideen attacks. They never captured any city that we held. That is why Gulbuddin [Gulbuddin Hekmatyar, the Hisb-i-Islami leader] is frightened of us. We killed many of his mujahideen.'

Kilim Jam means literally 'roll up the carpet' in Farsi, and by extension, 'to make disappear'. Because of their prowess in looting as well as fighting – the Kilim Jam pillaged half of Kabul when the city fell to the mujahideen, cleaning out one whole street in the carpet bazaar – they became known as the 'carpet stealers'. The Russians trained and armed them well, and despite looking and behaving like wild tribesmen, the Kilim Jam were highly professional when it came to handling Russian tanks, APCs and artillery. Their alliance with Masud's Panjsheri veterans was to prove an unstoppable force and after a short, sharp battle, Mazar-i-Sharif fell to them on the afternoon of 18 March. It was a mortal blow to the crumbling Najibullah regime and, in its speed and consequences, reminded me forcibly of the collapse of the South Vietnamese regime in 1975. There, it was the northern city-base of Danang which went first, and quickly led to a general rout. In Afghanistan, curiously, it was another northern city-base, Mazar-i-Sharif, which was the first to go, bringing down the rest of the dominoes in rapid succession. But whereas it was the Communists who triumphed in Vietnam, here it was the anti-Communists who won the day. In both cases, the final collapse was surprisingly swift.

Despite the Kilim Jam's reputation for looting, General Dostam was quick to stamp it out in his own 'capital' of Mazar-i-Sharif. Three looters were hauled before a drumhead court and hanged in public. This was seen by some United Nations personnel in the city, who recounted the incident to Christopher Thomas, the Delhi correspondent of *The Times*. I asked Dostam much later if it was true. 'Yes,' he said, and held up three fingers. The UN men also told Thomas that Dostam ordered an alleged rapist to be staked down on the ground and run over by a tank, from the feet up so that the wretched man could see his own death approaching. I do not know if this is true, but no more looting or raping was reported in Mazar-i-Sharif after that.

At the beginning of April, Masud's forces began to topple the dominoes on the road to Kabul. First to go, on 13 April, were the government posts south of the Salang Tunnel, one of the highest road tunnels in the world and the vital link between Kabul and the north of Afghanistan. Whoever held the Salang controlled the fate of Kabul. The next day Masud's men captured the big army base at Jebel Seraj, and ten miles to the south the busy town of Charikar, capital of Parwan Province, only thirty miles from Kabul. It was on that day, a Tuesday, as it happened, that I had arranged to see Mike Jermey, ITN's Foreign Editor, at ten o'clock in his office in Gray's Inn Road. Over breakfast that morning I had, as usual, read *The Times*, my eye being caught particularly by a report from Christopher Thomas in Kabul. In it he described very clearly what I had only sensed had been happening; that since the fall of Mazar-i-Sharif in March, the Najibullah regime had been stumbling from one disaster to another, and that after all these years of patient, piece-meal plodding, it really looked as if Masud was on the brink of capturing Kabul.

I concluded a brief resumé of the situation by saying, 'We ought to get to Kabul as soon as possible because, in my view, the situation is changing very fast and the fall of the city is now a very real possibility.' Mike Jermey needed very little persuading; he had also read the reports in that morning's papers, and jumping up from his desk with me following, marched over to the Foreign Desk and gave the orders which launched the ITN operation. It was to turn out

287

to be a big one: three reporters and crews, two video editors plus editing equipment, a producer, and a full complement of engineers: about twenty people in all, plus one and a half tons of satellite equipment. Our own satellite ground station, complete with portable generators, ensured we had instant communications, regardless of the situation in Kabul. This turned out to be a wise move because, when fighting started in the city, it became impossible to reach the local TV station and the entire foreign media corps, including the BBC and CNN, had to rely on ITN's communications.

Despite the initial speed of the response, my team and I did not reach Kabul until ten days later, partly because of visa and other delays, and partly because of the ITN foreign desk's concern that my unpopularity with the Najibullah regime might queer the pitch of the other reporter and crew who were alerted the first day. It was therefore decided, rightly or wrongly, that Paul Davies and his team, Chris Squires and Russell Padwick, should head straight for Delhi, where they would hope to pick up an Ariana Afghan Airways flight – a route they had used before – while Nigel Thomson, Patrick O'Ryan Roeder and I should fly to Dubai on the very dubious chance of being able to charter to Kabul. When that turned out to be impossible, we flew to Islamabad, where I thought, wrongly as it turned out, that we might be able to wangle a seat on a Pakistan Air Force or United Nations plane. Next day, Sunday, having considered and rejected the possibility of trying to reach Kabul by road over the Khyber Pass, we rang ITN's efficient travel expert, Jay, at home and sought his help. 'Give me a couple of hours,' he said, 'and I'll call you from the office.' He did, to say that since Delhi seemed to be the only way in, we should fly immediately to Karachi where we could catch a late evening flight to Delhi. We did so, arriving in Delhi early on Monday, having been travelling almost continuously for more than forty-eight hours, via five different airports: Heathrow, Dubai, Islamabad, Karachi, and Delhi.

When we reached the Taj Palace Hotel at two in the morning I was upset to discover that the other team of Davies, Squires and Padwick had managed to get on one of the few flights to Kabul and had flown in the previous day. Worse news was to follow: the next flight from Delhi to Kabul was heavily oversubscribed and we were so far down the waiting list that the disagreeable Indian clerk in the Ariana office informed us smugly that we had no chance at all of getting on. We started dropping hints about paying in dollars, which produced a flicker of interest. Tuesday came and went with no news and then on Wednesday the Ariana clerk, now slightly less disagreeable, said there would be a flight the next day. 'What about the waitlist?' we asked. 'There is no waiting list,' came the airy reply. 'This is special plane for the press.' That evening, ITN reinforcements arrived in the shape of Penny Marshall, with Paul Carleton, whom I had last seen in the Gulf, one of ITN's most experienced cameramen, and his sound recordist, and Peter Heeps, the chief engineer, with his satellite team and one and a half tons of equipment.

That night, we passed a convivial evening together, knowing it would be the last for some time, and drove to the airport at six next morning to make absolutely sure we were on the Ariana flight. A scrum of television crews and journalists was already shoving hard against the Ariana desk, struggling to catch the attention of two harried-looking officials, one of whom was our now fairly agreeable friend. Eventually, after half an hour of pushing and arguing, we managed to check in. We took off at ten in a rickety old Antonov: Ariana then had only three ageing airliners, two Antonovs and a Boeing 737.

It is a short but spectacular hop to Kabul by way of Pakistan, the Khyber Pass and the snowy peaks of the Hindu Kush. I looked down at them with awe and amazement, wondering how on earth I had ever managed to walk and climb over their vast and utterly hostile expanse for weeks on end, not only in summer but once in winter as well. In little over an hour we were descending towards the Afghan capital which sits in a wide green saucer-shaped valley, surrounded by a ring of mountains, eight to ten thousand feet high, all white from a recent snowfall. In the final stages of the descent, the plane went into a steep dive, a trick learned by pilots in the war to dodge missiles and anti-aircraft fire. We stepped out into bright sunshine and were met inside the terminal by Peter Read, an old friend and senior editor, and Nick Atkins, a young producer.

It was twenty-one years since I had been in Kabul, but at first glance it did not look very different: more battered and bruised, undoubtedly, the taxis even older and more decrepit, and the airport bore the scars of many rocket attacks. As we stood in line to show our passports to a non-existent immigration official – the only one on duty had gone off to attend to the party of a minister who had been on the same plane – I saw my first members of the Dostam militia, two young Uzbeks. They walked with a devil-may-care swagger, Kalashnikovs dangling loosely from one hand, long hair flowing from beneath their turbans, their bare feet thrust into sandals. They looked what they were, tough and simple tribesmen from the northern plains, descendants of the Mongol hordes who rode with Genghis Khan to lay waste half of Asia and raze its cities in one of the most ruthless campaigns of conquest the world has seen. They and Masud's men, who looked like the Brigade of Guards by comparison, jointly controlled the airport, and much of the city. I was glad they were on our side.

We drove into Kabul, raddled by twelve years of occupation and war, with only the Royal Palace, which looked like a Swiss resort hotel, lending a note of Ruritanian glamour. Then up the hill to the Intercontinental, where I had stayed for a night in 1971 on my way home from the Indo-Pakistan war. It seemed little changed, perched on a ridge with a superb view of the city, and crowded with journalists. At the entrance we were greeted by a splendidly-attired, mous-tachioed doorman, two liveried porters and a small boy dressed in mujahideen uniform, toting a Kalashnikov almost as big as himself. I was anxious, after all these delays, to get to grips with the story as soon as possible. My assignment was to find Masud and stick to him, while Paul Davies and Penny Marshall covered the Kabul story. Over mediocre lamb kebab and a glass of beer, I discovered, to my enormous relief, that Masud was still outside Kabul, in the Charikar area. I had been desperately worried that, after all these years reporting the Afghan war I would, because of all the delays, miss the finale: the fall of Kabul and Masud's entry into the city.

At half past three, having been found transport by Nick Atkins, and acquired some afghanis, the local currency, Nigel, Patrick, Nick and I left for Charikar. We took Nick and Patrick with us, but not his large edit suite, since it looked highly likely that we would have to operate a shuttle service from wherever we found Masud to the satellite point in Kabul. Nick and Patrick would act as couriers for the material and Patrick would edit when they got back to Kabul. Editors normally spend their time sitting in hotel rooms in front of an edit machine, seeing little of the world outside, so Patrick was delighted to come with us.

Our driver was called Rashid, an ingratiating young man in his mid-twenties who said he wanted to work for us so that he could improve his knowledge of English, although I suspect the real reason was the large amount of money he hoped to make out of us. Owing to the shortage of taxis and an even more acute shortage of drivers who were prepared to risk their lives and vehicles driving television crews, journalists and photographers around, prices were sky high. The daily rate was $100 for Kabul; $200 for the airport; and $300 for places outside the capital, such as Charikar. In normal times, of course, it would have cost only a few afghanis, but Kabul was on the brink of civil war. Rashid had a battered old orange Volkswagen Kombi which, although roomy, had the disadvantage of being unable, except with great difficulty, to exceed thirty miles an hour. We had been told to take the old road to Charikar, avoiding the new Salang Highway because of unfriendly roadblocks, but when Rashid lost his way leaving the city, we realised he not only did not know the old road from the new but clearly had never been outside Kabul before. His total ignorance, coupled with the dreadful state of the roads, made our progress painfully slow.

We passed through a number of roadblocks manned by Masud's men, which presented no difficulty, and had no trouble until we reached the outskirts of Bagram, thirty miles north of Kabul, once renowned for its archaeological sites, but now better known for its air base, the biggest in the country. Here we were stopped by mujahideen belonging to Gulbuddin Hekmatyar, Masud's bitterest rival. Their weasel-faced commander stuck his head through my window and after sizing us up and asking where we were going, demanded money. I shrugged and said, 'Sorry, no money.' He clearly did not believe me and switched his attention to Rashid. Not being a proper Kabul taxi driver, Rashid gave in and handed over 5000 afghanis (about $5). Perhaps he felt he had no choice, for we knew that a number of journalists had been turned back at this particular road-block and at least the sweetener got us through.

When we reached the Bagram crossroads, things became more serious. Several armed mujahideen lounging beside an APC demanded to know where we were going. While Rashid was doing his best to satisfy their curiosity, an *exalté* with wild hair and unkempt beard appeared and started shouting at us, eyes rolling. Rashid translated as best he could. 'He says they don't want foreign journalists here, in Afghanistan, and we must turn back.' As the man continued to pace up and down in front of the Kombi, several bystanders approached and, making apologetic noises, tapped their foreheads with their forefingers. Rashid sniggered. 'They say this man is . . . madman. Take no notice. He is, how you say, crazy.'

Others now joined the argument, some saying we should get a permit from Farah, the local Hisb commander; others that we should go on. A new man appeared and, perfectly politely, asked once again, where we were going.

'To Charikar.'

'Why do all you foreign journalists want to go to Charikar, to see Masud.' It was a statement, not a question. 'Are we not just as good? Are we not mujahideen too? Why do you not take pictures of us, too?'

We protested that we did want to take their pictures as well. 'We will take your picture when we come back, tomorrow,' I said not altogether convincingly.

We reached Charikar as the sun was setting, threading our way through a stream of traffic, Russian army jeeps packed with bearded mujahideen, lorries, horse-drawn carts, heavily-laden donkeys and crowds of people. The shops were open, the teahouses full, Charikar buzzed with the excitement of its recent liberation. At the big roundabout in the centre of the town, Rashid asked where we could find Masud. Someone pointed to the left and we drove up the hill until we saw about a dozen mujahideen in camouflage uniforms – Panjsheris – standing outside a big iron gate. 'This must be it,' I said to Rashid. 'Park anywhere you can.'

Among them I recognised an old friend, Abdul Azim, who had been wounded in the Salang early in the war, losing his left arm. I had met him in 1983 when he came to London to get an artificial replacement with another of Masud's commanders, Abdul Wahid, who had had a foot blown off by a mine. He was later captured by the Russians and executed in Pul-i-Charkhi prison in Kabul. But Azim survived to become one of Masud's most important commanders, described by Masud himself as being 'très dur'.

293

Azim pointed to the house and said we should go inside, and wait for Masud. Not long afterwards the gate swung open, revealing a new, black Japanese jeep with a six-foot aerial, from which stepped a smiling Masud dressed in Russian fatigues, with a Chitrali cap perched on the back of his head. I found him virtually unchanged since our last meeting two and half years before, slightly older perhaps, but with all his old charm. 'Comment allez-vous?' he asked me. 'Je suis très heureux de vous revoir. Quand êtes-vous arrivé?'

'Aujourd'hui même,' I said, and introduced the rest of the team to him. He beckoned us to follow him inside and as soon as I had the chance, I explained we were very anxious to satellite a report to London the next day. Could he therefore give me an interview before midday? He said, yes, and invited us to have supper, although he did not join us. After a very good Kabuli *palau* of rice, pieces of lamb and raisins, cooked in a light vegetable oil, we were taken to a nearby villa belonging to a rich merchant where we were to spend the night in the large and comfortable guest room. We slept on mattresses on the floor, of course: outside Kabul, few Afghan houses have beds.

Our host, a tall, distinguished-looking greybeard, came to welcome us, complained of a headache and asked if we could give him something. This is normal practice in Afghanistan, since throughout the war drugs were scarce and any foreigner was always presumed to be well-supplied. Nick produced one tablet and gave it to him, which he clearly thought was not enough. But Nick refused to be bullied, and after inspecting our sleeping bags with interest, our friend retired. I had already crawled into mine, an act which nearly always afforded me a moment of unalloyed bliss, and was soon asleep. It had been a long and eventful day.

Next morning, a week after we had left London, I rose early and started drafting my script for that night's *News at*

Ten report, because I knew there would be little time later. For the same reason Nigel, Nick and Patrick went off filming with Rashid before breakfast: there was plenty of material in Charikar, crowded as it was with mujahideen, packing out the *chaikhanas* and driving their tanks through the town with the snow-covered mountains in the background. These were the outrunners of the Hindu Kush, rising steeply from the Shomali plain, across which I had trudged ten years before before on my way to the Panjsher Valley and my first meeting with Masud. At that point, the last stage of our twelve-day trek from the border, we had travelled mostly at night to avoid being spotted by Russian helicopters, or ambushed by a patrol; it would have been nerve-racking had we not been almost too exhausted to care. We often went without breakfast, but now, alone in the guestroom, I had a copious and delicious breakfast of fried eggs, *nan*, cheese and plums in syrup, and finished off my script.

Masud had said he would arrive between eleven and twelve for the interview but instead he sent a message summoning us to Jebel Seraj, the army base he had captured recently on his drive south from the Salang. Thinking we would have an exclusive, we tried to give the slip to the only other journalist who appeared to be in Charikar, Jean-Paul Marie of the *Nouvel Observateur*, whom I had met in the Gulf. But he was clearly suspicious we were on to something and followed us in his taxi to the base, about ten miles north of Charikar. Twenty or thirty Afghan Army T55 tanks, with their crews, were parked just off the road, another clear sign that Masud was concentrating his forces for the final push on Kabul. After half an hour vainly trying to find Masud, I discovered he was inside an APC, talking on the radio to Gulbuddin Hekmatyar. We caught up with him just as he was coming down the hill from the APC to his headquarters. Falling into step beside him, I explained in French we wanted to satellite the interview from Kabul that evening, so we would like to do the interview straight away. By now

295

we were walking into the headquarters, a rather shoddy collection of temporary buildings.

'Where?' he asked.

'Here,' I said, pointing to a corner.

But he did not like the idea and disappeared into an office with a group of mujahideen commanders and Afghan army officers. The door shut in our faces and we were left there, firmly excluded. As we waited a white Land Rover suddenly drew up outside and, killing stone dead all remaining hopes of an exclusive, disgorged a producer, reporter and crew from BBC *Newsnight*. With civility which you do not normally find in the competitive world of television news, the producer came up to me and said since they were not in any hurry, they had no intention of interfering with whatever we were doing. I was still thanking him when the door of the office into which Masud and his commanders had disappeared was flung open. Immediately, everyone surged forward, the BBC crew well to the fore. Confronted with this barrage, Masud hesitated and then retreated, allowing everybody to follow him into the office. At the back of the queue by this time, we were forced to stand and listen while an impromptu press conference started.

Nigel, seeing the story slipping away from him, became extremely agitated, urging me to do something. But what? Nick and I tried to get a young official who spoke some English to intervene, but he was too overawed to do so. Finally, as the minutes ticked up to and past our deadline, and Nigel became more and more agitated, I interjected in French, asking if we might interrupt the press conference for ten minutes to do our interview with Masud. There was a startled pause, then Masud said.

'It's up to your colleagues.'

No one said anything, so I repeated. 'It will take only ten minutes, and then you can resume the press conference.'

Still no one objected, so Masud got up and followed us outside the room to where Nigel, somehow, had pushed a

296

sofa into the corner. I gestured for Masud to sit down, while I squatted in front of him. Everyone else had followed us out, and they crowded round. Someone produced a chair, I sat down and the interview started. It was not an easy interview for anyone and perhaps because of that Masud was exceptionally cagey – usually he is extremely frank. He refused to be drawn on whether the formation of a mujahideen government would go ahead without the co-operation of Gulbuddin, but was clear about one thing. He, Masud, would not enter Kabul himself unless Gulbuddin 'attacked' it, or sent his troops into the city. If, however, Gulbuddin did, he would oppose him.

While we had been waiting for Masud, I bumped into Commander Panna, a fellow Panjsheri and one of his most dashing commanders, and asked him when he expected Masud to enter Kabul. 'Soon, very soon,' he replied with a grin. I wondered if he was indulging in wishful thinking, but I had known Panna as long as I had known Masud; he was brave and honest, and I was inclined to believe him.

Immediately after the interview with Masud, we left for Charikar, where I recorded my commentary and voiced-over the interview. This did not take long and within an hour Nick and Patrick were ready to set off for Kabul, leaving Nigel and me behind. At the last minute, Rashid started prevaricating, saying he wanted to talk to me. Since I was sure it was about money, I refused, saying it was vital that he get back to Kabul as soon as possible. He was already being paid $300 a day, plus food and petrol, and that was quite enough. Temporarily thwarted, Rashid drove off reluctantly and I prayed they would be in time for the feed: it was our first story and the first time, as far as I knew, that anyone from the British media had spoken to Masud since the start of his victorious march south.

Chapter
19

We installed ourselves in the Jamiat office, a former headquarters of Khad, the Afghan secret police, making ourselves as comfortable as possible on the floor in the corner of the guest room, where visitors came and went at all times of the day and even, sometimes, night. That is one of the drawbacks of life à l'Afghan. But the house did have two advantages: a kitchen downstairs, which produced huge quantities of rice twice a day for the ever hungry mujahideen, and a nice garden. Masud, who had a bedroom-cum-office at the far end of the garden, suddenly appeared that evening, and after talking to the local worthies who had gathered to greet him came into the guest room where Nigel, Jean-Paul and I were sitting. Without preamble he launched into an extraordinarily frank account of the day's events.

When we had seen him earlier, he told us he had spoken to Gulbuddin Hekmatyar, but not that he had given him an ultimatum. 'We had a long talk, on the radio, and I told him, "Stop your men attacking Kabul or I will enter Kabul myself."' I asked if the ultimatum extended to Gulbuddin agreeing to join the new mujahideen government. He had after all, been nominated as prime minister, while Masud had been appointed defence minister. Masud's answer was, 'If Gulbuddin does not co-operate with the new government, if he continues to attack the city, and if he does not

298

withdraw his troops, I will enter Kabul myself tomorrow morning.'

Did he have the forces to do it?

'Yes, I have 6000 troops in Charikar and tanks and jets in Mazar-i-Sharif and Bagram which I can use against him.' Masud went on, 'During our conversation, Gulbuddin asked me if I was angry. I said, "No, not as angry as you will be later,"' meaning if Gulbuddin ignored the ultimatum. Masud said that he was going to radio Peshawar to find out if Gulbuddin had accepted. We discovered next day that he had been unable to get through and had gone to bed.

Next morning, we heard on the BBC World Service that 'a prominent guerrilla leader', presumably Gulbuddin, was still objecting to the plan for a mujahideen government. It sounded as if confrontation was inevitable. While we hung around waiting for Masud to appear, I sat in the garden writing my diary and enjoying the warm spring sunshine. Sparrows were noisily busy, chasing one another amorously among the bushes, and a swallow or swift darted overhead. Only a few feet in front of me, a plum or apricot tree was thickly covered with the tenderest pink blossom. The long, harsh Afghan winter was over, the fragile beauty of spring was all around us: but, I wondered, would the spring bring with it a bloody offensive?

At about ten, a whole new batch of journalists, along with Rashid, arrived from Kabul, so Nigel and I decided to drive up to Jebel Seraj to see if we could find the elusive Masud. As we were standing outside his headquarters, several helicopters came clattering in from the direction of Bagram and swooped down to land. At first we thought they were bringing people in – VIPs possibly – but one of Masud's staff insisted they were empty. They landed above the headquarters and shortly afterwards Nigel spotted a group of people, who turned out to be soldiers, marching up the hill. We followed and suddenly realised that Masud was

299

about to start airlifting troops to Kabul, as he had said he would the day before if his ultimatum was rejected. A few minutes later, the troops started boarding under the directions of Commander Panna. While Nigel was filming I tried to find out from the pilots where they were going, but could get very little sense out of them. The crews spoke Russian, not English, and my Farsi is almost non-existent, so it was not until Masud arrived that we knew it was definitely Kabul.

I asked him in French, 'Ou envoyez-vous vos troupes?'

'À Kaboul.'

'Aujourd'hui? Maintenant?'

'Aujourd'hui! Maintenant!' He gave a little smile. Then, after a brief talk with the crews, Masud said a prayer and the helicopters started their engines. We retreated down the hill, away from the dust cloud, and watched the Mi8s climbing up towards the sunlit, snow-covered Hindu Kush mountains, before turning south towards Kabul. As we walked down the hill together, Masud explained. 'I'm sending my men to Kabul, not to attack the city, but to control it. Gulbuddin does not agree with my proposals.' In other words, Gulbuddin had rejected the ultimatum calling on him to stop attacking the capital and to join the interim government. Masud was holding a press conference for all the journalists who had driven up from Kabul, but we already had the story, so we told Rashid to take us back to Kabul as fast as he could, which he managed in an hour and a half, arriving at the Intercontinental at three. Patrick cut a very good, if brief, story which, added to the Kabul material, gave our coverage a completeness which no other organisation, including the BBC, could match. We had Paul Davies and Penny Marshall reporting from Kabul itself, where battle was about to be joined, while Nigel Thomson and I provided the other, vital, half of the equation; we were the only media team with Masud throughout the final days of the war.

300

Gulbuddin's latest attempt to take Kabul relied on his usual combination of intrigue backed by force. Having tried to engineer a *coup d'état* against Najibullah with the help of his Defence Minister, Tanai, and the Pakistani ISI in 1990, and failed, the wily Pathan was now attempting a *coup de main*. In these last days of Najibullah's tottering regime, he infiltrated several hundred of his men into Kabul where, with the connivance of the Interior Minister, they were armed and sent out to seize key points in the city. It was this attempt to take Kabul from within which provoked Masud's ultimatum and the decision to fly in troops. Masud also alerted his ally General Dostam in the north and persuaded him to fly several hundred Kilim Jam to Kabul.

In the weeks preceding this final, hectic period, the United Nations special envoy, Benon Sevan, had been desperately trying to arrange the resignation of Najibullah and a transfer of power to a group of 'the great and the good', mainly exiled Afghan intellectuals. This scheme had the flaw of having been devised by Benon Sevan and his United Nations team without reference to the main players, the mujahideen commanders in general, and Masud in particular. Benon Sevan's journey to Kabul in early April was doomed to failure. The list of 'the great and the good' he carried in his pocket had no legitimacy in the eyes of people like Masud. For one thing, they had without exception sat out the war in Pakistan or the West, in California or Cologne; for another they were mainly Pashtuns, and Masud like his closest allies, Momen and Dostam, were northerners; Tajiks, or Uzbeks. But most fatal flaw of all, neither Masud nor any other mujahideen leader was prepared to see Najibullah, who had the blood of thousands of mujahideen on his hands, escape so easily.

Benon Sevan returned from Kabul empty-handed, and on the night of 15 April, as the noose tightened, Najibullah made a run for it. He did not even get as far as the airport, where a United Nations plane was waiting to fly him to

Delhi. Warned by one of his generals that the airport was in the hands of General Dostam's green-turbaned militia, the Kilim Jam, Najibullah ordered his driver to take him to Benon Sevan's office, one of the UN's many compounds in Kabul, where he sought political asylum. When he heard the news, General Yaqubi, his Minister of State Security, drew his pistol and shot himself, and the rest of the government either fled or went over to the mujahideen. The collapse which had been so long in coming was in the end as swift as a dagger thrust. Not so Najibullah's own fate: he lingered on in Benon Sevan's office, an embarrassment to the UN and a symbol of the utter defeat of his brutal and unpopular regime.

I was aware of some but not of all these developments that afternoon. My main priority was to get back to Charikar where I had left Nigel Thomson, to make contact with Masud again, since I was determined, after all these years, not to miss the denouement of the Afghan war; and I knew that Masud was the key. I found Rashid having lunch in the dining-room. 'Rashid, I want to leave in half an hour for Charikar. Will you take me?'

'Go to Charikar?' he wailed. 'Now? But it is too late. There is a curfew now. It is too dangerous.'

'Nonsense,' I said. 'The curfew doesn't start until six, and there is no danger. You know that, you've just driven in.' I could see fear and greed struggling for supremacy in his face. Fear won. 'No, the mujahideen will shoot the car. Tomorrow morning we will go.'

'No, I've got to go tonight. I'll get someone else.' As I walked away, angrily, I heard his wail pursuing me. 'Nobody will go tonight. It is too dangerous.'

I went to the front of the hotel where the taxis were parked and said, 'Charikar? Who'll take me to Charikar?' There were not many volunteers. Then, a fat, loutish-looking man approached. 'You want to go Charikar?'

'Yes. How much?'

302

'Four hundred dollars to Charikar. But if we stopped at roadblock and have to turn back, $200.'

'No, $100 if we get turned back.'

'No, $200 if turn back.'

'Sorry,' I said. He turned on his heel and waddled off bad-temperedly. Mr Sakhi, the head receptionist, a distinguished-looking man in his early fifties who could have passed for an ambassador, now appeared. I had taken the precaution of tipping him $100 on arrival. 'Mr Sandy Goll, you need some help?' I explained my predicament, and within a few minutes he had produced a tall, wild-looking character in an extremely dilapidated taxi who agreed to the terms: $400 to Charikar, and nothing if we were stopped and turned back. We left at five – I had acquired a young Englishman, Jason Elliot, who also wanted to go to Charikar and told me could speak Farsi, which he had studied at the London School of Oriental and African Studies. We soon realised that Mr Sakhi's choice of driver was inspired. Wild-looking he may have been, but he was a genuine Kabuli taxi driver who knew all the back doubles and handled the mujahideen on the roadblocks with just the right mixture of firmness and good humour. After the egregious Rashid, his professionalism came as a great relief and, despite the terminal condition of the taxi, he deposited us safely in Charikar at 6.45, just as it was getting dark. He wanted to get back to Kabul as soon as possible, so I paid him his $400 and watched his old rattletrap grind off into the dusk.

Nigel was quite surprised to see me back so soon and reported that all the other media people had left, but that during the afternoon about fifteen tanks had driven up past the house to the hill above. We found out why a little later when tanks and MBRLs started shelling and rocketing Hisb-i-Islami targets, presumably, on the road to Kabul; and then, in the night, I heard a lot of heavy traffic, including tanks, going through Charikar, heading south. Next day, Sunday 26 April, over scrambled eggs and tiny pots of sweet green

303

tea in an extremely dirty *chaikhana*, I suggested Nigel should wait for Peter Heeps and Patrick who were coming to see if it was worth transferring the satellite dish to Charikar, while Jason and I went to Jebel Seraj, which was clearly Masud's base now. Infuriatingly, Masud was not there and one of his wireless operators who spoke some English told me he was in Charikar. When he added that Commanders Panna and Azim were in Kabul, I thought for a horrifying moment that we had missed the boat; the tanks will be in Kabul now, I told myself despairingly. We rushed back to Charikar and, having picked up Nigel who said Patrick and Peter Heeps had not arrived, spent the rest of the morning scouring the town for the elusive Commander. At one point we managed to talk our way into the local Governor's office who summoned an aide and instructed him to find us a jeep and driver.

Thinking that at last we were getting somewhere, we set off in a shiny, new Russian army jeep with high hopes – until the young mujahid driver stopped outside the same Jamiat house from which we had begun our search earlier that morning.

'No, not here,' I exploded. 'This is the Jamiat house. Tell him, Jason, for God's sake.'

Jason, who admitted that his Farsi was rusty, began a rather hesitant explanation. 'He says this is where he was told to take us.'

'Bloody hell. Tell him we want to find Masud. Where's Masud?'

Jason did his best, but without success. 'He doesn't know where Masud is. He wants us to get out here. He has to go somewhere else.'

Beaten, we abandoned the search long enough to have lunch of lamb, beans and rice with the mujahideen and set off again, with Rashid driving now, for Jebel Seraj, where our persistence was finally rewarded. Although Masud was not there, one of his radio operators who recognised me said helicopters were on their way to airlift more troops to Kabul. I asked him if he could call up Masud and ask permission for us either to join him, wherever he was, or to fly on one of the helicopters. 'Wait,' the friendly operator said, and we waited rather anxiously, although as Nigel said, 'the vibes' were good. The answer came in half an hour.

'Commander Masud says he is not going to Kabul at the moment, but you are free to go when you like.'

'Yes, but can we go by helicopter?'

The radio operator went back to Masud's operator and put the question. Although I could not understand exactly what he was saying I could distinguish the words 'Sandy Goll', and 'elicoptair'. In a few minutes the response came back. 'Yes, you can go by helicopter.'

Soon afterwards, eight Afghan Air Force Mi8 troop-carrying helicopters flew in across the plain from Bagram, sending clouds of dust spiralling up from the pad above us. Several hundred of Masud's tough-looking, well-equipped Tajik troops in flat Chitrali caps and camouflage battledress began to move up the hill, ready to board. I went over to tell Rashid that we were going to fly to Kabul in one of the helicopters, so he could leave as soon as he liked. He became extremely agitated. 'You not all going in the 'elicoptair, are you?'

'Yes, we're all going. You'll have to drive back on your own, Rashid.'

'No, no, it is too dangerous. The Hisb will murder me if I go by myself.'

'Don't talk nonsense, Rashid. Why should they murder you?'

'These are very bad men,' Rashid wailed. 'Please, Mr Sandy, send your friend with me.' He pointed at Jason.

But Jason wanted to go in the helicopter. I became impatient. 'Rashid, we must go now. We'll see you in Kabul.' In his anxiety not to let us go, Rashid jumped out of the Kombi, cutting his finger quite badly on the door. It bled profusely until I gave him my handkerchief to wrap round it. For a moment I felt sorry for him, until he trailed after me up the slope, whining.

'Look, Rashid,' I said roughly. 'If you're scared to drive back to Kabul tonight, get a bed here, in Charikar. There are plenty of *chaikhanas* in town. And then you can drive down in the morning.'

'But, Mr Sandy. These people will kill me. They are very bad people, the people in Charikar . . .' His voice pursued me up the hill, but I had had enough.

We made for the lead helicopter, an Mi8 gunship with silvered rocket pods on either side of the fuselage, parked at the left-hand side of the pad. I remembered vividly being rocketed by Mi8s beside the main road from Kabul to the Khyber Pass eight years before, and thought it ironic that we – and Masud's troops – should now be flying in one. About twenty heavily-armed Panjsheris clambered aboard and squeezed themselves on to the canvas seats ranged on either side of two large fuel tanks which occupied most of the floor space. I studied their unhappy faces, and guessed it was the first time any of them had flown in a helicopter. The pilot and co-pilot, wearing Russian-style flying suits boarded last, and shortly afterwards we were airborne, heading for the mountains. It was a dramatic ride, and certainly proved that the pilot had been well trained. We started by flying straight down a narrow funnel of a valley with the great wall of the Hindu Kush ahead of us. The valley narrowed to not much more than a river bed and then to a perpendicular thread of water, the mountains towering above us like skyscrapers. Glancing out of the small window beside me I saw the ground racing to meet us and, with a swoop that left my stomach behind, we skimmed over a jagged ridge of naked rock and went hurtling down the far side. The sense of speed and risk was more exhilarating than anything I had ever experienced, except for riding the

306

Cresta in St Moritz. I glanced at our companions; some of them had turned a faint shade of green and one was rolling his eyes in terror. Down, down we went, following a new valley, right down to the plain where the pilot flattened out and sent us roaring across green meadows only ten feet above the ground. A few minutes later, the lights of Kabul appeared through the dusk, and deciding we were now safe from hostile ground fire, the pilot abandoned his kamikaze style and made a conventional landing.

It was now dark, and after standing about for quarter of an hour not knowing quite what to do, we bumped into a friendly Afghan general who invited us to his office, in what looked like the airport police station. Half an hour later we were sitting drinking tea and making desultory conversation with the general and his men when two Panjsheris came in. I introduced myself and asked for Commander Panna, who I had been told was in charge of the airport. They reacted very quickly, offering to take us to Panna and hinting, as soon as we were outside, that we were not 'very safe' with the general because, I imagine, of the threat of rocket attack.

Panna turned out to be only five minutes' walk away, perched up on the roof of a draughty outpost, from which he sprang down nimbly to give me a cold hand. We knew that Gulbuddin Hekmatyar's men had been rocketing the city on a daily basis and that there had been fighting in and around the Bala Hissar, the great fort which guards the southern approaches to Kabul.

I told Jason to ask Panna if we could see some of the fighting. Panna promised to send someone to pick us up at six the next morning. It sounded like a typical piece of Afghan prevarication, and indeed turned out to be such. Having placated us for the time being, Panna was clearly determined to move us to a less exposed environment. Summoning several young, green-turbaned Kilim Jam, he gave them instructions to take us to what turned out to be military headquarters. As we drove along the unlit airport

307

roads, terrifyingly fierce Kilim Jam sentries sprang out of the darkness to point Kalashnikov rifles and scream challenges in Uzbek at us. As we got out of the jeep and walked towards the headquarters an ear-splittingly loud salvo of rockets roared off into the night from a nearby battery. They were so close and so unexpected that I jumped, involuntarily. Inside, a bevy of Afghan army brigadiers and colonels in regime uniform debated what to do with us. An hour or so and another cup of tea later, one of them informed us, via Jason, 'It is not safe here. We will take you now to another place where you can spend the night.'

Feeling rather weary now, we got back in the Uzbeks' minibus and drove around the airport for another hour, finally drawing up outside an army mess. There, to our surprise we found one of the colonels we had seen at the original headquarters. He introduced himself. 'Colonel Sayed Jalal, Sayedi Commander of the 25th Transport Regiment, National Guard.' All I wanted was a cup of tea and a bed, but he insisted on ushering us into his office where he and his fellow officers held us in relentless conversation for another hour. By the time dinner – the inevitable rice, lamb, beans, bread and tea – arrived, I was almost asleep. The Colonel and his men, all Pashtuns as far as I could make out, were friendly but worried. In the space of a few short weeks, they had seen the Communist system they had served for years crumble into dust and be swept away by a whirlwind from the north; the Kilim Jam and the Panjsheris. Ironically, the man who was rocketing Kabul from his positions south of the capital was not a northerner, not an Uzbek nor a Panjsheri, but a fellow Pashtun, Gulbuddin Hekmatyar.

'Nobody here wants Gulbuddin. His people have been shooting rockets into the city for years now,' the colonel said. 'Nobody in Kabul wants him. They all hate him.'

I asked the colonel what he thought would happen if Gulbuddin succeeded in taking Kabul.

308

'If Gulbuddin takes Kabul,' he said, 'there will be a bloodbath.'

As soon as decency permitted, I struggled to my feet, hardly able to conceal my yawns, and followed an orderly outside to a flimsy Russian-style Nissen hut where I collapsed gratefully into a camp bed. Next morning, we were roused at six by the sound of shelling from a hilltop five miles to the south, previously occupied by Gulbuddin Hekmatyar's rocket batteries, which had now been pushed back. It was a beautiful morning and the battle seemed remote and harmless, too far away to interfere with breakfast of tea and *nan*, brought to the hut by the friendly orderly, a Kabuli, who turned out to speak quite good English. The colonel and his fellow officers were nowhere to be seen.

At seven a MiG 21 jet fighter took off with a scream and a roar, climbing up into the perfect, pale blue of the morning sky. We were only a couple of hundred yards from the runway, so Nigel shouldered his camera and we walked over to the perimeter wall, climbing onto the top of a damaged APC for a better view. At eight, three more MiG 21s took off from just the other side of the wall, climbing and banking against the spectacular backdrop of a sunlit mountain, and circling back over our heads, sharply outlined against the cloudless sky.

Shortly after the third jet had disappeared into the azure, a mortar shell landed on the far side of the airport, well away from any aircraft and apparently causing no damage. A puff of brown smoke rose lazily. I looked at my watch: 8.15. Minutes later, we heard another mortar being fired, from what sounded quite close by. It landed near the first, again without causing any obvious damage, and was followed by a third. In the distance, on the far side of the ridge of green hills that form a rampart to the south of Kabul, the jets were bombing, the dull thunder of the explosions carrying clearly in the still air. Minutes later, we could see

309

the dust and smoke rising like a haze and the mortaring stopped, although whether as a result of a hit, or tactical withdrawal, we could not tell. Soon afterwards the jets came back, roaring over our heads in victory rolls before dropping down the runway like sated birds of prey, trailing their brake parachutes like trophies and taxiing away to their revetments. Peace descended again on the bright, sunny morning and it was time for us to leave.

But it was not to be. As we passed a village not far from the airport in our large lumbering bus, we heard a lot of shooting, mainly mortars, I thought. Stopping the bus, in which we were the only passengers, Nigel – never one to pass up a shoot-out – and I got out, leaving Jason to watch the equipment, and walked towards the village. We threaded our way down the narrow streets, the high mud walls of the houses blank and silent above us, until on the far side, a friendly householder with a very pretty young daughter invited us to climb up on to his balcony. From there, looking over the last few houses to the green hills beyond, Nigel took several shots of mortars dropping on the ridge in front of us. I had promised I would go back for Jason when we had decided if it was worth filming and on the way back, a well-dressed elderly villager with a well-combed white beard and long *chapan* waved his arms and shouted at us in Farsi.

'What does he say, Jason?'

Jason chuckled. 'Well, in effect he's saying "bugger off."'

We arrived at the house of our friend just in time for tea, brought up by his pretty daughter and small son. When the girl was inclined to linger, examining us with her huge, lustrous black eyes, the father quickly shooed her away. She was probably only ten or twelve, but as soon as puberty approaches all Afghan village women disappear behind the veil. Their beauty is legendary, but no strangers – not even fellow villagers – are allowed to feast their eyes on it, Afghan men being intensely jealous of their womenfolk. During the

310

first Anglo-Afghan war, and possibly in the later ones too, the British officers who occupied Kabul had a high old time, living like kings and forming numerous liaisons with the local belles. This loose behaviour, of course, infuriated the mullahs and tribal elders and further inflamed the already intense resentment of the invaders, for which they had to pay, many of them with their lives.

My train of thought was rudely interrupted by four loud cracks, rather like ice breaking on a frozen lake, and four rockets landed beside and behind us, in salvoes of two. After the first pair landed, only fifty yards away, people started running in terror. The second salvo hit a house behind us and we could hear someone screaming. They sounded like Chinese-made 122 rockets, with a range of five to eight miles. Our host said the village often came under attack from Gulbuddin Hekmatyar's rocket teams and a number of villagers had been killed and wounded. It had been going on for years and had given all the mujahideen a bad name, although Gulbuddin, supplied by the Pakistani ISI, was the only leader who pursued this policy. Nigel had been filming from the top of the flat roof and, it occurred to me, would have been clearly visible to anyone with field glasses on the ridge in front of us. The same thought must have occurred to our host, and although too polite to say so, I could see our presence was making him nervous, so we took our leave.

Our driver dropped us on the airport perimeter, saying he was not allowed to go any farther, and as we were wondering how to complete the journey to the Intercontinental, a taxi drew up and out stepped one of the other ITN crews, Paul Carleton, David Prime and the reporter, Penny Marshall. We told them where we had been, and in return for our information they let us take their taxi back to the hotel – provided we sent it back for them. While Patrick was editing our report of Masud's reinforcements being flown in by helicopter, and the morning's bombing and rocketing, I

311

had to stand on a balcony overlooking the city to be interviewed by Sonia Russeler in London. Unfortunately the sound was so bad that I could barely hear her and I had to guess at her questions.

As soon as that was over Nigel and I went back to the airport to try to get a lift on a helicopter back to Charikar or Jebel Seraj, since Masud remained my overriding concern and I worried constantly about losing contact with him. As we drew up at the gate outside the passenger terminal, three Mi8s flew low across the airport in front of us, but it was now 5.30 and I suspected they would be parking for the night and not flying off somewhere. I asked for Panna and they gave us a mujahid who took us to one of the offices we had visited the night before. But of Panna, alas, there was no sign. Eventually, it now being almost dark, we gave up and drove back to the Intercontinental where two pleasures awaited: a bath, and a large glass of whisky, neither of which was obtainable in Charikar. I discovered that not only taxi prices were hugely inflated in Kabul: a bottle of Johnny Walker Red Label cost US$100 across the bar.

Next morning, Nigel Thomson, Jason Elliot and I went back to the airport to see if we could find a helicopter to take us north. While we were waiting with a few other journalists for Panna, who was somewhere in the terminal, an office door suddenly opened and through it we saw half a dozen United Nations personnel, their distinctive blue berets giving them away immediately, deep in discussion. They seemed equally surprised and not altogether pleased to see us. The door was quickly closed again and we were left wondering if they had come to negotiate the release of President Najibullah. A few minutes later Panna appeared and led us down the corridor to his large new office. I said we wanted to go north to see Masud but, to avoid running the gauntlet of Hisb roadblocks, wondered if we could find a seat in a helicopter. Panna said he would inquire, and to

312

wait for him, which we did in the warm spring sunshine outside the terminal.

Ten minutes later I was standing with Jason by our taxi when half a dozen mortar shells came whistling over our heads and landed 200 yards in front of us in the middle of the airport. The dirty brown smoke from the explosions had barely drifted away when three or four more mortars came shrieking in to land all round us. Jason and I threw ourselves on the ground beside the taxi as one hit the arrival building to our right and another landed just in front of us, next to a parked car and only a few yards from where Nigel was standing. He had the camera on his shoulder, looking towards the runway where the first stick had landed.

Luckily, the car was between him and the point of impact, otherwise he would have been either killed or seriously wounded. The blast blew out the whole plate glass front of the terminal, which collapsed like an ice fall, but by the time I looked up, Nigel had disappeared. I did not realise until five minutes later – nor did he – that he had been hit. The car had burst into flames and Jason and I ran, crouching, towards the terminal building, expecting the petrol tank to explode. After a few more minutes I moved from the side of the terminal building round to the front to find Nigel. Inside the doorway, a soldier lay motionless, slumped against the wall. I discovered later he was dead. Then I caught sight of Nigel. He was wearing, as he always did, a plain white T-shirt. The whole of the back was drenched in blood.

'Nigel, you're hit. Are you all right?'

'Fine. I've just seen the blood myself. I felt something hit me in the back. I thought it was a stone, or something like that. Could you get me my rucksack from the taxi? There's a first-aid kit inside.'

I went outside to the car, made our elderly taxi driver open the boot, and was wrestling with the rucksack when Nigel came up and said, 'Let's get out of this bloody place. I'm losing quite a bit of blood.'

'I think we better get you to the Red Cross hospital rightaway.' Then, trying to be reassuring, I said, 'They'll soon fix you up.' As we drove off, I said loudly to the driver, 'Spital! Spital! ICRC, yes? Red Cross, yes?'

But the old man, who came highly recommended by Mr Sakhi, the head concierge, seemed to be too shell-shocked to understand, even when Jason translated.

After what seemed an excessively long time, we found ourselves drawing up outside what was clearly not the ICRC but an Afghan hospital, and a very dirty-looking one at that. We took one look and then turned and marched right out again, to the silent disapproval of an Afghan doctor or nurse in a grubby white coat.

'Back to the Intercontinental,' I ordered. As we went in we met a charming young American journalist with some first aid knowledge who took us up to her room, wiped the blood away and lent Nigel a clean shirt, but wisely left the wound alone and suggested we go to the ICRC hospital. Explaining this is what we had meant to do in the first place, we thanked her, descended to the ground floor and had the doorman get the message through to the driver.

'Ah hah!' he nodded wisely, as if to imply 'Why didn't you say that in the first place?' This time, it took us all of five minutes.

The ICRC hospital, run by the Swiss-based International Committee of the Red Cross, was the only well-equipped and well-run hospital not only in Kabul but in the whole of Afghanistan. They were extremely busy – having had a record number of eighty-five wounded the day before – but after a short wait Nigel was X-rayed, and after another, longer wait the Italian surgeon who the previous day had successfully removed a piece of shrapnel from the forehead of an Italian cameraman, performed the same service on Nigel's left shoulder. Afterwards, over a stiff drink in the hotel bar, he showed me the offending object which the surgeon had given him as a souvenir. It was about half the length of a cigarette, viciously jagged and quite clearly part of the mortar shell casing. Unwisely, I said that it looked quite small.

'The surgeon said it was quite big, actually. He had quite a job getting it out. It was quite deeply embedded in the muscle and I could hear this sort of tearing sound as he pulled it out.' Nigel made a face and laughed. 'I didn't feel anything, because he had given me a shot, but I could hear it.'

'Very unpleasant,' I said.

'Not nice!' That meant, in anyone else's book, extremely nasty. That evening, after dinner, while we were still trying to kill the ache in Nigel's shoulder, the barman announced he was closing. There was a curfew, and he had to get home. So on purely medicinal grounds, I bought a bottle of whisky across the bar. It certainly helped me, and I think Nigel, to sleep soundly, but not so soundly as to be unable to plan ahead. Nigel would clearly be *hors de combat* for some time, and I remained very much aware that Masud's entry into Kabul was only a matter of days away: it turned out to be only one day away but, of course, I did not know that. I therefore suggested to Nick Atkins, the producer, that I should 'borrow' Paul Carleton, who was working with Penny Marshall. Paul was very experienced, and this was the big story, so he was the natural choice. His place could be taken by David Prime, who had recently graduated from sound recording to filming, so Penny would not be left in the lurch. Nick agreed and Paul, Jason and I arranged to leave the hotel at six the following morning.

Chapter
20

Wednesday 28 April 1992 turned out to be a historic day, although it started in routine enough fashion. Paul and I left half an hour late without Jason who, unfortunately for him, overslept. Having heard a rumour that the road to Charikar was closed, we went first to the airport in the hope of finding a helicopter, but failing to find Panna, were directed to the *garneson*, the army headquarters. There, in the guard room by the gate, we located Masud's political deputy and representative in Kabul, Dr Abdul Rahman. Chubby, bearded and bespectacled, he was a difficult man to reach, being almost completely submerged in a knot of people who swarmed round him like midges, all vying for his attention. Way was finally made for us and we entered his office to find two Iranian-born photographers from Paris, one called Abbas from Magnum, and the other Reza from Gamma. This was lucky, since the doctor spoke little or no English and we were without Jason.

Through the good offices of Abbas and Reza I was able to establish that no helicopters were available and that we would have to 'take our chances' on the road. I did not particularly like the sound of that but Reza spoke to the doctor again and came back with the information that it should be 'possible'. An idea was forming in my mind.

'Reza, have you got a car?'

316

'I'm afraid not.'

'Why don't you come with us, then? There are only the two of us, there's plenty of space.'

As it happened, I had hired one of Kabul's better taxis, an old but solid-looking Russian Volga saloon. To my relief, Reza accepted. I knew with him on board, we had a sporting chance. Without him, and with no Farsi between us, the odds would be heavily against. Reza turned out to be charming, intelligent – and quick-witted, as he proved at the first roadblock. Ironically, it was a roadblock manned by Jamiat, Masud's party, and therefore should have presented no problem. We waited beside the road while they summoned the commander, a rather dour individual who listened to Reza's explanation without a hint of enthusiasm. He was still looking negative and had just opened his mouth to say something when Reza seized his hand, shook it warmly, thanked him and climbed back in the car. As we drove off, he laughed.

'Did you see that? I shook hands with him before he could say no. He wasn't at all happy about letting us through.'

The Hisb roadblocks were frequent but remarkably friendly, which surprised me. With all the fighting in Kabul, I thought they would have been hostile, but here was a perfect example of Afghan unpredictability. At one road-block, a long discussion and a mile-long detour off the main road turned out to be nothing more serious than a request for a lift from two commanders. As we all made ourselves small in order to accommodate the large, hairy, heavily armed and strongly smelling commanders, we became aware that three or four other mujahideen were climbing into the boot, also intent on going for a ride. The driver was too frightened to say very much, but Paul and Reza soon made it plain their presence was unacceptable, guns or no guns. Surprisingly, the mujahideen vacated the boot with great good humour, rather like naughty children who have been caught misbehaving. At the next roadblock it became even more of a squeeze when we were asked to take two small boys and a car battery to Bagram, presumably for recharging. On the outskirts of Bagram, near another Hisb outpost, we saw a group of local men digging trenches on both sides of the road, as if in anticipation of an attack, but they did not stop us.

We reached Bagram at about one. Just outside the base, we passed a long line of Masud's tanks, BTMs (Russian-made APCs) and lorryloads of troops drawn up at the side of the road, pointing south. I counted nearly one hundred vehicles, the crews enjoying the sunshine, or having lunch beside the road. I strolled over to where a group of Panj-sheris were sitting cross-legged on the grass round a huge pot of rice. Waving welcoming hands, they invited us to join them, but we politely declined. I asked where Masud was and they pointed in the direction of the base, only a mile or so up the road. Fifteen minutes later we were outside his headquarters and I was able to snatch a quick word with him before he drove off.

'Are you going to Kabul today?' I asked in French.

'Yes, later.'

'Can we come with you?'

'Yes, of course.'

'How will you travel, in a BTM?'

'Yes, probably.'

'Can we come with you?'

'I will give you a BTM for yourselves.' He grinned and the jeep shot off. We followed, bumping our way across what had been the Russians' biggest base in Afghanistan. We finally caught up with him as he was standing on a flat roof, peering through his binoculars in the direction of Kabul. As soon as he saw us, he called Reza up to join him and questioned him closely about the road. When Reza said we had seen trenches being dug, Masud looked 'very serious', pacing up and down on the roof, weighing up the risks.

Finally he climbed down and I said I would like to interview him.

'Not now, a little later,' he said.

I knew that on a day like this there was no time like the present, so I kept talking, and Paul, being an old pro, started walking backwards with the camera on his shoulder, filming. This is what used to be called *cinéma vérité*, and is now known as a walking interview. Walking backwards holding a television camera steady is not only difficult but can also be dangerous, unless there is someone, ideally the soundman, to guide the cameraman. We did not have a soundman and at one point we walked along a path with a deep ditch on one side, so it was really a *tour de force* on Paul's part. With Reza translating as we went, I asked Masud if he anticipated any trouble in Kabul. He said there might be some trouble on the road, but he did not think there would be any in the city.

'Kabul is free,' he said, 'and I am going to see my troops there.'

I asked him if he ever thought, when he began his resistance struggle in 1979, that one day he would march into Kabul?

'I always thought this government would collapse and we would be the first people into the city.'

'This must be a very happy day for you,' I said in conclusion. We had run out of space and come to a halt. He did not reply, but his smile was radiant. Then, after giving two young mujahideen what seemed to be last-minute instructions, he led the way into another headquarters building where a group of Afghan army officers, including General Momen, were waiting to receive him. At first we were shown to a separate room and offered tea there, but a few minutes later, obviously on Masud's instructions, we were ushered into the big office next door. Masud sat on one side of the room, with his back to the window, and one of his senior Panjsheri aides beside him, and the Afghan

319

army general whose office this presumably was, occupied the desk at the far end. It was all very informal, Paul sitting down beside Masud and Reza and I opposite him. Various army officers including Momen came and went, all showing Masud a friendly deference. I asked him if reports that he had been appointed Defence Minister were true, but he good-naturedly dodged my questions, insisting that the only official post he held was as head of the Committee for the Security of Kabul, to which he had been appointed by all the mujahideen leaders in Peshawar.

I knew Masud well but his remarkably relaxed manner amazed me. Here he was, on one of the most important days of his life, the day on which he would, after all these years, enter Kabul in triumph without, he hoped, firing a shot; and yet he had time to sit down and talk for an hour, about the war past and present. No doubt the presence of Reza, a fellow Persian speaker and someone he knew well, was a help, and I was an old friend too. But it was almost as if he wanted to put the record straight, describing how from the start he had been in close touch with various officers in the army. I asked him when he had first started talking to General Momen?

'Four years ago.'

'And to General Dostam?'

'Two months ago.'

It was the alliance with General Dostam which led to the crucial success, the fall of Mazar-i-Sharif, in March. After that, the final stages of the war went very quickly. 'In the first place, Najibullah thought I would move my forces south, through the Salang, the direct route to Kabul. So he planned to give Charikar and Jebel Seraj to the Hisb-i-Islami [of Gulbuddin Hekmatyar] so that they would fight us. But we took them by surprise, bringing in our forces from east and west.

'The second reason was that Najibullah appointed a new general to the Charikar-Bagram area, what they call the

"Iron Gate to Kabul". It was because of this general that we were able to take Charikar and Bagram virtually without a fight. When the people saw that there was no killing and no looting in Charikar, they did not want to fight any more. They realised the mujahideen were just like everyone else.' At this point General Momen came in, and sat smiling beside Masud as he delivered the punch line of the story.

'When Najibullah received the news that Jebel Seraj and Charikar had fallen, he thought Hisb-i-Islami had taken them. But when he learnt that it was Jamiat that had captured them, he began to shake.' Masud laughed.

I took advantage of his expansive mood to ask him about the coup he and Gulbuddin Hekmatyar had tried to mount against President Daoud in 1975: it failed and both men had to flee to Pakistan. Masud grinned. 'Dr Abdul Rahman [whom we had seen in Kabul] told me "Don't include Gulbuddin Hekmatyar."'

It was during his exile in Pakistan that Masud studied guerrilla warfare, reading Mao Tse-tung, Che Guevara, Regis Debray and a number of other writers on the subject, including an American expert whose name he could not remember. Then in April 1978, the Communists overthrew Daoud and seized power in Kabul.

I asked him when he had left Pakistan and gone back to Afghanistan to fight the *jehad*? 'In June 1979, before the Russian invasion.'

He crossed the border into Kunar (Nuristan) with only twenty-seven comrades-in-arms, armed with a motley collection of weapons: five shotguns; one G4 American carbine; two AK47 Kalashnikov automatic rifles; nine old-fashioned .303 rifles, made in Darra, on the North-West Frontier; two RPG7s (Rocket-Propelled Grenades) and seven rockets; fifty to sixty hand-made grenades, also from Darra; and five thousand rounds of ammunition. They divided into two groups, and started fighting in July, in the Panjsher and in

321

Tagab. 'From the very beginning we started talking to officers in the army, through our Urban Committee.'

His verdict on the defeat of the Communist regime was simple. 'The government collapsed because it was hollow.'

On the future he was prophetic. Speaking of his old enemy and rival, Gulbuddin Hekmatyar, Masud said, 'Having failed militarily to capture Kabul, he will accept the prime ministership and then try to achieve politically what he has failed to achieve by force.'

And did he see Gulbuddin winning an election in Afghanistan?

'No, never. He is in a minority.'

'Who do you think would, then?'

'It is obvious that Jamiat would. They are the biggest party.'

But it was time for action. Just outside the base, the convoy for Kabul was forming up under the joint supervision of General Momen and one of Masud's young commanders, Homayoun. There must have been close on 200 Russian tanks, BTMs and lorries so loaded down with troops they tilted over alarmingly, axles groaning, as they climbed up the slope onto the road. Three more or less equal elements made up the convoy: Masud's Tajik troops, based on his own crack Panjsheris; Dostam's Kilim Jam militia; and part of General Momen's division. Dostam's men, easily recognisable with their flowing locks and blue and green check turbans, and General Momen's soldiers in their mud-brown army uniforms, provided most of the armour, and Masud's men most of the infantry. But each vehicle carried a mixture of all three forces in an obvious and apparently successful demonstration of unity. Masud refused to say how many men he had in the column, but I guessed about 5000; they carried a lot of firepower.

At six, Masud appeared, climbed into his dark green Russian jeep and the column started to move. Homayoun, young and dashing, with a few words of English, had told us he would arrange a lift for us but, in the final scramble to depart, he was nowhere to be seen. So much for Masud's blithe promise of our own BTM, I thought bitterly. There was nothing for it but to stick to our own tortoise-like taxi.

The advance party had already gone ahead, presumably radioing back that the road was clear, and now the main column set off at a cracking pace. Despite our repeated exhortations to the driver, who retorted testily that his old Volga diesel could go no faster, we fell further and further behind. Overtaken by BTMs, and a variety of jeeps, including a smartly-painted Japanese model driven by Peter Juvenal, a freelance working for the BBC, accompanied by Richard MacKenzie, a formidable Australian writing for the *National Geographic*, I began to think we would be the last to arrive in Kabul, without any pictures of the column on the move.

We passed several groups of Hisb villagers standing expectantly by the side of the road, all waving as if they were the best of friends, their roadblocks conveniently forgotten. It would soon be dark, which would make filming difficult, and in the mountains to the west, lightning flashed and rain clouds gathered. To add to the sense of drama, a solitary MiG 21 made two low passes over the convoy, in salutation of the victor.

I was becoming more and more agitated when fate, or rather Allah, intervened. The column stopped. Immediately, Paul and I leaped out of the taxi, clutching our equipment, and ran a hundred yards or so up the road, threading our way through the column, towards Homayoun's BTM. The reason for the halt soon became clear. Masud and his entourage were on their knees, in the middle of the road, offering up evening prayers. Our attempt to climb onto what I took to be Homayoun's BTM was rebuffed by an unfriendly mujahid; so instead, Paul and I ran to the next one, an older and more battered model manned by the

Kilim Jam. They had a fearsome reputation, and for a second I wondered what sort of reception we would get. In fact, two grinning Uzbeks, each with five RPG rockets strapped to his back, hauled me and our equipment up on to the flat space behind the turret, while Paul ran back to get a wonderfully atmospheric shot of Masud praying. He only had about thirty seconds, and I admired both his professionalism, and his turn of speed as he sprinted back to be hoisted on board just as we started with an almighty jerk.

If we had been near the end of the column before, we were now at the head of it, roaring into the night with the lights of the column blazing behind us. Paul began to get some marvellous pictures, with Masud's jeep only ten or twenty yards away and the long line of tanks and BTMs rocking and swaying at full speed behind us through the darkness. After ten or fifteen minutes of this exhilarating progress, we caught up with the advance column, strung out across the road in three lanes, like a traffic jam on the M25. A few minutes later the convoy started off again, but we remained obstinately stuck in the right-hand lane, while the rest of the column roared past us into the night. It finally dawned on us that we were stuck behind a BTM which had broken down and I began urging our driver in my best Farsi to pull out and pass it.

'*Bera bekhair*,' I kept shouting, 'Move on,' and eventually, he did as instructed. Briefly, we hurtled at top speed through the darkness again but, as soon as we caught up the main column, we had to slow down almost to walking pace. At one point, as a lorry crept past, an old man with a long grey beard and ankle-length blue *chapan* held up two Kalashnikov rifles, one in each hand, grinning happily at the camera. Soon afterwards, we came to the top of the ridge that surrounds Kabul like the rim of a saucer, the lights of the city twinkling sparsely in front of us. The Kilim Jam in the nearest BTM went wild, firing bursts of 30

324

millimetre cannon into the sky in jubilation. All round us, as the mujahideen celebrated their arrival in Kabul, the sky was full of red tracer. The din was terrific.

At the foot of the hill, outside the gates of Khairkhana barracks, we and the rest of the BTMs stopped for a moment. Then the lead BTM revved its engine noisily, and swung sharply left up the hill, with the rest of us following. I wanted to shout out that we did not want to go to the barracks, but no one would have heard and it would have been pointless in any case. I was reduced to cursing the lack of any 'press relations' on the part of the mujahideen and then told myself to stop being absurd. In the general excitement, I had taken it for granted that the column, and we as part of it, would enter the city with Masud. But owing to the vagaries of the journey, Masud and Homayoun had long since vanished, their promises with them, and we were stuck with a wonderful piece of television reportage 'in the can', in the middle of a blacked-out army camp, without any transport.

I had a vague idea the Intercontinental was not very far away, but how were we going to get there? Our only hope lay in the main road, where we might find a taxi willing to risk breaking the curfew, or better still, a friendly Panjsheri with a jeep. We started to walk down the hill in the dark, lugging Paul's camera equipment, which had become surprisingly heavy by the time we reached the main road. But there was little traffic and after ten or fifteen fruitless minutes, we were accosted by a young man who spoke some English, and who offered to help.

'Please, you come with me,' he said with perhaps too convincing an air of authority. 'I will take you to officer house.'

This turned out to be another jerry-built Russian office block, like the ones we had seen in Jebel Seraj and Bagram, only more dilapidated. It was three years, of course, since the Russians had left, but it was hard to believe this had been one of their principal barracks, the springboard for all those offensives the Red Army launched against Masud and the Panjsher in the early and mid-1980s. Having handed us over to the sentry on the door, the young man departed, and we were led along a dimly-lit corridor to a room where three or four Afghan army officers sat sprawled on chairs and sofas, smoking and drinking tea. The vibes, as Nigel Thomson would have said, were not good.

After the usual preliminaries, I explained to the major, a young smart alec who seemed to be in charge, in a mixture of English, pidgin Farsi and a kind of home-made Esperanto, that we had just arrived from Bagram with Masud and urgently needed a lift to the Intercontinental. Perhaps misguidedly, since the major and most of his fellow officers were Pashtuns and probably pro-Moscow, I added that Masud's arrival in Kabul was a historic event and needed to be satellited to a waiting world immediately. So would he please let us have a jeep to take us to the hotel as soon as possible? The argument went on interminably, with the other officers joining in, often in Russian. One, by turns silly and malevolent, kept asking infuriatingly 'Do you speak Russian?' when it was clear that we did not.

Eventually, at eleven o'clock, after two hours of pleading, cajoling, browbeating and even attempted bribery, it became clear that we were getting nowhere. The smart-alec major reiterated for the umpteenth time, 'Tomorrow. Tonight, too dangerous. Tomorrow you go to Intercontinental.' I stood up in a fury and announced that Paul and I were going to walk up the hill to find the mujahideen commander. Outside, a jeep was parked by the front door, and behind the wheel was one of the officers who had been in the room earlier. He spoke a few words of English, and I could not resist saying, 'Hotel Intercontinental. How much?'

'You have dollars?'

'Yes. You take my friend and me to Intercontinental, now, I give you $500. US'

His voice shook with disbelief. 'Five hundred dollars? Show me now!'

I did not trust him. I patted my pocket. 'I have, here. You take us to Intercon, I give it you. Sure.'

There was a long pause, and then he shrugged. 'Sorry, not possible go Intercontinental.'

As we walked up the hill in the darkness, I inwardly cursed all Afghans. But I was also increasingly worried that the opposition, in the shape of Peter Juvenal, an old Afghan hand, would have been back in the Intercontinental for several hours, and might well have already sent the first pictures to London. Our only hope was that he would not have access to the ITN satellite, and would have been too late for Kabul Television.

At the top of the hill, near the spot where our BTM had deposited us three hours before, we found the *qarargah*, mujahideen headquarters, and after being challenged by an Uzbek sentry, were led to a small room where two men were asleep in bed. The sentry woke one, the commander, who immediately got up. He was very tall, about six-foot-four at a guess, and had an uncanny resemblance to Clint Eastwood, despite being dressed in a long white night-shirt.

He listened sympathetically to our story, seemed to recognise my name and immediately rang up someone on his field telephone. Ten minutes went by, while we sat waiting and the other occupant of the room slept on as if drugged. The commander rang again, had a brief conversation, and then slipping on a pair of sandals, beckoned us to follow him outside. He walked with a long, lithe stride, like a sheriff in a Western, and my hopes began to soar. I felt sure that, like Clint, he would get the better of the bad guys. Among the BTMs and jeeps parked in front of the *qarargah*, one jeep had just arrived, with lights on and engine running. The commander spoke to the driver, in army uniform, who made it very clear he was not going to co-operate.

Abandoning a lost cause, Clint, as I now thought of him, walked over to another jeep, and began to talk to its driver. For a moment, my hopes were rising again, when, suddenly, another officer we had met in the first headquarters materialised out of the darkness. I recognised him immediately as being a particularly unhelpful shit. He had not changed, telling our tall friend, unmistakably, 'No, it is not possible.'

He may have added that the commander should consult headquarters, because Clint turned on his heel abruptly and strode off down the hill at such speed that we had almost to run to keep up with him. We took a slightly different route, a sort of *direttissima* in the dark, but as the familiar shape of the hut-like headquarters loomed in front of us, my heart sank. It sank even lower a few minutes later when the commander marched determinedly along the still dimly-lit corridor and we found ourselves back in the same room, confronting the same smart-alec major.

Clint said his piece and then, without more ado, quickly departed, leaving us to continue the battle on our own. I felt a pang of disappointment, betrayal even, that our hero had failed to beat the bad guys, and even worse, left us in the lurch. There followed another acrimonious hour with the major, which ended at midnight in deadlock, with his final dictum. 'Not possible tonight. Eight o'clock tommorrow morning.'

Paul had already stretched himself out on the floor in disgust at the whole proceedings but the major, having won his point, summoned an orderly to take us to our quarters. These were in an adjoining, even more ramshackle hut occupied, in considerable squalor, by what are known in the British Army as other ranks. The room contained four two-tier, metal frame bunks. All the bottom berths seemed to be occupied, so we had to climb, with the whole contraption swaying, to the vacant top ones. It was cold and dark – they did not seem to believe in electric light in Khairhana – which

328

was perhaps just as well as I suspected the mattress was both filthy and flea-ridden. But wrapping my Barbour tightly round me, I stretched out and immediately fell fast asleep.

I woke at about six and after making a brief tour of the not very attractive grounds, went to call on the major at seven. He did not present quite such a smart-alec appearance at this time of the morning, being tousled and unwashed and clearly having slept in his uniform. But he was still so deliberately unhelpful that, in a surge of contempt and anger I walked out on him, taking Paul with me. Outside we found a mujahideen commander I knew slightly, and asked him for help. As we stood looking down on the road below, I suddenly saw a taxi, and desperation lending my Farsi fluency, persuaded the commander to lend me his jeep for five minutes to drive down and hire it. Unlike the smart-alec major, he agreed without discussion, and leaving Paul to watch over the camera equipment, I drove down the hill, commandeered the taxi, and made him follow me up again to collect Paul. Fifteen minutes later we drove out of the main gate of Khairkhana, which I now hated with passion, and half an hour later arrived at the Intercontinental. It was a lovely morning, the sun already warm, and good news awaited us.

After all my worrying, it turned out that we had not been scooped. Over breakfast, Nick Atkins, our producer, told me that to his knowledge no pictures of Masud's arrival in Kabul had been seen in London, and inexplicably, Peter Juvenal did not seem to have done a 'voicepiece', or telephone report, which the BBC could have used on television. In other words the field was still clear, which made my breakfast taste twice as good. Afterwards, I sat down with Peter Read, a delightful man and an editor of genius, and watched him cut a four minute forty second piece for the lunchtime news. Paul's pictures were brilliant and the walking interview with Masud remarkably successful: I

329

marvelled again at how he had managed to hold the camera so steady and avoid falling into the ditch.

There was one other bonus. If we had managed to get the story on air the previous night, it would inevitably have been a rush job. As Peter pointed out, with plenty of time in hand, we were able to turn out a polished performance. It ran all day, Peter cutting it back for the early evening news and then recutting it at about four minutes for *News at Ten*. It led a seven minute belt on *News at Ten*, which I 'linked' on camera, as if live. This was Paul Davies's idea, which London accepted and which, as it happened, was the last report I did for ITN.

We heard later that 'it all ran as planned', and that London were so enthusiastic about our entire coverage that they broke out the champagne. I wrote in my diary for 30 April 1992, 'We murdered a few bottles of whisky at our end too. All in all, a very successful operation, ITN at its best, and the long Afghan war seemed to be really over! Historic and astonishing that Masud had so brilliantly brought off a coup few ever thought he would come close to. I think most Afghans, certainly in Kabul, were happy.'

Looking back, this may have been over-optimistic, although I think it was right at the time. But the sense of euphoria was short-lived. The Kilim Jam were busy looting everything they could lay their hands on, as we soon discovered personally. Mr Sakhi, the head concierge, had offered to arrange lunch for us in the Baghibala Palace, a graceful, nineteenth-century pleasure dome set in gardens below the Intercontinental, to which it belongs. All we had to do was to tell him what food we wanted and he would arrange the rest. We ordered grilled chicken and salad and said we would get the caviar and wine. Alas, by the time Paul and his helpers had descended on the Chicken Street shops, all the wine had disappeared, either under the counter or into the gutter, smashed by Islamic zealots. Worse was to follow. On Saturday morning, Mr Sakhi rang

330

me to say the lunch was off: the Baghibala Palace had been looted and destroyed by the mujahideen, presumably the Kilim Jam, who also stripped one whole section of the carpet bazaar. Such is war.

On Monday 4 May we were all due to fly to Delhi, en route for London. I was rather late leaving for the airport, having run into complications over my hotel bill, paid partly in dollars and partly in afghanis. I found myself short of afghanis, and was sitting with Paul, wondering what I was going to do, when one of the room boys appeared holding a key. Did it belong to one of us? 'Yes,' said Paul, 'that's mine.'

'You leave this in room,' the Afghan said, holding aloft a huge wad of afghanis.

'Christ! Did I really?'

Paul was so impressed with the man's honesty that he gave him one of the wads, worth 10,000 afghanis [$20], as a reward. The man went away beaming – it was a fortune, locally – and Paul kindly solved my problem too.

We need not have worried about being late for the plane. We arrived at the airport at ten, and left at three. We were lucky to take off at all. Around midday, while we were sunning ourselves outside the terminal building – not far from where Nigel, Jason and I had been mortared a few days before – Gulbuddin Hekmatyar made his own comment on Masud's capture of Kabul. Ten or twelve shells crashed into the city a mile away, not far from the Presidential Palace. A little later a single rocket exploded near the end of the runway, and we all thought: there goes our flight. But Ariana are made of sterner stuff. As if nothing had happened, the plane came in shortly afterwards and forty minutes later we were airborne.

As I looked down at Kabul and its ring of snow-covered mountains, a whole cavalcade of thoughts and images went through my mind. I thought again of my first long, long trek through the Hindu Kush to find Masud ten years

331

before; the fear of the helicopters with their hornet's sting; the long grind of the war and then, suddenly, the Russian withdrawal, and the collapse of the Soviet Empire, in which mujahideen resistance played such a prominent part. I thought too of my first sight of the great blue wall of the Hindu Kush; the beauty of the high valleys; the elixir of green tea after a fourteen-hour march; and the unforgettable picture of a lammergeyer vulture, with its yellow chest and cruel beak, its mighty wings outspread as it soared along a jagged ridge, 14,000 feet up in Nuristan, the symbol of Afghan courage and independence.

Index

Gorbachev, Mikhail 160
Greene, Graham 65
Groslier, Henri 100
Groslier Henri jr 100, 104
Gul, General Hamid 171,
    175–6
Gulbuddinn Hekmatyar
    (leader of Hisb-i-Islami)
    162, 172, 173, 176, 177,
    286, 292, 321
  ruthlessness 123, 172–7
  Pakistan and American
    support for 172, 176–7
  rivalry with Masud 297,
    298–9, 300, 322
  attacks on Kabul 298–9,
    300–1, 308, 311, 331
Gulf War 61, 183, 186–90,
    193, 201–83. *See also* Iraq
    Kuwait
    Saudi Arabia

Hackworth, Colonel David H.
    235–7, 239
Hafar-al-Batin 240
Hairatan 284
Hancock, Nigel 194–5, 241–2
Hanoi 30, 35, 37, 42–62, 71
  during Vietnam war 43,
    61–2
  filming in 45, 48, 49–51, 59,
    60
  black market 45–6
  Ho Chi Minh's house and
    tomb 54–5

Paul Doumer Bridge 45, 48,
    49–50
  Thanh Loi hotel 43, 44, 51
Haq, Abdul 111
Harrow, Steve
  during Gulf War 219,
    221–5, 239, 241, 250–65
  drive to Khafji 242–8
  driving through roadblocks
    242–4, 253, 256, 258–60
  and allied entry to Kuwait
    250–3, 255–65
Heeps, Peter 289, 304
Heng Samrin 57
Hickey, Fred 165, 170
Hindu Kush 162, 289, 295,
    300, 306, 332
Hisb-i-Islami 123, 303, 320,
    321, 323
  gangsterism 173, 174, 176,
    177
Hissarak, intended attack on
    125, 144–6, 151–2, 154,
    158
Ho Chi Minh 54–5, 61
Ho Chi Minh City – *see*
    Saigon
Ho Chi Minh Trail 29, 52
Homayoum (Afghan
    commander) 322, 323,
    325
Horobin, Don 31, 32–3, 35, 37
Hu Nim 83–4
Hughes, Ed 3
Hunt, Jon 122, 135, 139, 146,
    147
Hussein, King of Jordan 3, 5,
    184–7, 197